CHILDREN OF THE RAVEN AND THE WHALE

Children of the Raven and the Whale

VISIONS AND REVISIONS IN AMERICAN LITERATURE

Caroline Chamberlin Hellman

UNIVERSITY OF VIRGINIA PRESS

Charlottesville and London

University of Virginia Press
© 2019 by the Rector and Visitors of the University of Virginia
All rights reserved
Printed in the United States of America on acid-free paper

First published 2019

ISBN 978-0-8139-4359-6 (cloth)
ISBN 978-0-8139-4360-2 (paper)
ISBN 978-0-8139-4361-9 (e-book)

9 8 7 6 5 4 3 2 1

Library of Congress Cataloging-in-Publication Data is available for this title.

Cover art: Lithograph from *The Naturalist's Library*, edited by William
Jardine. (Visipix)

For my parents,
Maria Chamberlin-Hellman and Gerard Hellman

Nothing changes, though much be new-fashioned: new fashions but revivals of things previous. In the books of the past we learn naught but of the present; in those of the present, the past. All Mardi's history—beginning, middle, and finis—was written out in capitals in the first page penned.

—Herman Melville, *Mardi, and A Voyage Thither* (1849)

The great flood-gates of the wonder-world swung open, and in the wild conceits that swayed me to my purpose, two and two there floated into my inmost soul, endless processions of the whale.

—Herman Melville, *Moby-Dick* (1851)

Contents

Acknowledgments   xi

Introduction   1

1. "A Walker in the City": Chang-rae Lee's *Native Speaker*,
    Jonathan Lethem's *Motherless Brooklyn*,
    and Walt Whitman's Cartographic Legacy   21

2. Literary Custom House: Nathaniel Hawthorne's
    The Scarlet Letter and Jhumpa Lahiri's *Unaccustomed Earth*   43

3. Short Happy Palimpsest: Ernest Hemingway's "The Short
    Happy Life of Francis Macomber" and Junot Díaz's
    The Brief Wondrous Life of Oscar Wao   66

4. New York Unearthed: Excavating the Works of
    Washington Irving, Walt Whitman, and F. Scott Fitzgerald
    in Colum McCann's *Let the Great World Spin*
    and Joseph O'Neill's *Netherland*   88

5. Black Boys and White Whales: Ta-Nehisi Coates's
    Conversations with Herman Melville, Richard Wright,
    and James Baldwin   112

    Conclusion   139

    Notes   145
    Works Cited   157
    Index   171

Acknowledgments

THE FOCUS OF THIS BOOK, literary influence, is a reminder of the many individuals who contribute to the genesis of any accomplishment. At New York City College of Technology/CUNY, I am grateful to President Russell Hotzler, the Office of the President, the Office of the Dean of Arts and Sciences, the City Tech Foundation, and the Professional Staff Congress for their financial support of this undertaking. Thanks to Eric Brandt, my editor at University of Virginia Press, for his belief in and stewardship of this project. Thanks to Evelyn Cohen, Michael Colvin, Jay Deiner, Marc Dolan, Jane Feder, Paul Fisher, Cori Gabbard, Laura Kodet, Jaime Marsanico, Ann Masters, Mark Noonan, David Reynolds, Johannah Rodgers, Stephen Soiffer, Neal Tolchin, and the Baltimore Hellmans for kind encouragement. Thanks to my City Tech students, whose remarkable insights and diversity brought so much to class discussions and helped inspire this work. Thanks to Bill Cain, my Wellesley College thesis adviser, for continued conversation and wisdom almost two decades later. Thanks to my family—Mary and Jo Chamberlin, Dorothy Hellman, Maria Chamberlin-Hellman and Gerard Hellman, and Matthew and Nicole Hellman—for love and constancy. Finally, as this book examines notions of inheritance, I especially wish to acknowledge two writers whose voices helped shape my own: my grandfather, Jo H. Chamberlin, and my mother, Maria Chamberlin-Hellman.

A version of chapter 1 appeared in *Studies in American Culture* (October 2013), and an earlier version of a portion of chapter 4 appeared in *The City Since 9/11: Literature, Film, Television,* edited by Keith Wilhite (Fairleigh Dickinson UP, 2016). I am grateful for permission to reprint.

The Great Gatsby by F. Scott Fitzgerald © 1925 by Charles Scribner's Sons. Copyright renewed 1953 by Frances Scott Fitzgerald Lanahan. Reprinted with the permission of Scribner, a division of Simon & Schuster, Inc. All rights reserved.

The Short Stories of Ernest Hemingway © 1936 by Ernest Hemingway. Copyright renewed 1964 by Mary Hemingway. Reprinted with the permission of Scribner, a division of Simon & Schuster, Inc. All rights reserved

Let the Great World Spin by Colum Mccann © 2009 by Colum Mccann. Used by permission of Random House, an imprint and division of Penguin Random House LLC, and Bloomsbury Publishing PLC. All rights reserved.

The Brief Wondrous Life of Oscar Wao by Junot Diaz © 2007 by Junot Diaz. Used by permission of Riverhead, an imprint of Penguin Publishing Group, a division of Penguin Random House LLC, and Faber and Faber LTD. All rights reserved

Native Speaker by Chang-rae Lee © 1995 by Chang-rae Lee. Used by permission of Riverhead, an imprint of Penguin Publishing Group, a division of Penguin Random House LLC, and Granta Books. All rights reserved.

Unaccustomed Earth by Jhumpa Lahiri © 2008 by Jhumpa Lahiri. Used by permission of Alfred A. Knopf, an imprint of the Knopf Doubleday Publishing Group, a division of Penguin Random House LLC, and Bloomsbury Publishing PLC. All rights reserved.

Between The World and Me by Ta-Nehisi Coates © 2015 by Ta-Nehisi Coates. Used by permission of Spiegel & Grau, an imprint of Random House, a division of Penguin Random House LLC, and Anne Bielby Text Publishing Company. All rights reserved.

CHILDREN OF THE RAVEN AND THE WHALE

Introduction

SEPTEMBER 2017, RAVEN USED BOOKS, Cambridge, Massachusetts. On a bookshelf: F. O. Matthiessen's *American Renaissance: Art and Expression in the Age of Emerson and Whitman*. Signed, First Edition. ~~$45~~. $8.95. "For Charlie and Lee, / Affectionately, / from Matty. May 1941."

Appreciating Matthiessen's inscription from so many moons ago, contemplating the poignant history that existed beyond the page, I paid for the book and brought it home with care. What might have been a routine bookstore visit became a sort of synecdoche for many of the issues associated with this project: the still considerable legacy of an American Renaissance writer, evidenced in the name of the shop; the store's location near Harvard University, where much of the early work establishing the field of American studies took place; and the book's discounted price, reflecting the value more recently assigned to American literary scholarship from this era. *Children of the Raven and the Whale* builds on the foundational contributions of Matthiessen and his contemporaries to posit the existence of a new American Renaissance, expansive in its reach.

During a recent family excursion in Florence, my father and I embarked on a pilgrimage to the Torre Montauto, where Nathaniel Hawthorne wrote *The Marble Faun*. On a gray morning spattered by torrential rain, we ascended into the Florentine hills, past cypress trees, olive groves, villas, and monasteries, the twenty-first century receding with the clamor of the city below. The downpour persisted on our climb up Bellosguardo Hill, where Henry James resided almost thirty years subsequent to the Hawthorne family's occupation of the proximal tower. With few signs and fewer Florentines visible, we continued trudging in what we supposed to be the right direction. Eventually the Torre Montauto rose before us, and our cheers resounded against the hillside.

On the descent, I thought of Hawthorne writing in the tower. I thought of Jhumpa Lahiri, who was profoundly influenced by Hawthorne and who had recently published a contemplation of her own experience of Italy as muse. With my father kindly slogging along beside me, I thought not only of literary ancestors but also of actual ones. The pseudonymous "Virginian Spending July in Vermont" was similarly associative about matters of lineage. "Would that all excellent books were foundlings, without father or mother, that so it might be, we could glorify them, without including their ostensible authors," Herman Melville wrote in "Hawthorne and His Mosses," in the *Literary World* of August 17 and 24, 1850. In his exuberant review of Hawthorne's *Mosses from an Old Manse,* Melville acknowledged that books are not orphans and that authorship is intrinsically derivative. His conception of literary influence rendered familial is also evident in *Moby-Dick,* whose Epilogue concludes with the "devious-cruising Rachel, that in her retracing search after her missing children, only found another orphan" (427).

This book is about literary genealogy, influence, and inheritance. *Children of the Raven and the Whale: Visions and Revisions in American Literature* examines ways in which contemporary ethnic American writers have responded to nineteenth- and early twentieth-century texts historically central to the American literary canon. The title alludes to a classic of American literary criticism, Perry Miller's *The Raven and the Whale: The War of Words and Wits in the Era of Poe and Melville* (1956), which examined disparate visions of the direction of American letters. Each chapter of *Children of the Raven and the Whale* looks down the roads American literature ultimately traveled, examining pairs and constellations of texts in conversation. The presentation of these literary relationships illuminates the widening of the canon; these adoptive family trees reflect the ability of American literature to elide, enlarge and extend, reinterpret, revere or reject, depart from and return to what has come before.

As Miller's title references the two most identifiable and anthropomorphized animals in American literature, the book itself is a metonym for the historical period and literary tradition it explores. Miller invoked the larger-than-life symbols of the raven and the whale not to focus expressly on Poe and Melville but rather to frame the literary culture of a time and place: the periodical, editorial, and publishing networks of mid-nineteenth-century New York. In the event there was any confusion regarding his intentions, the author issued a disclaimer on the first page of his Prologue: "The present book, let me say once and for all, is only incidentally concerned with *Moby-Dick* or even with Herman Melville: it is preoccupied with Melville's America (in several respects the America with which we have still to deal)" (3). The (new) present book is preoccupied with the descendants of Melville's America (in several respects the America with which we have still to deal). The purview of this project is not Poe's and Melville's literary influence, though Poe makes an appearance in the first chapter and Melville is discussed in the last. Like Perry Miller's book, my project concerns literary networks and relationships, the difference being that I examine these legacies across time and ethnic background. How, and why, do the twentieth- and twenty-first-century Korean, Jewish, Dominican, Indian, Dutch Irish, and African American authors discussed here respond to and revise texts long considered American literary classics? In its attention to these intertextual relationships, this project presents a new adoptive family tree for American literature, which future scholars will no doubt expand upon, complicate, and enrich.

To trace these relationships, we must bear in mind the idea that literature is inherently palimpsestic. Prior scholarly studies have sought to restore textual traces. David Reynolds's landmark text *Beneath the American Renaissance,* which examines sensational and reform texts underlying those more celebrated, reveals how popular ideas that permeated the culture and time found expression in more canonical work. The present work looks at the traces of texts by American Renaissance writers such as Walt Whitman, Herman Melville, and Nathaniel Hawthorne, in addition to mid-twentieth-century texts by writers such as F. Scott Fitzgerald, Ernest

Hemingway, Richard Wright, and James Baldwin, lying beneath works of contemporary American literature by Chang-rae Lee, Jonathan Lethem, Jhumpa Lahiri, Junot Diaz, Joseph O'Neill, Colum McCann, and Ta-Nehisi Coates.[1] In their rewriting and layering of new stories over older ones, these writers forge ahead in their interrogation of a spectrum of American experience, whether they or their characters are native to the United States, first- or second- generation immigrants, or transnational.

It should be noted that while the authorial constellations of influence in the following chapters happen to take up earlier white male writers and contemporary more diverse authors, innumerable other combinations and permutations of influence could have been included in this study. In *Literary Inheritance* (1984), Roger Sale writes, "My argument can be simply stated: in recent centuries literary tradition has been made, or unmade, primarily by the relations authors have established with important writers in the immediately preceding generation. Since my aim has been to illustrate rather than to argue this point, and to avoid fighting its battles in favor of suggesting what can be seen when looking from its point of view, I have engaged little in polemics and have not sought to emerge with a theory" (vii). Sale elaborates that some readers may find this to be a disappointing or evasive tactic, but it is an approach with which I concur; this book is by no means an exhaustive study, nor do I mean to suggest that the later works are derivative or that any single pattern of influence is ubiquitous. To offer just a sampling of myriad possible alternatives, a reader of Elizabeth Strout's Pulitzer Prize–winning short story collection *Olive Kitteridge* (2008) might recall Sarah Orne Jewett's similar exploration of small-town Maine denizens in *Deephaven* (1877). Roxane Gay's *Bad Feminist* (2014) and Colson Whitehead's *The Underground Railroad* (2016) are distinctive legacies of Harriet Jacobs's *Incidents in the Life of A Slave Girl* (1861). Maxine Hong Kingston's *Tripmaster Monkey: His Fake Book* (1989) features a protagonist by the name of Wittman Ah Sing. Sherman Alexie's short story collection *Ten Little Indians* (2004) is a nod to Hemingway's "Ten Indians," in the collection *Men Without Women* (1927). In Alexie's story "Flight Patterns," the protagonist, William, speaks to dominant and marginalized cultures in the United States. William "wanted to know all of the great big and tiny little American details. He didn't want to choose between Ernie Hemingway and the Spokane tribal elders, between Mia Hamm and Crazy Horse, between *The Heart Is a Lonely Hunter* and Chief Dan George" (*Ten Little Indians* 102).

Alexie's words are relevant here because the literary constellations featured in the project do not subscribe to this sort of binary, instead considering these stories as a single dialogic narrative.

This book advances several working premises about literary inheritance to inform how we read, write, and teach. First, we must consider literary influence across ethnicity and notions of national tradition. In "A Critique of Pure Pluralism" (1986), Werner Sollors called for American literary history to recognize alternative family trees without the constriction of heredity:

> Do we have to believe in a filiation from Mark Twain to Ernest Hemingway, but not to Ralph Ellison (who is supposedly descended from James Weldon Johnson and Richard Wright)? Can Gertrude Stein be discussed with Richard Wright or only with white women expatriate German-Jewish writers? Is there a link from the autobiography of Benjamin Franklin to those of Frederick Douglass and Mary Antin, or must we see Douglass exclusively as a version of Olaudah Equiano and a precursor to Malcom X? Is Zora Neale Hurston only Alice Walker's foremother? In general, is the question of influence, of who came first, more interesting than the investigation of the constellation in which ideas, styles, themes, and forms travel? (257)

Sollors fleshed out these concepts more thoroughly in his landmark text, *Beyond Ethnicity: Consent and Descent in American Culture* (1986), in which he confronts "the conflict between contractual and hereditary, self-made and ancestral, definitions of American identity—between *consent* and *descent*—as the central drama in American culture. . . . Descent language emphasizes our positions as heirs, our hereditary qualities, liabilities, and entitlements; consent language stresses our abilities as mature free agents and 'architects of our fates' to choose our spouses, our destinies, and our political systems" (5–6). A decade later, in *Was Huck Black? Mark Twain and African-American Voices* (1994), Shelley Fisher Fishkin concurred with Sollors: "With some notable exceptions, scholars of American literature have been curiously reticent about addressing, in all their rich concreteness, the mixed literary bloodlines of American fiction" (27). In the years since Sollors and Fisher Fishkin contributed these contentions, there has been comparatively little scholarship in this area, though the study of multiethnic literature has grown in other directions.[2] *Children of the Raven and the Whale* aims to further the discussion of literary influence outside the confines of descent.

Another significant premise of this book is that the consistent division of the American literary canon by ethnicity or immigration status is not useful. These arbitrary delineations impede conversations between texts and scholars alike, and promote the study of American literature as so many disparate threads instead of a continually unfurling narrative. While multiethnic and immigrant literature designations were crucial for the recognition of a much-belated field of study, continued isolation of these literatures is problematic. As Jhumpa Lahiri noted in a 2013 *New York Times* interview, "I don't know what to make of the term 'immigrant fiction.' . . . If certain books are to be termed immigrant fiction, what do we call the rest? Native fiction? Puritan fiction? This distinction doesn't agree with me. Given the history of the United States, all American fiction could be classified as immigrant fiction. Hawthorne writes about immigrants. So does Willa Cather" ("Jhumpa Lahiri"). The conversations about classification in literature and the arts speak to larger, national conversations about the classification of individuals—and, indeed, about the identity of the United States. Discussing the decrease in Melville's readership during his lifetime, Miller noted that "there are often more complicated reasons for an author's loss of readers. These may have less to do with his voyaging alone into dangerous seas of thought than with confusions within the culture itself: less with his boldly adventuring into heresy than with the nation's distraction over the problem of comprehending its own identity, wherefore it renders itself incapable of telling what is or is not heretical" (4). Miller's comments regarding readership and national identity pertain to the way in which we approach the American literary canon today. As antithetical notions of the American project loom ever larger in a divided national psyche, it is no surprise that U.S. literature suffers similar indignities, including artificial borders (walls) erected between "American" literature and multiethnic or "immigrant" literature. Academic conferences, scholarly journals, and college courses tend to segregate and differentiate these fields. In an era during which many old debates concerning what it means to be American are being reignited, the question of how these beliefs are formed is especially relevant. Literature, as always, is inherently political. Its study is better served by focusing less on the composition of a canon and more on the polemics motivating such debates.

Contemporary writers engage with texts historically central to the American canon in order to actively position their own work as part and parcel of the same tradition. To be clear, this is not a singular tradition; to quote Richard Brodhead, who in turn invokes Richard Chase, "I do not believe that the American novel has (in Richard Chase's words) 'its tradition.' It has a wealth of competing and interpenetrating traditions; no one of these is more American than the others, and no author draws strength from one American vein alone" (viii). As Sollors states in *Beyond Ethnicity*, "Most striking in a great variety of American texts are the persistent attempts to construct a sense of family cohesion in the new world, especially with the help of naturalizing codes and concepts such as 'love' and 'generations'" (6). Sollors's observation about these early texts can be applied to the intertextual relationships discussed here: contemporary authors' responses to older American texts mirror the construction of an adoptive family. Decades or even centuries after the texts to which they are responding were published, these contemporary authors take measure of ideas integral to the American project: democracy, transplantation, exploration, colonization, pluralism, marginalization, destruction, and displacement. As with all parent-child relationships, the younger generation determines its degree of concurrence or dissent, the nature of which leads to a variety of transtextual relationships. As Edwidge Danticat writes in her *New York Times* essay "New York Was Our City On the Hill" (2004), "It is the burden of each generation to embrace or reject the dreams set out by those who came before."

These contemporary multiethnic U.S. literatures are not only a part of the American literary tradition, they form its core. F. O. Matthiessen defined the American Renaissance as the mid-nineteenth-century flowering of a distinctively American literature in which Emerson, Thoreau, Melville, Whitman, and Hawthorne explored the possibilities of democracy and secular humanism. Despite its marked exclusion of women writers and writers of color, Matthiessen's *American Renaissance: Art and Expression in the Age of Emerson and Whitman* (1941) was groundbreaking. In the 1948 collection *Literary History of the United States,* Robert Spiller argued that the second American Renaissance occurred during the modernist period of the 1930s and included authors such as Hemingway, Fitzgerald, Faulkner, Frost, and Dreiser. Spiller's contention never gained much traction and perpetuated the lack of diversity in Matthiessen's text. While working on this book, I was struck by the sense that we have experienced another American Renaissance, dating from the last thirty years of the twentieth century to the first decade of the twenty-first. The term is perhaps even more applicable than in its initial use since these contemporary works actually include revivals of earlier texts. Together, the ethnic American writers discussed here, along with others, have brought about a new American Renaissance whose literature investigates the trajectory of the American self as it negotiates more than one culture, place, and language. Whereas the first canonical American writers were marked by being born in America, the contemporary American Renaissance writers have the freedom of other birthplaces and writing places. In *Global Matters: The Transnational Turn in Literary Studies* (2010), Paul Jay advocates a "global reframing" of the English and American literary tradition. He argues against studying it "through the lens of conventional national histories, guided by the sometimes unconscious assumption that the history of these literatures began with the history of *nations* and with relatively little attention paid to the transnational forces at work in their production" (5). Many of the authors discussed in this study can be, and are, claimed by other countries. Visit bookstores in Dublin, The Hague, and New York, and you will find Joseph O'Neill's work housed respectively in the Irish, Dutch, or American literature corner.

The *New Yorker* issue of June 21 and 28, 1999, titled "The Future of American Fiction," took notice of a pronounced eruption in American literature and featured work by twenty writers under forty, including some I consider here: Lee, Díaz, and Lahiri. The magazine included group photographs of the authors conversing and laughing, interspersed with their work. Viewing the photographs almost twenty years later, one is struck by the youth and diverse ethnicity of the cohort, half of whom are immigrants. The issue was fairly prophetic: the venerable authors featured would go on to win PEN/Hemingway recognition, National Book Awards, American Book Awards, and Pulitzer Prizes.[3] In *The School of Hawthorne* (1986), Richard Brodhead notes that editor, publisher, and critic Evert Duyckink "sought to establish a national literature by building various kinds of institutional support" and, among other strategies, by "bringing American authors into regular association with one another" (54). In 1850 Duyckink arranged one of the most momentous and mythologized meetings in American literary history when he brought Hawthorne and Melville together for a hike up Monument Mountain in the Berkshires. The *New Yorker* photographs document a contemporary iteration of Duyckink's nineteenth-century efforts to bring into relief a national literary culture. In his introduction to the "Future of American Fiction" issue, *New Yorker* editor Bill Buford notes that there is "a certain kind of story being told: the story of becoming American," and observes that many of the writers chronicle stories of immigration to the United States. Cognizant of contemporary writers returning to material that their turn-of-the-century forebears recorded, Buford suggests that "there is an appeal in the symmetry" (68). A distinctive feature of these texts is their addendum to the ideas, characters, and plots evident in the texts that we think of as nation-making, as a way to appraise the nation's progress in racial, ethnic, class, and gender relations, and in the democratic possibility Matthiessen underscored. As such, the new American Renaissance, like the old one, is marked by both embrace and criticism of the American project, channeling the speaker of Langston Hughes's "Let America Be America Again" (1936).

Whether literary influence is overt, in the form of an epigraph or literary allusion, the reappearance of a character or story line, or the adoption of a recognizable genre or form, or covert, found in the echo of language, the invocation of particular themes, or the familiarity of a setting, grasping such intertextual nods enriches a reader's understanding and experience of a text. When a writer revives an earlier author, text, character, form, or language, whether explicitly or implicitly, the nature of the textual relationship, and the resulting metacommentary, are codes for the astute reader to interrogate and decipher. Will the later text echo, challenge, revise, refute, reframe, or resist ideas of the predecessor text? Both identifying an intertextual nod and determining the nature of the intertextual relationship require prior reading. As Hans Robert Jauss argues in *Toward an Aesthetic of Reception* (1982), readers approach a given text with all they have read before; in the background are subconscious processes of memory and association that await ignition, akin to all that Proust's madeleine calls to mind. Jauss deems this subjective experience of a text the "horizon of expectation" (88).[4] As Jauss notes, a predecessor text and later ones participate together in the "continual founding and altering of horizons. The new text evokes for the reader (listener) the horizon of expectations and 'rules of the game' familiar to him from earlier texts, which as such can then be varied, extended, corrected, but also transformed, crossed out, or simply reproduced" (88). What are the consequences of these textual relationships? As Paul de Man writes in his introduction to

Jauss's work, the subjective reception of a text, or horizon of expectation, "complicates, but also enriches, the process of historical description to a considerable degree. A dialectic of understanding as a complex interplay between knowing and not-knowing, is built within the very process of literary history. . . . The individual work becomes part of a landscape against which new works will, in turn, be silhouetted" (xii–xiii). Regarding the dialectical nature of a reader's reception of a text, de Man writes, "Translated from spatial metaphors into epistemological categories, the process can be stated in terms of question and answer: the question occurs as an individual disruption of an answer that has become common knowledge but which, under the effect of this new question, can now be seen to have itself been an individual response to an earlier, collective question" (xiii). This is a useful framework for understanding the stimulation resulting from awareness of intertextuality. The individual, private reception of a text supercedes any notion of a public, collective, or objective understanding. The intertextual relationships considered in this book matter because they take stock of ideas long central to national definition, entreating the reader to consider the nature of U.S. literature past and present, as well as of the United States itself. Insofar as its contemporary authors span nations and cultures, the national literature is ultimately one without national boundaries.

As critics have devoted ample thought to theories of literary influence and intertextuality, the definitions and applications of these terms have evolved.[5] Some theorists and historians use them interchangeably, while others posit influence as one-directional transmission and intertextuality as a more neutral, dialogic conception of textual production. Influence, in particular, finds broad definition and application. As Robert Douglas-Fairhurst notes in *Victorian Afterlives* (2009), "Its applications include the impact of climate, locale, historical events, literary movements and conventions, social and cultural traditions, and individual writers or works; its forms include borrowings, forgeries, debts, and literary aftermaths, side-effects, and residues of many other kinds" (3). Perhaps the most notorious work in the field is Harold Bloom's *The Anxiety of Influence* (1973), which examines the burden of literary precursors and the various ways in which writers may transcend it or succumb to its pressures. In *The Anxiety of Influence* and its sequel, *A Map of Misreading* (1975), Bloom posits the existence of six different revisionary ratios (relationships) a later text may possess with an earlier one. He applies these ratios to the work of British and American poets. Bloom's reading of later authors inhibited by the anxiety surrounding perceived master texts or urtexts encountered considerable resistance to its psychoanalytical approach and restriction to male writers.[6] The study of literary influence was out of vogue for some time, in part owing to perceived paternalist or imperialist presumptions with regard to issues of race and gender. In recent years, intertextuality has replaced influence in some discussions of literary transmission. Influence supposes conscious borrowing from a master author, dominant source text, or tradition, whereas intertextuality is less concerned with hierarchies of textual relations. In their edited collection, *Influence and Intertextuality in Literary History* (1991), Eric Rothstein and Jay Clayton note, "One may see intertextuality either as the enlargement of a familiar idea or as an entirely new concept to replace the outmoded notion of influence. . . . Intertextuality might be used to oust and replace the kinds of issues that influence addresses, and in particular its central concern with the author and more or less conscious authorial intentions and skills" (3).

Yet it is possible to examine issues of influence and intertextuality through a less defensive lens.[7] For more egalitarian frameworks, we can turn not only to more recent models of scholarship on intertextuality but also to its early theorization. Julia Kristeva, who introduced the term "intertextuality" in *Semeiotike* (1969), explicates it as "a mosaic of quotations; any text is the absorption and transformation of another. The notion of intertextuality replaces that of intersubjectivity, and poetic language is read as at least double" (85).[8] Kristeva's positioning of intertextuality as the dialogic space of texts is a less combative, more productive model for exploring textual transmission. Gerard Genette's *Palimpsests: Literature in the Second Degree* (1982) takes up this subject exclusively to expound the many possible ways in which a text relates to its predecessors. He posits five subcategories of transtextuality: intertextuality (allusion, plagiarism, quotation), paratextuality (titles, headings, prefaces, footnotes), architextuality (genre), metatextuality (implicit or explicit response to another text), and hyper-/hypotextuality (transformation or modification of another text). These categories are not exclusive and often overlap in a single given text. Though his terminology is at times abstruse,

Genette's work inspired further consideration of the conceivable types of intertextual relationships.

My study builds on several works that apply theories of intertextuality. Like other prior texts that examine issues of literary influence and inheritance, this project focuses on the "mosaic," the networks of textual relations, not on anxiety or inhibition but on inspiration drawn from textual transmission. While most work on literary influence concerns British literature (in particular, the Romantic poets, with a few stray American writers (often expatriates such as James or Eliot) thrown in for good measure), there is also a burgeoning body of work on American literary influence.[9] Richard Brodhead's *The School of Hawthorne* offers a classic model of examining authorial influence. Especially useful has been the work of David Cowart, whose scholarship sheds light on the varied and vast filial relations Sollors urges American literary criticism to acknowledge. In *Literary Symbiosis: The Reconfigured Text in Twentieth-Century Writing* (1993), Cowart examines the ways in which postmodern fiction, drama, and poetry texts are explicitly attached to source texts. He notes that this investigation uncovers how "contemporary writers engage in a kind of 'epistemic' dialogue with the past, meanwhile forcing readers into a recognition of the historical or diachronic differences between the voice of one literary age and that of another" (1), as well as how these relationships are mutually beneficial. He concludes that all literary production entails reproduction, which does not necessitate burden or anxiety but effects renewal. Cowart's *Trailing Clouds: Immigrant Fiction in Contemporary America* (2006) is a multiethnic study that defines literary immigrant generations and enumerates features of immigrant fiction. The author notes his resistance to organizing his project by the ethnicity or national background of writers, and underscores the number of immigrant writers at the forefront of American literature today. The concept of filiation is one Cowart takes up further in his latest work, *The Tribe of Pyn: Literary Generations in the Postmodern Period* (2015), which compares how writers born in the mid-twentieth century work both within and outside the earlier postmodern tradition.[10] Bonnie TuSmith's groundbreaking *All My Relatives: Community in Contemporary Ethnic American Literatures* (1993) is an excellent early model of a cross-ethnic study. TuSmith is interested in notions of ethnic family and community both within and across ethnic groups, and refutes the idea that American literature is defined by a tradition of individualism. "It is rarely the case," she writes, "that a people exist in isolation without outside influences. . . . Writers who identify themselves with a nonwhite culture in America are necessarily engaged in some form of cross-cultural debate" (15). A relevant, more recent insightful study is Cyrus Patell's *Emergent U.S. Literatures: From Multiculturalism to Cosmopolitanism in the Late Twentieth Century* (2014), which historicizes the marginalization of Native American, Asian American, Hispanic American, and gay and lesbian American literature. Patell employs Raymond Williams's theory of dominant, residual, and emergent cultural forms to establish a dialog between foundational texts that have dominated the canon and emergent (what Williams defines as "new meanings and values, new practices, new relationships and kinds of relationships . . . continually being created") literatures (qtd. in Patell 4). Patell explains, "An emergent literature is therefore the literary expression of a cultural group that defines itself either as an alternate to or in direct opposition to a dominant mainstream. What makes the literature emergent is the fact that it portrays beliefs and practices that are taken to be new by the dominant culture, though in some cases they may in fact be thousands of years old" (5). His argument is useful to understanding the segregative practices that affect not only the American literary canon but also entire swaths of cultural identity in the United States. While each of these studies serves as an informative archetype, illuminating explorations of literary influence as well as the place of immigrant fiction in the American literary canon, my book differs in its convocation of multiethnic literature of the United States and earlier canonical texts, combating the scholarly tendency to isolate them in unique fields.

Although this is not a book about canon formation per se, writing about twentieth- and twenty-first-century authors returning to texts that formed the foundation of the American literary canon asks for a consideration of some of the works of literary criticism that positioned them there. Just as the writers discussed here felt compelled to respond to texts considered foundational to American literature, I found it equally compelling to reread foundational texts of American literary criticism, as they testify to the politics, tensions, and general evolution of the field.[11] In *F. O. Matthiessen and the Politics of Criticism* (1988), William Cain writes, "Matthiessen's choices in *American Renaissance,* it seems plain, were undemocratic. But though we are being more inclusive as editors, anthologists, and teachers, we may not be doing a better, more disciplined and exacting job in working for democracy than he did" (206). Cain contemplates what we can learn from the history of literary criticism, as well as the need for connection between politics, scholarship, and teaching. In the decades since Cain's study, impressive work has been done in this realm, with scholars recovering, teaching, and writing about lost or lesser-known works by women and minority authors. But the result of atoning for past deficiencies can be overly corrective in that it can promote the complete denigration or dismissal of earlier work (both the literature itself and its literary criticism) instead of including its important tenets in the conversation. As Sollors writes in "A Critique of Pure Pluralism," "In this scholarly drama of diversity and pluralism versus traditionalism and prejudice there is emotion and prophecy just as there are heroes and villains" (251). Here he underscores the limitations that result from this flawed oppositional relationship.

My teaching at New York City College of Technology within the City University of New York system has offered me unique opportunities to deconstruct this idea and investigate seemingly incongruous texts within the same space and conversation. Our college's annual Literary Arts Festival, which has featured writers such as Colson Whitehead, Junot Díaz, Willie Perdomo, Sapphire, Dinaw Mengestu, and José Olivarez, among others, influenced my syllabi and my thinking. I began folding the authors' works into American literature surveys and subsequently developed courses that featured constellations or pairs of writers responding to the ideas of earlier ones. Throughout this process, my City Tech students were not passive recipients of knowledge but active contributors to this endeavor. At an institution where it is common to have twenty nationalities in a single classroom, our conversations regarding American identity and experience, transnationalism, and what constitutes immigrant fiction were especially rich. In a class discussion of Junot Díaz's *The Brief Wondrous Life of Oscar Wao* (2007), a Dominican American student educated classmates about the importance of the Mirabal sisters and shared anecdotes from a youth spent in a house near the National Palace, once occupied by Generalissimo Rafael Leónidas Trujillo. In a class discussion of Edwidge Danticat's *Brother, I'm Dying* (2007), several Haitian students shared their experience of the devastating 2010 earthquake, which had set in motion their emigration to the United States and enrollment at CUNY. Class discussions of Ta-Nehisi Coates's *Between the World and Me* (2015) led to fruitful exchanges among African American, Muslim, and nonbinary students about counteracting different forms of bias. A discussion of transplantation in Nathaniel Hawthorne's *The Scarlet Letter* (1850) and Jhumpa Lahiri's *Unaccustomed Earth* (2008) led a Russian American student to acquire a beet tattoo, roots and all, which she explained represented the connections between her two worlds.

I have realized that what lies beneath my literary scholarship is CUNY itself, whose diverse student body has transformed my ideas and indeed my career. While my doctorate in English equipped me to write about these texts, my teaching at CUNY has equipped me to listen to and learn from my students, to recognize what each brings to the classroom and what I cannot. Just as the textual constellations illustrate cultural debates and national limitations, teaching these texts illustrates my own limitations as a professor. While I introduced students to these works and informed their reading with literary context, students brought a vast spectrum of cultural knowledge into the classroom, enabling a far richer understanding of these texts. The City Tech attendance rosters make me recall a passage from Chang-rae Lee's novel *Native Speaker* (1995), in which Leila pronounces her students' names "each one as best as she can, taking care of every last pitch and accent . . . speaking a dozen lovely and native languages, calling all the difficult names of who we are" (349). It is one thing to talk about the value of diversity but another to have global representation in a single classroom. This book is ultimately a testament to my students, and the truth that literature, and indeed higher education, do not simply concern texts or pedagogy but also what is learned in their interstices, at the times one least expects a worldview to be altered.

Today we are almost two hundred years past Emerson's call for a distinctive American literature in his address, "The American Scholar" (1837). "Each age," Emerson writes, "it is found, must write its own books; or rather, each generation for the next succeeding. The books of an older period will not fit this." Of equal importance is Frederick Douglass's 1859 speech "Self-Made Men," in which he interrogates this concept. He defines self-made men as those "who are not brought up but who are obliged to come up, not only without the voluntary assistance or friendly co-operation of society, but often in open and derisive defiance of all the efforts of society and the tendency of circumstances to repress, retard and keep them down. . . . They are in a peculiar sense, indebted to themselves for themselves" (38). Douglass makes the crucial point that class and race have much to do with the probability of distinction. "We have all either begged, borrowed or stolen. We have reaped where others have sown, and that which others have strown, we have gathered. It must in truth be said, though it may not accord well with self-conscious individuality and self-conceit, that no possible native force of character, and no depth of wealth and originality, can lift a man into absolute independence of his fellowmen, and no generation of men can be independent of the preceding generation," he asserts (37). The debts that Douglass acknowledged can be applied to our understanding of literary inheritance.

Today we have a much broader definition of what constitutes American letters, with a canon that reflects the turn toward the transnational. In *Through Other Continents: American Literature across Deep Time* (2006), an illuminating study of American literature and global exchange, Wai Chee Dimock writes, "For too long, American literature has been seen as a world apart, sufficient unto itself, not burdened by the chronology and geography outside the nation, and not making any intellectual demands on that score. . . . Rather than being a discrete entity, [American literature] is better seen as a crisscrossing set of pathways, open-ended and ever multiplying, weaving in and out of other geographies, other languages and cultures" (2–3). Dimock proposes looking beyond territorial borders, nation-states, and time periods to see "planetary" cross-pollination and circulation of ideas. These connections are important as well; I do not believe one has to choose between studying national or global influence, as both are instructive. It is time to recognize the dialog between the texts that once defined the canon and the texts that currently shape it. I hope that this book will appeal to scholars of all facets of American literature, undergraduate and graduate students grasping connections between texts across eras, ethnicities, and literary movements, as well as a broad readership intrigued by the voices lying beneath contemporary texts and interested in the present impact of the works of long-admired writers from the past.

The chapters that follow explore unique taxonomies of influence. Some of these intertextual relationships are overt, while others are more subtle. Chapter 1, "'A Walker in the City': Chang-rae Lee's *Native Speaker*, Jonathan Lethem's *Motherless Brooklyn,* and Walt Whitman's Cartographic Legacy," considers the influence of Whitman's *Leaves of Grass.* The chapter examines how Whitman's perambulation of nineteenth-century New York is recreated as voyeuristic in two twentieth-century American texts. At the same time that *Motherless Brooklyn* and *Native Speaker* map late twentieth-century Brooklyn and Manhattan, respectively, each work recalls Whitman's "I Hear America Singing" and "Crossing Brooklyn Ferry" in celebrating the sights and sounds of New York thoroughfares, experimenting with language, and featuring shapeshifting, quintessentially American narrators. Lethem and Lee return to Whitman's interest in a spectrum of American identity in order to historicize difference as native.

Chapter 2, "Literary Custom House: Nathaniel Hawthorne's *The Scarlet Letter* and Jhumpa Lahiri's *Unaccustomed Earth*," appraises Lahiri's appropriation of Hawthorne's language in "The Custom-House" chapter to address the promises and challenges of immigration, diaspora, and generational difference in her collection of short stories, many of which address literal and metaphorical acts of transplant. The author's invocation of Hawthorne illuminates characters' navigations of the tensions between transcendentalist ideas of self-reliance and familial tradition. Lahiri's concurrence with Hawthorne positions the immigrant experience as inherently, historically American.

Chapter 3, "Short Happy Palimpsest: Ernest Hemingway's 'The Short Happy Life of Francis Macomber' and Junot Díaz's *The Brief Wondrous Life of Oscar Wao*," examines Díaz's addition of ethnicity to the crisis of identity and masculinity in Hemingway's story. Díaz's nod to Hemingway is fairly overt: two adjectives precede a life and a name. The biographical subjects of both works experience happiness only briefly, and rather desperately, before meeting their respective ends. This chapter proposes a new intertextual relationship, that of literary colonialism, in which an author responds to occupation of the canon—the idea of the white American canon as the colonizing force whose space must be reclaimed. In giving voice to the marginalized and displaced, Díaz combats Hemingway's tale of violence and humiliation.

Chapter 4, "New York Unearthed: Excavating the Works of Washington Irving, Walt Whitman, and F. Scott Fitzgerald in Colum McCann's *Let the Great World Spin* and Joseph O'Neill's *Netherland*," examines the ways in which McCann and O'Neill unearth New York cultural and literary strata to come to terms with the tragedy of 9/11. *Let the Great World Spin* (2009) pays homage to the poetry of Walt Whitman and the prose of F. Scott Fitzgerald's *The Great Gatsby* (1925), while *Netherland* (2008) takes up the legacy of Washington Irving's *A History of New York* (1809) and revisions *Gatsby* with multiethnic characters and a transnational plot. While both contemporary

novels nostalgize earlier New York literature, McCann uses intertextuality to offer a calming counternarrative to recent trauma, whereas O'Neill
illuminates extant iterations of a time, place, and ideology thought to be
long extinct.

While the aforementioned chapters plumb contemporary fictional
responses to canonical works, chapter 5 examines the presence of such
texts in two contemporary memoirs. In the same way we consider the
stories that fiction tells us about ourselves and about our country, we can
apply these considerations to nonfiction. Chapter 5, "Black Boys and White
Whales: Ta-Nehisi Coates's Conversations with Herman Melville, Richard
Wright, and James Baldwin," combines a discussion of more expected literary influences with one that is less so. Coates's *Between the World and Me,* a
letter to his son about race relations in the United States, has been deemed
the twenty-first-century equivalent to James Baldwin's *The Fire Next Time*
(1963), in which Baldwin tackles the same topic in a letter to his nephew
James. Baldwin is not the only literary predecessor Coates enfolds; the title
alludes to Richard Wright's poem of the same name. The chapter examines
how Coates invokes the work of Baldwin and Wright to reiterate their prescience some fifty years later and reflect on a traumatic history that has
not been fully acknowledged or overcome. The chapter also establishes a
connection between Coates's insights into the nineteenth-century existential threat to the white whale and twenty-first-century race relations. In
considering Coates's conversations with Melville, Baldwin, and Wright, the
assessment plumbs issues of race, masculinity, paternity, and inheritance.

This book argues for the study of American literature as a diachronic whole
rather than a series of discordant fragments. In fact, this conception has
found expression in other spheres. In a 2014 *New Yorker* interview with
David Remnick, President Obama noted,

> I think we are born into this world and inherit all the grudges and rivalries
> and hatreds and sins of the past. But we also inherit the beauty and the
> joy and goodness of our forebears. And we're on this planet a pretty short
> time, so that we cannot remake the world entirely during this little stretch
> that we have. . . . But I think our decisions matter. And I think America was
> very lucky that Abraham Lincoln was President when he was President. If he

hadn't been, the course of history would be very different. But I also think that, despite being the greatest President, in my mind, in our history, it took another hundred and fifty years before African-Americans had anything approaching formal equality, much less real equality. I think that doesn't diminish Lincoln's achievements, but it acknowledges that, at the end of the day, we're part of a long-running story. We just try to get our paragraph right. ("Ten Days in June")

This notion of a continual story reflects a unified approach to the canon and rejects the historical fallacy of deciding which peoples, texts, and histories find inclusion. Ultimately, in its argument for the acknowledgment of a third American Renaissance, *Children of the Raven and the Whale* suggests a restructuring of what, historically, has been considered to be the center versus the periphery.[12] Even as contemporary writers return to foundational texts, they resituate and rewrite these ideas to reflect new residents, new cultures, and new territories. This is not a privileging of a dominant past but a claim and an amendment to it. In American literature—indeed, American life—there is, in fact, no central culture, author, or text but dialog and dissent, a succession of paragraphs, an ever-evolving "long-running story."

1

"A Walker in the City"

Chang-rae Lee's *Native Speaker,* Jonathan
Lethem's *Motherless Brooklyn,* and Walt
Whitman's Cartographic Legacy

Manhattan's streets I saunter'd pondering,
On Time, Space, Reality—on such as these, and abreast with them Prudence.
—Walt Whitman, "Song of Prudence" (1881)

WHITMAN'S TEMPORAL, GEOGRAPHIC, AND ontological contemplations
in these lines from "Song of Prudence" suggest that despite his speaker's
assertions in "Crossing Brooklyn Ferry" (1860) that time, place, and distance avail not, the poet was still thinking through these conceits years
later. To conceive of a self wholly independent of time and place is a fallacy; after all, as Lionel Essrog tells us in the first line of Jonathan Lethem's
Motherless Brooklyn (1999), "Context is everything" (1). Whitman's contention in "Crossing Brooklyn Ferry" that neither time nor distance divides his
speaker from future generations is contingent on a self who exists relative
to others, through geographic alliance ("I was Manhattanese, friendly and
proud!" [line 81]), physicality ("I too had receiv'd identity by my Body; /
That I was, I knew was of my Body—and what I should be, I knew I should
be of my body" [lines 66–67]), and identity ("I was call'd by my highest name

by clear loud voices" [line 82]). Though geography and temporality are hero-
ically dismissed as nondeterminative factors, they contribute significantly
to the speaker's self-portrait, for it is in the streets that he locates himself.
Through these Manhattan peregrinations "among crowds of people" and
in his "walks home late at night" (line 64), the poet feels "the abrupt ques-
tionings stir within [him]" (line 63). He is able to decipher answers about
existence and articulate hierarchies of value by distinguishing himself from
the crowd; through social and positional relation he combats the nightmare
of a wandering indeterminate self, "blank and suspicious" (line 70). The
title of this chapter alludes to Alfred Kazin's memoir *A Walker in the City*
(1951). Kazin himself invokes Whitman in an epigraph culled from "Crossing Brooklyn Ferry": "The glories strung like beads on my smallest sights
and hearings—on the walk in the street, and the passage over the river"
(line 9). The lines Kazin invokes focus on the composite portrait created by
successive visual and aural vignettes in the street.

Whitman reveled in the idea that he did not travel alone, that in his
day he was one among many who crossed Brooklyn Ferry, and that many
more would cross in his wake. I am interested in the literary wake, as it
were: how Whitman's nineteenth-century words concerning the elucidation of subjectivity through walking in New York resonate in two
twentieth-century American texts, Jonathan Lethem's *Motherless Brooklyn* and Chang-rae Lee's *Native Speaker* (1996).[1] Lee identifies himself as
one of Whitman's progeny immediately in *Native Speaker* with an epigraph
from "The Sleepers." Lethem, too, acknowledges Whitman's influence; in
an interview, he declared Whitman one of the greatest New Yorkers. Even
as *Motherless Brooklyn* and *Native Speaker* map late twentieth-century
Brooklyn and Manhattan, respectively, each text recalls Whitman's "I Hear
America Singing" and "Crossing Brooklyn Ferry" in its navigation of New
York streets, its experimentation with language, and the serial identities
of its protagonists.

Mapping the Fictional and Geographic Family Tree

Lethem's decision to set his book in downtown Brooklyn in the waterfront
neighborhoods that attracted Whitman in the nineteenth century and
authors ranging from Hubert Selby to Arthur Miller in the early twentieth

century demonstrates that literary inheritance extends to geography, history, and intangible culture: the writer burning the midnight oil in the office of the *Brooklyn Daily Eagle,* the briny air around the water, the shouts of the dockworkers. Like other Brooklyn texts, such as Betty Smith's *A Tree Grows in Brooklyn* (1943) and Arthur Miller's *A View from the Bridge* (1956), *Motherless Brooklyn* concerns itself with absent parents. The novel features four orphaned boys who are removed from the trials of a group home by Frank Minna, a mysterious Brooklyn character who ultimately employs the group at his car service, a front for a sort of private investigation firm. Frank Minna cavalierly informs the ragtag group of orphans that he "probably know[s] all your parents, if you think about it" (66). The protagonist and narrator, Lionel Essrog, then tells the reader, "So it was, with this casual jaunt . . . that Minna appeared to announce what we already half suspected—that it was not only his life that was laced with structures of meaning but our own, that these master plots were transparent to him and that he held the power to reveal them, that he did know our parents and at any moment might present them to us" (67). Yet in the first pages of the novel, Minna is murdered, his would-be children left to solve the crime and in the process write their autobiographies. That the main characters of the novel are orphans in a borough puzzling over its own heritage and identity is not an accident. As James Peacock notes, "The eruptive fragments of the past are comforting to Lionel as an orphan. . . . In trading incessantly between past and present, between myth and fact, Brooklyn allows a glimpse of those longed-for connections" (77). Who are Brooklyn's native sons—and what is their parentage? As Evan Hughes notes in *Literary Brooklyn,* "If you're a writer . . . you know that there's an American mythology about the borough, suffused with nostalgia though it may be . . . that newcomers in thrall to the American idea have come through Brooklyn for generations, perhaps including your own parents or grandparents—up to a quarter of all Americans can trace their family tree through Brooklyn" (275). How are the literary voices of Brooklyn inherited and transformed across a century and many generations? Lethem dedicates *Motherless Brooklyn* to his father; in the literary family tree, that figure is Whitman.

Though Whitman is a clear literary forebear for Lethem, Lethem's fictional characters exhibit anxiety regarding issues of origin and heritage. This uncertainty results in many characters, including the protagonist,

Lionel Essrog, constructing multiple selves. For Whitman's speaker and *Motherless Brooklyn*'s narrator, the parent is the borough itself. This is tantamount to Whitman's vision of nation: strangers rendered blood brothers through the mere fact of residence and citizenship. Whitman's guardian is found in the streets, shops, ships, and sights that love and welcome him. Lionel finds his most reliable routine in ordering sandwiches at the neighborhood deli, on an account in Frank's name. Lionel attempts to locate his lineage, calling various Essrogs every so often without identifying himself beyond his verbal tics, yearning for his audience's acknowledgment. The ultimate betrayals in *Motherless Brooklyn* are familial—brotherly, to be specific. Gerard betrays Frank, Tony betrays Frank, Tony betrays Lionel. The existential anxiety surrounding ancestry also manifests itself in the characters' dubious occupations (inherited from Frank Minna, surrogate father) as private investigators/double agents.

The attention to inheritance is not only familial but also occupational. Prior to *Motherless Brooklyn*, the evolutions of the Brooklyn waterfront were represented in literature. Fiction, nonfiction, and drama depicted the transition of the port from working to nonworking and from sail to steam; water as a means to exit, a ticket to see the world beyond the borough and a way to progress from the working class to the middle class; and the role of the water in exhibiting class, racial, and ethnic strife. New York's literature testifies to the complex history of residence and displacement, affirming tension between natives and immigrants and the more diffusive, international history of its waterfront and port. This tension between the domestic and the diasporic finds expression in ideas of containment—and containerization: what is contained in a community dually known for its residentiality and its participation in work that extends beyond its borders? Phillip Lopate writes in *Waterfront: A Walk around Manhattan* (2004), "We can expect the waterfront to remain for decades an unresolved zone, in which polished sections and decrepit shards of the old industrial port coexist in an unsettling or perversely pleasing disharmony" (400). As the waterfront is unresolved, so too are the destinies of the men who in an earlier era would have been dockworkers or deckhands. The mystery Lethem poses in *Motherless Brooklyn* extends beyond Minna's murder to the history of work and masculinity in the borough and its unsure future. The work of the Minna Men, or private investigators, consists of surveillance: watching others work and feigning legitimate, legal work themselves.

While Whitman ponders the Brooklyn-Manhattan commute in "Crossing Brooklyn Ferry," a work originally titled "Sun-Down Poem," as it testifies to the workday routine, the denizens of *Motherless Brooklyn* require no commute. "On the ferry-boats, the hundreds and hundreds that cross, returning home" (line 4), Whitman writes. Late nineteenth-century and early twentieth-century Brooklyn waterfront jobs are thus replaced by work as masquerade, a front for amorphous assignments and makeshift jobs shadowed by corruption.

Mapping Language, Identity, and Occupation

Lethem also conjures Whitman in the protagonist's experimentation with language, though in a framework of disability. In his experiment with language, Lethem deploys two forms of Genette's transtextuality: architextuality, an extratextual association made clear through the text's relationship to its genre, and hypertextuality, in which "text B [is] not speaking of text A at all but being unable to exist, as such, without A . . . which it consequently evokes more or less perceptibly without necessarily speaking of it or citing it" (5). Whitman's catalogs of people and sights manifest as verbal compulsions, in a late twentieth-century interpretation of exchange between the world of the mind and the world outside. As Lionel explains, "Assertions and generalizations are, of course, a version of Tourette's. A way of touching the world, handling it, covering it with confirming language" (307). Whitman's poetry and Lionel Essrog's verbal tics are both methods of comprehending, explicating, and attempting to control the exterior environment. Whitman's experimentation comes in the form of free verse, while Lethem's arrives in the verbal tics of his narrator. The tics are a version of free verse, varied in meter, recreating rhythms, and mimicking the cadences of natural speech in the invention of words. After comparing Gerard Minna to Brando in both *Apocalypse Now!* and, jauntily, *On the Waterfront,* Lionel tics "Thehorrorthehorror" and "Icouldabeenacontender," then affirms, "It was like a couplet" (229). One character tells Lionel that he has an "utterance problem"; Lionel's tics, like Whitman's lines, break with conventional speech patterns.

Both the speakers of "I Hear America Singing" and "Crossing Brooklyn Ferry" and the narrator of *Motherless Brooklyn* are large, containing multitudes. Lionel tells the reader: "I'm a carnival barker, an auctioneer, a downtown performance artist, a speaker in tongues, a senator drunk on filibuster. I've got Tourette's" (1). Bennett Kravitz underscores the importance of language to these occupations, writing that "all of these social functions rely on language to reach fruition, though most of them function in the realm of linguistic distortion" (174).[2] Though Barnum was Whitman's contemporary, the carnival, the circus, the hoaxes and the funhouse mirrors also resonate with Lethem. The man who does Gerard Minna's corrupt bidding is a giant. One of Lionel's tics is "barnamum," and he is routinely called "freakshow" by his compatriots, conjuring Coney Island's famed boardwalk attraction Shoot the Freak. The characters populating *Motherless Brooklyn* represent the lowbrow cultures that fascinated Whitman. And while Whitman celebrates the diversity of everyman by adopting alternative personas, Lethem introduces the question of narrative reliability if the self undergoes constant change. Another way to read Lionel's serial identities is through Whitman's lens. In "I Hear America Singing," Whitman is the mechanic, the carpenter, the mason, the boatman, the shoemaker, the woodcutter. Lethem offers analogous catalogs of occupations and of humanity. Lionel tells us, "My life story to this point: The teacher looked at me like I was crazy. The social services worker looked at me like I was crazy. The boy looked at me like I was crazy and then hit me. The girl looked at me like I was crazy. The woman looked at me like I was crazy. The black homicide detective looked at me like I was crazy" (107). Here, however, it is inverse Whitman: the spectrum of humanity dismissing the subject instead of the subject embracing the spectrum of humanity.

Mapping the City and the Self

Long before geospatial tagging, people attempted to locate themselves in time and space, participating in ambulatory pilgrimages more oriented toward self-discovery than toward indices of longitude and latitude.[3] Henry David Thoreau tells us in his essay "Walking" (1862) that it is an autobiographical act: whether one nostalgically traces steps already taken or discovers novel sights or sites, walking is a tourism of the self, visiting it in different places. This cartographic impulse travels beyond physical location to psychological associations with the past, present, and even the potential future. Thoreau's peregrinations around Concord present him with natural vistas devoid of human inhabitants and public property that offers the walker boundless freedom as he contemplates his own movement through space and time. In language that echoes the value Whitman accords walking, Thoreau writes, "I have met with about one or two persons in the course of my life who understood the art of Walking, that is, of taking walks,—who had a genius, so to speak, for *sauntering*." He goes on to explain that saunter is derived from Sainte-Terrer, pilgrims on their way to the Holy Land, but that some "would derive the word from *sans terre*, without land or home, which, therefore, in the good sense, will mean, having no particular home but equally at home everywhere" (632). To saunter is to move slowly, deliberating on not only the destination but also the journey. This comfort in vagrancy is noticeably absent from *Native Speaker* and *Motherless Brooklyn*, whose respective protagonists are comfortable neither with their anchors nor with their sails. Their walks are motivated by grief, loss, and unease with their current life stations, which entail suspect careers and failed loves.

Walking was central to Whitman's work as a writer and editor. In his cultural biography of the poet, David S. Reynolds chronicles Whitman's day. He "typically wrote editorials in the morning, took a walk after sending them to the composing room, and read proofs upon his return. After work in midafternoon he perambulated Brooklyn or took the ferry to Manhattan for entertainment or to see the city sights, walking sometimes with literary types like the *Evening Post* editor William Cullen Bryant" (114). Walking was a democratic means of transportation that entailed encounters with people from all walks of life. Exposure to individuals, sights, and sounds not necessarily gleaned from other methods of transport nourished Whitman's work.

Just as Kazin described the process of memory salvation in *A Walker in the City,* chronicling his returns to his Brownsville, Brooklyn, neighborhood in order to recall the sights, sounds, and smells of his Jewish youth, Lethem walks his protagonist around the city for purposes of narrative recovery. It is in navigating the Brooklyn streets that Lionel is most at home. *Motherless Brooklyn* begins outside the borough, outside a Zendo on Manhattan's Upper East Side, which is presented as foreign territory. The exoticization of the Zendo foreshadows the suspect dealings of the enigmatic Fukisaki corporation, which attempts to control New York's most valuable commodity, its real estate. As Lionel tells the reader, "Here on the Upper East Side we were off our customary map" (3). He and Gilbert bicker and helplessly munch hamburgers as Frank disappears inside the building and is then kidnapped. Lethem juxtaposes the Zendo with the prototypically American food, a cross-cultural junction common in New York. As Rebecca Solnit observes in an essay about perambulating San Francisco, "Just as a bookshelf can jam together Japanese poetry, Mexican history, and Russian novels, so the buildings of my city contained Zen centers, Pentecostal churches, tattoo parlors, produce stores, burrito places, movie palaces, dim sum shops" (171). In the car chase that ensues, Lionel and Gilbert attempt to decipher coded exchanges over the wire but become successful cryptographers only when they exit Manhattan territory. They sail across the Pulaski Bridge, "into the mouth of Brooklyn" (20), where narrative recovery and Lionel's autobiographical quest begin.

This Brooklyn may not be Whitman's mast-hemm'd, thronged locus of commerce and vitality, but even so, Lethem conveys the characters' appreciation of the landscape in their celebration of the streets. Just as Whitman revels in the quotidian excursion and sees "many I loved in the street, or ferry-boat, or public assembly, yet never told them a word" (line 84), the last advice that Lionel gives the reader is to "tell your story walking" (311).[4] We are given a veritable street map of downtown Brooklyn, weaving through Smith, Warren, Bergen, Montague, Hoyt, Joralemon, Court, and Schermerhorn Streets. Though the neighborhood is dotted with underground dealings, the Minna Men are not afraid, even in the shadow of crime and death, even in the shapeless, shadowy modernity that has replaced the workday routines of the waterfront. Familiarity constitutes home; the mapping of the streets injects narrative authority and therefore credible subjectivity.[5]

In *A Walker in the City*, Kazin endeavors to speak for a generation of Brownsville residents, rather than himself. However, the *New York Times* reviewer seemed to miss the indefinite article of the title and the intentional evasion of singular experience. Critic Orville Prescott wrote, "Although *A Walker in the City* is exceedingly well written for the most part, sensitive and perceptive throughout, it is vague and elusive in its impact. Mr. Kazin has cited numerous specific details, but he nevertheless conveys an abstract and generalized impression. . . . There are few anecdotes about particular events. . . . Mr. Kazin doesn't even convey a clear idea about what kind of little boy he was himself, beyond his conscientious industry, his passion for books and his powers of observation and memory." Kazin's memoir offers both a self-portrait and a portrait of the masses. Similarly, the portrait Lethem paints of his protagonist is cumulative, encompassing all the streets and landmarks en route, and collective, including all the people encountered along the way. The portrait is of the character and his surroundings, seemingly accessible to all on foot but in fact exclusive to the protagonist in his knowledge, ritual, and routine. The idea of chronicling this travel is almost antiquated and departs from texts that render invisible characters' transitions from place to place. The urban condition is conceived quite differently in *Motherless Brooklyn;* the borough is portrayed as a rough inner city loaded with racial antipathy and the uneasy coexistence of a spectrum of ethnicities and religions. As Solnit argues, walking around such an area is unique: "Urban walking has always been a shadier business, easily turning into soliciting, cruising, promenading, shopping, rioting, protesting, skulking, loitering, and other activities that, however enjoyable, hardly have the high moral tone of nature appreciation" (174).

New York's physical structure influences the linguistic structure of the novel. The distinction between the defunct Brooklyn waterfront and the functional one in Maine is characterized in terms of both language and architecture. Lethem conveys Lionel's distance from the New York streets as a separation anxiety. In a variation on Whitman's joyous greeting in "Crossing Brooklyn Ferry," "Flood-tide below me! I watch you face to face" (line 1), Lionel gazes down at the rocky coast of Maine, confessing,

> I was off the page now, away from the grammar of skyscrapers and pavement. I experienced it precisely as a loss of language, a great sucking-away of the word-laden walls that I needed around me, that I touched everywhere, leaned on for support, cribbed from when I ticked aloud. Those walls of language had always been in place, I understood now, audible to me until the sky in Maine deafened them with a shout of silence. I staggered, put one hand on the rocks to steady myself. I needed to reply in some new tongue, to find a way to assert a self that had become tenuous, shrunk to a shred of Brooklyn stumbling on the coastal void: Orphan meets ocean. Jerk evaporates in salt mist. (264)

Lethem aligns the edge of language with the edge of the water; both are bodies constituting solidity and void, crashing against one another.

Lopate observes that "the empty harbor becomes, paradoxically, the zone revealing to us our own shallow impatience, alienation from nature, unattainable sexual desires, professional pettiness, the substance of our nattering inner monologue." (412). Here the empty harbor connotes not only the absence of language but also the paucity of cultural exchange. Lionel's assertion at the end of the novel that he is "off the page now" and needs "to reply in some new tongue" is a metaphor for a writer's negotiation of a precursor text, and for Lethem's application of Whitman, grounded in New York.

Mapping Ethnicity and Immigration

In "The Sleepers," Whitman writes, "I turn but do not extricate myself, / Confused, a past reading, another, but with darkness yet" (lines 81–82). These lines from *Leaves of Grass* form the epigraph to Chang-rae Lee's novel *Native Speaker* (1995), the story of a second-generation Korean American man's search for language, identity, and place in late twentieth-century New York. The epigraph is a paratextual signal that binds *Native Speaker* to a distinctly American text that Whitman revised many times over the course of his life. Lee includes Whitman's words to foreshadow his protagonist's attempt to decipher and distinguish multiple selves. Ultimately, the reader learns that Whitman's lines encompass both the main character's "past reading[s]," or interpretations, of himself, as well as Lee's "past reading" of an American literary forefather, more than a century after *Leaves of Grass* first saw the light of day. Moraru characterizes Lee's use of Whitman as an American map with an Asian legend. Though I believe that mapping is relevant in the context of New York's physical plan, helping to clarify the self in both writers' works, I interpret Lee's use of Whitman's words more broadly, as they speak to the challenge of comprehending someone else. It is fitting that Lee, a Korean American author, appropriates Whitman, a poet who celebrated the democratic promise of America and its many faces. Whitman's lines emphasize the problematic issues of identity, self, and other in the story.

Whitman begins "Crossing Brooklyn Ferry" with a reflection of the self: "Flood-tide below me! I watch you face to face!" (line 1), and employs this I/you dichotomy throughout the text. In contrast, *Native Speaker* begins with the protagonist's reception of a weathered, folded list of his own character attributes, enumerated by his wife. "The day my wife left she gave me a list of who I was" (1). Whitman's speaker actively asserts his identity himself, whereas Henry Park receives news of his identity from an outside source, in the passive voice. In the familiar poems such as "Crossing Brooklyn Ferry," "Song of Myself," and "I Hear America Singing," among many others, Whitman presents a free verse list to the reader of the personalities and occupations surrounding him. These catalogs of occupation, much like the early local city directories that listed a person's name, address, and occupation (e.g., Auer, Frederick, *milk,* 429 Cherry Street), acknowledge individuals' contributions to the fabric of society. They also distinguish between individual and collective identities, as Whitman employs the definite article "the" to speak about singular representatives of local industries. The list Lelia gives her husband is vague, indefinite not only in its lack of articles but also in its question marks. The list reads, in part: "sentimentalist / anti-romantic / _____ analyst (you fill in) / stranger / follower / traitor / spy" (5). This catalog is Lelia's poem in free verse.

Like *Motherless Brooklyn, Native Speaker* features a protagonist traversing the streets of New York in an attempt to piece together his heritage. Whitman's embrace of generations—"I am with you"—becomes an anxiety in Lee's text. The protagonist, Henry Park, must distinguish himself from other people in his life, chief among them his father. Henry Park's relationship with his father is fraught with tension; Henry and Lelia's son, Mitt, dies. The links between generations are uncertain, uneasy. "He was the definition of thick skin. For most of my youth I wasn't sure he had the capacity to love," Henry Park says of his father (58). But Henry and his father are actually very similar; as Henry's wife, Lelia, points out to him, "He's just a more brutal version of you" (58). At times their identities blur and cannot be "extricate[d]," or distinguished from one another. Henry's identity is in constant flux because of his job as a spy, his consciousness of his otherness, and his silence. In his study of contemporary Asian American literature, King-Kok Cheung notes, "Paradoxically, verbal withholding or indirection often goes hand in hand with multiplicity" (5). Because of Henry's fluid identity, he has trouble comprehending others, particularly his father. Henry's reluctant love, increased comprehension, and continuous endeavors to comprehend his father's language of silence are evident in Mitt's death and in Henry's attitude toward his father's relationship with his wife and, later, with his housekeeper. When Henry verbally attacks his father on the last night of the latter's life, however, it is clear that the communication barriers between the two men can only be overcome after his father's death. Henry must decode the voice present in his father's silence. In discussing the deaths both of a parent and of a child, Lee characterizes familial inheritance as loss.

Whitman's everyman persona and Lionel's serial identities are for Henry a requisite part of his work as a spy. As a result, he cannot distinguish between his invented and real selves. Henry seems to have double, triple, even quadruple consciousness; as he tells us, his "work is a string of serial identity" (33), of masked but merging personalities revealed in short succession. He is Korean and American, immigrant and native, Henry Park and other, yet these selves are not so different from one another. Lelia notes Henry's otherness in her list, a shadow version of Whitman's; in lieu of the mason, woodcutter, or shipbuilder, Lelia deems her husband an "illegal alien, emotional alien, stranger, follower, traitor, spy" (5). Henry makes three photocopies of the list. He tells us, "The original I destroyed. I prefer versions of things, copies that aren't so precious" (4). He attempts to make his identity a copy in order to distance others from his original. This threatens his relationships with all who surround him, including his father and wife. Henry admits that in seeing Dr. Luzan, the Filipino psychoanalyst, he becomes "dangerously frank, inconsistently schizophrenic" (22). As in *Motherless Brooklyn* with Lionel's various succession of identities, the multiplicity of self is recast as a disorder. As Luzan tells Henry, "We have our multiple roles like everyone else" (133), implying that transnational consciousness is no different.

Lee illustrates Henry's "multiple roles" through the characters of his father and Councilman John Kwang, in addition to Henry's father. As Chang-rae Lee noted in an interview, "There's something about *walking* around people who look like you. It shouldn't be that, but it feels like that. I'm different from them, but I look like them so it raises interesting questions" (Mong 2; emphasis added). This marks a departure from Whitman's clear distinction between himself and others as he heralds difference and diversity. Here subjectivity becomes confused by ethnicity and the self mimics others. Kwang tells Henry, "When you are someone like me, you will be many people at once" (293). With "like me," Kwang emphasizes the relation between the self and the other. He suggests that his American political role and his Korean origin result in different selves exposed to different people. After his work with Kwang, Henry observes, "I believed I had a grasp of his identity, not only the many things he was to the public and to his staff and to me, but who he was to himself, the man he beheld in his most private mirror. . . . Through events both arbitrary and conceived it so happened that one of his faces fell away, and then another, and another, until he revealed to me a final level that would not strip off. The last mask" (140–41). Lee poses the question of whether the immigrant must be perpetually masked. As David Cowart queries, "How could one's deepest self bear the visage of another? The insight seems predicated on a Lacanian view of the ego as merely a site from which to experience perpetual yearning for an illusory psychological wholeness" (*Trailing Clouds* 116). The speech monster mask that Henry Park dons is a conscious exploration of language and identity as performative—a version of Lethem's carnival costumes.. Earlier in the story Lee frames Henry's marriage as a circus act in a conversation that Henry has with Hoagland, his boss: "Marriage is a traveling circus. We're the performers. Some of us, unfortunately, are more like freak acts" (44). "So it followed," Henry as narrator responds to this characterization, "I must be the Wolf-Boy, Lelia the Tattooed Lady" (45). Both Lethem and Lee invoke Coney Island to explore difference.

That Kwang is Henry's foil is suggested when Henry rebels against drawing up his usual painstakingly careful reports for Hoagland. Henry reports to his boss less and less frequently. "It seemed like an unbearable encroachment. An exposure of a different order, as if I were offering a private fact about my father or mother to a complete stranger in one of our stores" (147). Henry does not want to betray John Kwang because he would be betraying himself. As Kwang notes, "The problem is our acceptance of what we loathe and fear in ourselves. Not in the other, not in the person standing next to you, not in the one living outside in this your street, in this your city, not in the one who drives your bus or who mops the floors of your child's school, not in the one who cleans your shirts and presses your suits, not in the one who sells books and watches on the corner" (152). Kwang's speech illuminates the voyeuristic problem of the protagonist, who routinely trains a lens on others rather than on himself. Like Whitman's speaker, Kwang invokes a list structure but negates each self instead of celebrating it, as he attempts to negate difference between self and other. As Benjamin contends, "The cycle of destroying the reality of the other and filling the void with the fantasy of a feared and denigrated object, one who must be controlled for fear of retaliation, characterizes all relations of domination" (94). By betraying Kwang and offering up the money club list, Henry in effect relegates Kwang to the category of other, immigrant, and foreigner. This double consciousness is present in his speech; he is painfully aware of the "mysterious dubbing" (179) that others perceive when he speaks. In the mirror he attempts not to discern a symbolic separateness but to unify his personality, body, voice, and reflection, to naturalize the immigrant in him.

While Lethem distinguishes his protagonist through excess verbiage, Lee steeps his protagonist in silence. When speech is not obstructed, Henry and his father wield it as a weapon. When his father lashes out at Henry's mother with nonsensical strings of English slang she cannot comprehend, Henry responds in turn, "hurl[ing]" (63) a cacophony of complex vocabulary that his father cannot understand. The excess of words is not unlike Lionel's verbal outbursts but here characterized as linguistic fluency rather than a speech disorder. Ultimately, however much Henry decries his father's lack of communication, he knows he shares this lack. He admits, "I celebrate every order of silence born of the tongue and the heart and the mind. . . . It finds hard expression in the faces of those who would love you most" (171). Here Whitman's celebration of the self takes the form of lack.

On his mother's death, Henry questions whether his father ever loved her at all. He considers their relationship and thinks his father acts out of duty rather than love. Henry remarks, "He showed great respect to my mother to the day she died . . . and practiced for her the deepest sense of duty and honor, but I never witnessed from him a devotion I could call love. . . . He never said the word, in any language" (58). Somehow, the signifier becomes all-important, its content secondary. King-Kok Cheung's observation regarding the Asian American writers Hisaye Yamamoto, Joy Kogawa, and Maxine Hong Kingston can be applied to Chang-rae Lee: "They articulate—question, report, expose—the silences imposed on themselves and their peoples, whether in the form of feminine and cultural decorum, external or self-censorship, or historical or political invisibility; at the same time they reveal, through their own manners of telling and through their characters, that silences—textual ellipses, nonverbal gestures, authorial hesitations—can be articulate" (4). By the time Ahjuhma dies years later, Henry is able to translate his father's language of grief. "I knew he had suffered in his own unspeakable and shadowy way," Henry states (81).

When Mr. Park is dying, however, it is evident that Henry's understanding of his father's personal language is still at war with his own repressed, shared identity. Foreshadowing Lelia's enumeration of Henry's character flaws, the last night his father is alive, Henry bombards him with another list—a list of grievances, even though Mr. Park can neither move nor speak. "I spoke at him . . . half-intending an emotional torture. I ticked through the whole long register of my disaffections, hit all the ready categories. . . . I thought he would be an easy mark, being stiff, paralyzed, but of course the agony was mine. He was unmovable," Henry confesses to the reader (49). Speech is wielded as a monologic weapon. Henry knows that "The truth, finally, is who can tell it" (7). "Old artificer, undead old man," he observes bitterly, acknowledging his father's great influence on his thoughts and personality, his inherited practice of silence (159). Other (literary) forbears are present here: Lee alludes to James Joyce's *A Portrait of the Artist as a Young Man*. In the novel, Stephen Dedalus lives by the codes of silence and exile. Lee invokes another ill-fated father-son relationship in the myth of Dedalus and Icarus, in which the son's disregard for the father proves fatal. In *Like Subjects, Love Objects,* Jessica Benjamin contemplates the child's struggle for recognition and separation from the parent. She writes, "The paradox of recognition is not solved once and for all but remains an organizing issue throughout life, becoming intense with each fresh struggle for independence, each confrontation with difference" (94). Henry and his father cannot confront each other on equal ground; in each of their interactions, either Henry or his father is subordinated by the other as their identities merge, lacking intersubjective space. This argument seems borne out in Henry's description of his father when Mitt dies: "And then my father came out from the sliding porch door and saw me, a cordless phone in his hand, and he yelled in Korean that the ambulance was coming. But before he made it to us his legs seemed to fold under him and he sat back unnaturally on the matted lawn, his face so small-looking, arrested, so short of breath," Henry describes his father's behavior when Mitt has suffocated (205). Here Henry merges his father's identity with that of his son, which suggests that the "paradox of recognition" is indeed ongoing. The nature of

Mitt's death by suffocation represents the problematic role of oral expression throughout the novel.

Mapping Diaspora

Whereas Lethem's protagonist travels widely, traversing and naming so many New York streets that the reader is provided with a veritable map, Lee's protagonist has specific destinations in mind, evident in his conversation with his estranged wife:

> "I decided to wander over."
>
> "I bet. . . . Though I doubt you've ever really wandered."
>
> "I wander a lot."
>
> "Oh, that's good," she replied. "But only in the place and time of your choosing. The word for that is *invasion*." (115)

Rather than wandering, Henry walks deliberately along planned routes, offering up to the reader his maps.[6] "I went to him this way," he describes his commute to John Kwang's office: "Take the uptown number 2 train to Times Square. Get off. Switch by descending the stairs to the very bottom of the station, to the number 7 trains, those shabby heaving brick-colored cars that seem to scratch and bore beneath the East River out of Manhattan before breaking ground again in Queens. They rise up on the elevated track, sneaking their way northeast to the farthest end of the county. The last stop, mine. Main Street, Flushing" (82). The passage recalls *A Walker in the City*, in which Kazin names subway stations on the IRT line—Clark, Borough Hall, Hoyt, Nevins—that take him deeper into Brooklyn and farther away from New York. Though Kazin laments his noticeable distance from the city during his Brownsville youth, the fictional Lionel and Henry are happy to exist outside Manhattan proper, whether in a Westchester suburb or in downtown Brooklyn. There isn't the same immigrant anxiety about desiring residence at the center of culture and commerce rather than on the cultural margins; Henry, for example, revels in traveling to Flushing, a neighborhood populated by immigrants and their descendants and street vendors proffering wares ranging from kimchi to cuchifrito. Kwang's campaign headquarters is in the Flushing streets, woven into the fabric of exchange rather than insulated in an austere office. Kwang walks the streets too, learning the people of the city through the speech reverberations of sidewalks and building and street corners. Solnit posits that "walking is only the beginning of citizenship, but through it the citizen knows his or her city and fellow citizens and truly inhabits the city rather than a small privatized part thereof" (176). Kwang's walks render the district his.

While Lionel lopes around the Brooklyn streets in an attempt to piece together Minna's past and thereby find his killer, Henry also attempts to solve a mystery, the dissolution of his marriage, through visiting and revisiting particular neighborhoods in and out of the city. He and Lelia return to past culinary routines in Flushing, escapes from the city on the Staten Island Ferry, and familial habits at Mr. Park's home in Ardsley. Each revisited routine traces familiar steps yet forges novel communications and discoveries about the marriage and each individual. Each trip with Lelia recovers a part of Henry's story and allows her to craft a narrative about him and his work, as well as about his relationships with others. Ultimately, these explorations also recover their marriage.

While the characters populating *Motherless Brooklyn* are uncomfortable outside their native borough, the characters in *Native Speaker* are uneasy in most of the spaces they occupy. After Mitt dies, Henry's father paints the room in which Mitt used to sleep stark white. Henry views this action as an attempt to erase Mitt and be finished with his existence. "My father— who could display amazing properties of emotional recovery—had long before cleared [the room] of any signs of our boy. . . . 'Now done,'" he imagines his father thinking (217). In an interview, Chang-rae Lee commented on his own life: "Maybe it's being an immigrant. You inhabit a place, but some part of you is always observing and self-conscious" (Mong 2). Lee's description of plural identity recalls W. E. B. Du Bois's concept of double consciousness. Henry Park lives in a space without boundaries; as he describes the loft, its wide white expanse makes it dysfunctional. Its lack of compartments and partitions dooms it because it is the antithesis of Henry's divided self. Like Henry and Lelia's cat, Henry prefers to slink along peripheries, in his work and in his daily interactions.

The failure of communication is expressed in the protagonist's silence instead of the verbosity of Lionel Essrog, but this silence does not dictate singularity. Henry's communication with his father is also unsuccessful because of Henry's many selves. When his father asks Henry to demonstrate his command of English at the store by casually reciting Shakespeare, Henry thinks sarcastically, "I, his princely Hal" (53). Lee invokes the tenuous relationship of Hal and his father in *Henry IV*, as well as a character who continuously evolves in order to manipulate others. Lelia once reveals to Henry, "I just know you have parts to you that I can't touch. Maybe I figured out I didn't want to get to them anymore. Or shouldn't bother" (127). These parts are the other selves in the novel: Councilman Kwang, Mr. Park, the other identities Henry takes on in his work as a spy. In Henry's belated love and attachment to his father, he misses what has ultimately come to be a part of himself. He views turning in the money club list as a betrayal of his father and his background. As Henry represents his father, so too do the people on the money club list. Instead of disconnecting himself from this emotion he wishes to speak with the people on the list, to be "spoke at"; he wishes to bear their hardship. He thinks in perpetual list form, categorizing people and things, dividing them into neat bullets on a page. The prominence of lists is another indication of Henry's insufficient communication; the isolated components of a list do not require any relationship to one another. The money club list is not only Lee's emphasis of Henry's naturalization; given extra dimension by the news of the sinking of the *Golden Venture* in 1993, it also relates back to Whitman.[7] The money club names, and the names of the dead, are additional catalogs of humanity. Moreover, the news program that Henry and Lelia watch on Staten Island after they themselves take a boat to their destination broadcasts the shipwreck of a boat smuggling hundreds of would-be Chinese immigrants. The commuters of "Crossing Brooklyn Ferry" become immigrants from a farther shore. Some drown in New York Harbor, while others are arrested and later deported.

In addition to employing Whitman's words in the epigraph, Lee also makes explicit reference to "The Sleepers" in the body of the novel. When Henry meets his wife, Lelia, at a party and they venture outside for some air, Lee writes, "We sat on a bench among the sleepers" (12), ostensibly alluding to people sleeping on park benches but also invoking Whitman's poem. In "The Sleepers," Whitman refers to lost swimmers and shipwrecks and invokes the casualties of the Revolutionary War's Battle of Brooklyn, in which the East River played an important role. In *Native Speaker*, Lee reimagines the shipwreck Whitman witnesses in his poem as a failed, tragic twentieth-century immigrant passage. Toward the end of "The Sleepers," Whitman writes, "Elements merge in the night, ships make tacks in the dreams, / The sailor sails, the exile returns home, / The fugitive returns unharm'd, the immigrant is back beyond months and years . . ." (lines 123–25). Cowart contends that Whitman's text "speaks obliquely to the self-exploration and 'past-reading' that Lee's narrator undertakes. . . . [Whitman] catalogs a whole world of sleepers (including immigrants, a catalogue within a catalogue), among whom the speaker wanders, perhaps dreaming himself" (*Trailing Clouds* 116–17). Lee invokes a poem that celebrates exiles, fugitives, and immigrants; unlike Whitman, Lee underscores that not all return home.

Mapping Departure and Return

Both books deal with the importance of language and multiple identity. In *Motherless Brooklyn,* Lethem presents this progression of voice by giving his main character Tourette's syndrome, one manifestation of which is an overabundance of language, beyond control, voicing different selves. In *Native Speaker,* Lee's main character is Korean American and bilingual, but he is also a spy who must inhabit different selves. Both Lionel Essrog and Henry Park inhabit serial identities. When Henry's father has a stroke and is rendered unable to speak, Henry capitalizes on the occasion to regale him with an exhaustive list of shortcomings and offenses committed, bombarding him with language. This is a version of Lethem's conception of the sudden, involuntary vocalizations of Tourette's syndrome—words shot at immovable, uncomprehending targets. Whereas Lionel grapples with the lack of control over his communication with everyone he encounters, Henry contends with a life of silence, both from within his ethnicity, in the lack of communication with his father, and outside it, a function of being an ethnic minority in the United States. Lee confronts prejudice directly, with an immigrant "Song of Myself." Henry tells the reader, "We are your most perilous and dutiful brethren, the *song of our heart,* at once furious and sad. For only you could grant these lyrical modes. I call them back to you. Here is all my American education" (320; emphasis added). This is not only a metaphor of the immigrant as spy, it is also Lee's sardonic acknowledgment of literary tradition. Christian Moraru writes that Lee employs a Whitmanesque system of legends, keys, and maps to identify himself as an American writer. "Whitman, the 'legendary' native precursor, helps Lee lay his own claim to American writer status; Korean-born Lee becomes a 'natural,' naturalizes himself into America and its letters via the emblematically American Whitman interlodged inside his novel. The writer wants his story to be heard through Whitman's voice, as a ventriloquial narrative that concurrently emulates and further dislocates the precursor's symbolically capacious idiom" (67–68). Other critics have discussed the weight of the precursor text. In *Literary Symbiosis,* David Cowart writes about potential perceptions of texts like *Native Speaker:* "The latecomer artist . . . would seem to run the risk of being perceived by readers as lacking in maturity and originality; readers may, indeed, assume that the production of a guest text is somehow less admirable than the production of a host text. Yet the latecomers with their 'stolentelling' rise above such residual cultural disquiet. Neither exhausted or effete, they prove agents of renewal" (26). Lee describes Henry Park's occupation as "ethnic coverage" (18) as he surveils first-generation Americans in their immigrant communities. If one steps back from the fiction, Lethem and Lee convey larger points about literary influence being perceived as imitative and voyeuristic, but ultimately emphasize that their language is not derivative or copied but native and original. Lee concludes his novel with Lelia "speaking a dozen lovely and native languages, calling all the difficult names of who we are" (349). Though Lee appropriates Whitman to signal a participation in the American literary tradition, he also refutes potential misreadings of ethnic American texts simply "call[ing] back" what has thus far been learned from the American canon.

This refutation is important, as the literary influences, and thus their attendant anxiety, extend beyond Whitman in both novels. Like *Motherless Brooklyn, Native Speaker* owes a debt to Edgar Allan Poe, who invented modern detective fiction with "The Murders in the Rue Morgue" (1841). Both *Motherless Brooklyn* and *Native Speaker* feature classic conventions of the genre: the detective figure, a murder, a puzzle, and an ultimate discovery. *Motherless Brooklyn* contains an additional hallmark of Poe's detective fiction, the narration by a close friend. And it is impossible to read *Native Speaker* in the context of American letters without thinking of Richard Wright's *Native Son* (1940), whose protagonist, Bigger Thomas, is expected to navigate the segregated neighborhoods of Chicago. Henry Park can also be compared to the protagonist of Ralph Ellison's *Invisible Man* (1952), which famously begins with a reference to Poe. "I am an invisible man. No, I am not a spook like those who haunted Edgar Allan Poe; nor am I one of your Hollywood-movie ectoplasms. I am a man of substance, of flesh and bone, fiber and liquids—and I might even be said to possess a mind. I am invisible, understand, simply because people refuse to see me. Like the bodiless heads you see sometimes in circus sideshows, it is as though I have been surrounded by mirrors of hard, distorting glass" (3). Ellison's language about his protagonist reminds us of the reflexivity of American literature. Daniel Kim points to Ellison as a dominant influence, yet argues that critics' likening of *Native Speaker* to *Invisible Man* is reductive: "A particularly convenient way for reviewers to praise Asian American literary works is to liken them to roughly comparable if more famous African American texts. It is easy to see how such compliments might seem double-edged: in this case, they laud Lee's novel not by suggesting its originality but rather by depicting it as an artfully executed 'reimagination' of a text widely regarded as a masterpiece of African American literature. If the value of writing is seen as driving solely from the inventiveness with which it reworks Ellison's, then Lee's literary performance risks being reduced to an act of authorial impersonation" (231). My argument here, and indeed, throughout the book, is that a response to an earlier text does not render it derivative; it does not lessen the literary value of the later work but instead enriches it.

As Henry Park observes, "Sometimes you have to meet the parents to figure out what someone really looks like" (256). Read alongside Whitman, these New York texts reflect twentieth-century adaptations of the multitudinous, diverse New York self, walking the city's streets and traversing its waterways. Perhaps it would please Whitman that at the close of *Motherless Brooklyn*, Lionel is still a pilgrim. "Tell your story walking," he advises the reader (311). And at the conclusion of *Native Speaker,* Henry Park wishes to hear his father's voice, demonstrating at least a partial resolution to the crisis of the self and the failure of intersubjectivity. Toward the end of the novel, Henry states, "Now, I think I would give most anything to hear my father's talk again, the crash and bang and stop of his language, always hurtling by. I will listen for him forever in the streets of this city" (337). Walking around New York, the respective protagonists of *Native Speaker* and *Motherless Brooklyn* travel similar distances from their parents (real and surrogate), just as Lethem and Lee depart from Whitman, mapping the self in distinctive trajectories. Yet characters, authors, and readers alike return to their origins: Lee frames Henry's departure from and return to the home of his father as "a long and lyric processional that leads me out from the city in which I live, to return me here, back to this place of our ghosts" (227). As Whitman writes near the final stanza of "The Sleepers," "I stay a while away O night, but I return to you again, and love you" (line 178).

2

Literary Custom House

Nathaniel Hawthorne's *The Scarlet Letter*
and Jhumpa Lahiri's *Unaccustomed Earth*

IN THE *LITERARY WORLD* of March 30, 1850, Evert Duyckink heralded the publication of Nathaniel Hawthorne's *The Scarlet Letter*. With enthusiastic praise, he noted, "Our literature has given to the world no truer product of American soil" (325). The story, imbued with American history, sprouted from American land. Duyckink, editor, publisher, and Hawthorne patron, borrowed the horticultural language from Hawthorne's "Custom-House" introductory, which he had already printed in his magazine. The same vernacular would prove useful many years later in the transnational context of Jhumpa Lahiri's short story collection, *Unaccustomed Earth* (2008), which chronicles the cultural negotiations of Bengali immigrants and their American-raised children. Resurrecting a familiar customs inspector laboring at the Salem port, Lahiri's epigraph hails from "The Custom-House": "Human nature will not flourish, any more than a potato, if it be planted and replanted, for too long a series of generations, in the same worn-out soil. My children have had other birthplaces, and, so far as their fortunes may be within my control, shall strike their roots into unaccustomed earth" (13). Hawthorne's words speak to the dual yokes of geography and ancestry in Salem, but they also portend the direction of American literature, whose children have had other birthplaces.

In an interview about the genesis of *Unaccustomed Earth,* Lahiri recalled revisiting *The Scarlet Letter:* "I remember . . . coming across that passage and I just stopped and everything stopped. I felt that these words were so beautifully expressing everything I was trying to write about, everything I was trying to do as a writer, from the very beginning, from the very first book, and I suspect, until the end of my writing life. I don't think that that particular phrase and what it conveys will ever not somehow reflect what I'm doing and what I've lived in some sense and what I am, and who I am." Lahiri's response reveals her own Hawthornian hybrid of autobiography and fiction. As she explains this memorable literary encounter, her child's murmurs are audible in the background, accentuating the idea of generations.By redeploying Hawthorne's words from *The Scarlet Letter,* Lahiri underscores the immigrant underpinnings of one of the most canonical texts in American literature and locates her own writing within the same tradition.[1]

Set largely in Massachusetts some 150 years after Hawthorne's Salem excavation, *Unaccustomed Earth* appropriates Hawthorne's warning regarding the consequence of provinciality to address twentieth-century immigration and generational difference in the collection's stories, many of which plumb literal and metaphorical acts of transplantation. *Unaccustomed Earth* surveys a spectrum of Indian American characters, some born in India, some in the United States, along with many iterations and ramifications of diaspora. Like the Puritans, the Bengali Americans must adapt to the New World. The collection contains eight stories and is divided into two parts, with the last three stories devoted to the trajectories of two characters, Hema and Kaushik, from childhood to middle age. This chapter focuses primarily on the title story, "Unaccustomed Earth," which chronicles the relationships between three generations of a family—a father, his grown daughter, Ruma, and her son, Akash—negotiating existence in the wake of several forms of unsettlement. After characters are planted and replanted elsewhere, Lahiri interrogates what may flourish in the aftermath of both personal and cultural loss.

Place, Memory

To more fully understand Lahiri's invocation of "The Custom-House," one must begin with Hawthorne's domestic misgivings. Four residences shaped Hawthorne's oeuvre: Salem and Concord, Massachusetts; Liverpool, England; and Florence, Italy.[2] In each location, the author engaged with, or rather battled, the anxiety of influence. Robert Milder notes that Hawthorne wrote both *about* and *from* the region that haunted him, observing that "Hawthorne never abandoned any of his habitations; he assimilated them into a self that deepened and expanded as he aged without finding, after the Salem period, a settled physical and metaphysical 'home'" (ix). Before visiting the Massachusetts Bay Colony, Hawthorne contemplates the weight of the Hathorne history.

In Salem, Hawthorne and his autobiographical narrator are surveyors of customs: social, civic, political, and domestic. With "The Custom-House" introductory, Hawthorne throws open the doors to the seemingly impenetrable "spacious edifice of brick" standing sentinel on Salem Harbor (*Scarlet Letter* 8). The reader walks up the steps past the aging denizens of the town, through the first-floor transactional offices, and finally up to the second-floor private offices, to gaze through the windows on the wharf below. The siting of the custom house overlooking the water enables Hawthorne to contemplate the arrival of his family's first representatives in the Massachusetts Bay Colony and explore the burden of ancestry. As this chapter discusses a twenty-first-century Bengali American author's engagement with *The Scarlet Letter,* it is worth adding here that the East India Company's imports traveled through Salem's world port before that entry point declined in the 1840s, when Boston and New York attracted more commerce.[3]

The tour also enables Hawthorne to lay bare contemporary political corruption and more general incompetence. The custom house is determinedly male, "a sanctuary into which womankind, with her tools of magic, the broom and mop, has infrequent access," aged, with the chairs, like many of the employees, "exceedingly decrepit and infirm" (*Scarlet Letter* 10), and inept, with many of its occupants "asleep, in their accustomed corners" (15), their chairs tilted back against the wall. "The Custom-House" introductory functions similarly to "The Old Manse," the preface to *Mosses from an Old Manse,* in that both employ a structure—one civic, one residential—to tell the story of an individual and the history of the surrounding area. The earlier narrative, however, is lighthearted in tone, written during a pleasant time in Concord, while the later text, reflecting on Hawthorne's time as a surveyor (1846–49), contains notes of despair and stagnation. On November 11, 1847, he wrote from the custom house to Henry Wadsworth Longfellow, "I am trying to resume my pen; but the influences of my situation and customary associates are so anti-literary, that I know not whether I shall succeed. Whenever I sit alone, or walk alone, I find myself dreaming about stories, as of old; but these forenoons in the Custom House undo all that the afternoons and evenings have done. I should be happier if I could write" (qtd. in Myerson 126). Hawthorne's letter speaks to the literal and metaphorical restrictions wrought by the bureaucratic dysfunction of the custom house; he yearns to light out for the territory. As Dan McCall contends, "'The Custom-House' is a record of Hawthorne's struggle to relocate those gifts which once enabled him to live as fully as he did in the Old Manse when he was a 'literary man'" (37). "The Custom-House" introductory alters the narrative framework of the book, as it inserts the narrator into the town's problematic history and aligns him with Hester in his desire to resist the arm of the state. Most pivotally, the tour allows the narrator to discover the scarlet letter and the story of Hester Prynne, establishing the fictional narrative by an author invested in the spaces of personal and collective history.[4]

It is in this vein that Hawthorne brings up his literary contemporaries and offers the reader wry commentary on the financial pressures with which the artist must contend.

> I took it in good part at the hands of Providence, that I was thrown into a position so little akin to my past habits; and set myself seriously to gather from it whatever profit was to be had. After my fellowship of toil and impractical schemes, with the dreamy brethren of Brook Farm; after living for three years within the subtle influence of an intellect like Emerson's; after those wild, free days on the Assabeth, indulging fantastic speculations beside our fire of fallen boughs, with Ellery Channing; after talking with Thoreau about pine-trees and Indian relics, in his hermitage at Walden; after growing fastidious by sympathy with the classic refinement of Hillard's culture; after becoming imbued with poetic sentiment at Longfellow's hearth-stone;—it was time, at length, that I should exercise other faculties of my nature, and nourish myself with food for which I had hitherto had little appetite. Even the old Inspector was desirable, as a change of diet, to a man who had known Alcott. (*Scarlet Letter* 22)

In dissociating himself from the New England transcendentalist lot, Haw-thorne seems to be channeling Edgar Allan Poe. In his November 1847 review of *Mosses from an Old Manse* in *Godey's Lady's Book,* Poe suggested that Hawthorne distance himself from this group, writing, "Let him mend his pen, get a bottle of visible ink, come out from the Old Manse, cut Mr. Alcott, hang (if possible) the editor of 'The Dial,' and throw out of the win-dow to the pigs all his odd numbers of the *North American Review* (qtd. in Sova 233). Pretending to dismiss his time in the literary community as an impracticable youthful indiscretion, Hawthorne ponders the direction of his life and the divergent roads of literary and corporate pursuit that face him. Again he employs the language of nutrition, here in the context of Brook Farm and Fruitlands. Yet he also admits that his Salem political appointment is nothing more than "a transitory life" (*Scarlet Letter* 22). He does not renounce his life as a writer but instead puts to work the tools of the trade in his new position.

His work as surveyor serves as a parable for American literature and the early disregard for American artistry. He laments the existence of the mundane documents that surround him.

> It was sorrowful to think how many days, and weeks, and months, and years of toil, had been wasted on these musty papers, which were now only an encumbrance on earth, and were hidden away in this forgotten corner, never more to be glanced at by human eyes. But, then, what reams of other manuscripts—filled, not with the dulness of official formalities, but with the thought of inventive brains and the rich effusion of deep hearts—had gone equally to oblivion; and that, moreover, without serving a purpose in their day, as these heaped up papers had, and—saddest of all—without pur-chasing for their writers the comfortable livelihood which the clerks of the Custom-House had gained by these worthless scratchings of the pen! (24)

The author impugns partisan politics and dysfunctional bureaucracy as a vehicle to contemplate lost authorial careers and neglected narratives. Hawthorne's own career was far from lost; Duyckink noted in his celebra-tory review of *The Scarlet Letter* that the author's ejection from the custom house was fortuitous, as "the city by his removal lost an indifferent official, and the world regained a good author" (325).

While the custom house is rooted in Salem, the institution is interna-tional in its function. Similarly, *The Scarlet Letter* is not a local or provincial story but an immigrant one that delves into the formation of American community. The three opening chapters feature civic structures: the custom house, market place, and prison. Hawthorne builds additional structures for the reader: Governor Bellingham's mansion, Hester and Pearl's cottage, and the pious widow's residence that Dimmesdale and Chillingworth cohabit. Each space exemplifies particular customs and behaviors. Hawthorne was a writer able to traverse local politics of space and place while also imbuing a narrative with the universality of human experience. The town's residents are immigrants, their origins both European and English. As John Carlos Rowe notes, "Despite James's denial in *Hawthorne, The Scarlet Letter* . . . embodies Hawthorne's own international theme in the local space of Puritan Boston, itself the crossing not only of Europe and America but also of established theological traditions (Reverend Wilson) and the new learning (Dimmesdale)" (33).

The final chapter reveals an increasingly international order: "But, through the remainder of Hester's life, there were indications that the recluse of the scarlet letter was the object of love and interest with some inhabitant of another land. Letters came, with armorial seals upon them, though of bearings unknown to English heraldry" (*Scarlet Letter* 165). Pearl resides abroad, while Hester chooses to return to Salem. "But there was a more real life for Hester Prynne, here, in New England, than in that unknown region where Pearl had found a home. Here had been her sin; here, her sorrow; and here was yet to be her penitence. She had returned, therefore, and resumed,—of her own free will, for not the sternest magistrate of that iron period would have imposed it,—resumed the symbol of which we have related so dark a tale" (165). Hawthorne concludes *The Scarlet Letter* on a global note, emphasizing the possibility of travel and departure, as well as on a note of choice rather than determinism. But if we return to the time in which he is writing, of course, we know that our narrator remains in Salem. He acknowledges the recession of the past, observing, "Gradually, they have sunk almost out of sight; as old houses, here and there about the streets, get covered half-way to the eaves by the accumulation of new soil" (12), yet it is clear this soil remains underfoot. Hawthorne positions both ancestors and domiciles as characters haunting the storied landscape.

In his biography of Hawthorne, Henry James writes that the burden of ancestry of which the author speaks in "The Custom-House" should not be surprising, as "a hundred years of Salem would perhaps be rather a deadweight for any family to carry, and we venture to imagine that the Hathornes were dull and depressed. They did what they could, however, to improve their situation; they trod the Salem streets as little as possible" (10). Hawthorne himself did not adhere to this dictum. In *Hawthorne and the Historical Romance of New England,* Michael Davitt Bell provides helpful context for understanding Hawthorne's role as a historian. He notes, "When Hawthorne began in the 1820s to turn to the history of New England as material for fiction, there was widespread interest in the New England past, and in the American past generally, on the part of American writers" (ix). Lahiri participates in this tradition, conjoining the periods of revolution and settlement with twentieth-century immigration. But both Hawthorne and Lahiri are interested not only in history but also in romance. In his study of Hawthorne's literary influence, Samuel Chase Coale writes that his aim is "to show that American romance is far more than a mere disguise for traditional allegory, as some critics of the term have suggested, that it embodies most of the great cultural and moral questions of American society. Romance also reveals the conflicts between the American notions of history and myth that continue to plague us" (viii). Through locating many of her stories in places of national historical significance, Lahiri investigates some of the same conflicts of American identity.

   Place is of central importance in *Unaccustomed Earth.* The Bengali American characters, having emigrated from a region that had been under British East India Company colonial rule in the eighteenth century, inhabit a spectrum of Massachusetts towns, while also traveling to and from Italy, India, and Southeast Asia.[5] In a *New York Times Book Review,* Liesl Schillinger writes that Lahiri "shows that the place to which you feel the strongest attachment isn't necessarily the country you're tied to by blood or birth: it's the place that allows you to become yourself. This place, she quietly indicates, may not lie on any map." However, it is difficult to think about the Massachusetts setting without invoking not only the American Renaissance but also pertinent earlier American history: the arrivals of the Pilgrims and the Puritans, the opening fire of the American Revolution. In "Hell-Heaven," Pranab Chakraborty, with whom the narrator's mother is in love, marries in Ipswich, one of the seats of the Massachusetts Bay Colony. Later in the story the Chakrabortys host Thanksgiving, where a guest jokes, "Here's to Thanksgiving with the Indians" (*Unaccustomed Earth* 78).

As the literature of nineteenth-century New England reflected on the legacy of earlier immigrants to the New World, it provides Lahiri with a helpful framework for understanding the continuous attempt to define what constitutes American literature independent of ethnicity and era. The collection's title is an allusion to Hawthorne's introduction to *The Scarlet Letter*, but, along with rereading Hawthorne's entire oeuvre when working on the short story collection, Lahiri revisited Thoreau and Emerson, too. The American Renaissance reverberates throughout the collection as characters discover the importance of self-reliance, visit Walden Pond, and search for real estate in Lexington and Concord. In "Unaccustomed Earth," the title story, Ruma's father, who is never named but exists only in filial relation, warns her against dependency, with a nod to Emerson. "Self-reliance is important, Ruma. . . . Life is full of surprises" (38). Lahiri suggests that the next generation must navigate the antithetical challenges of stasis and precarity, with the additional complication of transnationalism. In "Hell-Heaven," the narrator and her discontented mother retrace Thoreau in their trips to Concord. "As the weather grew hotter, we started going once or twice a week to Walden Pond. . . . [There] Pranab Kaku would coax my mother through the woods, and lead her down the steep slope to the water's edge" (66). On the shores of Walden Pond, in Thoreau's shadow, mother and daughter experience their first freedom from domestic routine. Revisiting these earlier texts gives Lahiri's work new meaning and new parameters. At the same time, the invocations help reframe older American literature as global and transnational.

Prior Plantation

Paul de Man writes in his introduction to Hans Robert Jauss's *Toward an Aesthetic of Reception,*

> Translated from spatial metaphors into epistemological categories, the process can be stated in terms of question and answer: the question occurs as an individual disruption of an answer that has become common knowledge but which, under the effect of this new question, can now be seen to have itself been an individual response to an earlier, collective question. As the answer metamorphoses into a question, it becomes like an individual, tree,

or portrait set within a stylized landscape and it reveals, by the same token, a live background behind its background, in the form of a question from which it now can itself stand out. (Jauss xiii)

The tree metaphor is useful in the context of Hawthorne and Lahiri. A text is an individual plant; it is also, simultaneously, one with roots in another text or texts. Lahiri participates in the American narrative tradition of plantation. Readers of American literature know that an interest in vegetation—the vernacular of roots, earth, and planting—predates *The Scarlet Letter*. William Bradford's "Of Plimoth Plantation" situated discussions of planting and migration early in the American consciousness. "But hear I cannot but stay and make a pause, and stand half amased at this poore peoples presente condition; and so I thinke will the reader too, when he well considers ye same. Being thus passed ye vast ocean, and a sea of troubles before in their preparation (as may be remembered by yt which wente before), they had now no friends to wellcome them, nor inns to entertaine or refresh their weatherbeaten bodys, no houses or much less townes to repaire too, to seeke for succoure." Bradford's words concern the connections between migration, shelter, and settlement in which Lahiri is still interested several centuries later. In the nineteenth century we have Hawthorne and his mosses, Whitman and his leaves. At the Old Manse in Concord, Emerson drafted his essay "Nature" (1836), Thoreau planted a vegetable garden for Sophia and Nathaniel before they arrived, and Hawthorne penned the short story collection *Mosses from an Old Manse* (1846).[6]

Equally famous is Melville's 1850 review of *Mosses*. Writing as a "Virginian Spending July in Vermont," Melville's nom de plume hails from two disparate regions, doubly qualifying the writer to weigh in on the American landscape that Hawthorne explores in his collection. Melville begins his impassioned review, "A papered chamber in a fine old farm-house—a mile from any other dwelling, and dipped to the eaves in foliage—surrounded by mountains, old woods, and Indian ponds,—this, surely is the place to write of Hawthorne." After situating himself in the American landscape (the reader cannot help but imagine the actual writer ensconced at Arrowhead, his Pittsfield dwelling), Melville goes on to argue for a distinct American literary tradition, and positions Hawthorne on the proud roster of American authors. "It is curious, how a man may travel along a country road, and yet miss the grandest, or sweetest of prospects, by reason of an intervening hedge, so like all other hedges, as in no way to hint of the wide landscape beyond. So has it been with me concerning the enchanting landscape in the soul of this Hawthorne, this most excellent Man of Mosses" (Idol and Jones 105). He connects his observations about the state of American literature to the beauty of the land and, in so doing, to the Salem author's interest in themes of wilderness and settlement. Melville continues, describing the literary recommendation of a cousin who "soon returned with a volume, verdantly bound, and garnished with a curious frontispiece in green,—nothing less, than a fragment of real moss cunningly pressed to a fly-leaf.—'Why this,' said I, spilling my raspberries, 'this is the 'Mosses from an Old Manse.' 'Yes,' said cousin Cherry, 'yes, it is that flowery Hawthorne.'—'Hawthorne and Mosses,' said I, 'no more: it is morning: it is July in the country: and I am off for the barn.' Stretched on that new mown clover, the hill-side breeze blowing over me through the wide barn door, and soothed by the hum of the bees in the meadows around, how magically stole over me this Mossy Man!" (Idol and Jones 106).

Melville employs Hawthorne's favored form of allegory here but repurposes it with humor, rendering the imagined cousin a cherry and both the real-life author and his book pieces of moss. In fact, the passage is replete with bounty—flowers and fruits, fertile and verdant land, with bees to assist with reproduction—that Hawthorne similarly appreciates in "The Old Manse." Melville writes tantalizingly of the orchard: "Throughout the summer, there were cherries and currants; and then came Autumn, with this immense burthen of apples, dropping them continually from his over-laden shoulders, as he trudged along. In the stillest afternoon, if I listened, the thump of a great apple was audible, falling without a breath of wind, from the mere necessity of perfect ripeness. And, besides, there were pear-trees, that flung down bushels upon bushels of heavy pears, and peach-trees, which, in a good year, tormented me with peaches, neither to be eaten nor kept, nor, without labor and perplexity, to be given away" (8). The American Eden that Melville describes is a far cry from potatoes in worn-out soil. He thus engages Hawthorne's dedication to place, as he pays homage not just to the writer's work but also his landscape. This attention to the natural world parallels the work of Hudson River School painters, who explored themes of settlement and wilderness in celebrating the American landscape.

In *The Scarlet Letter,* we have an actual planting, in the rosebush adjacent to the Prison-Door, in addition to untamed wilderness in the forest outside of town. The rosebush, connected to Anne Hutchinson, a woman banished to unaccustomed earth that would ultimately not serve her well, connotes exile. But most prominent in the text is the idea of human root and transplant. As "The Custom-House" chapter is a sustained meditation on the nature of a family "planted deep," it offers Lahiri, almost two centuries later, fertile ground for repurposing the metaphor of transplantation for later immigrants. The narrator explains, "And yet, though invariably happiest elsewhere, there is within me a feeling for old Salem, which, in lack of a better phrase, I must be content to call affection. The sentiment is probably assignable to the deep and aged roots which my family has struck into the soil" (11). Hawthorne employs the rhetoric of plantation to discuss his attachment, sometimes inexplicable, to Salem and its local, familial history. But he qualifies that this attachment is unusual, in part "the mere sensuous sympathy of dust for dust. Few of my countrymen can know what it is; nor, as frequent transplantation is perhaps better for the stock, need they consider it desirable to know" (11). That the very earth he treads is composed of the bones of his ancestors is both privileged and ponderous.

While the narrator extols the virtue of transplant in "The Custom-House," Hawthorne's comments elsewhere were ambivalent. From Villa Montauto in the Florentine hills, he reported, "This evening I have been on the towertop star-gazing. . . . From time to time the sweet bells of Florence rang out, and I was loath to come down into the lower world, knowing that I shall never again look heaven-ward from an old towertop in such a calm soft evening as this. Yet I am not loath to go away; impatient, rather; for, taking no root, I soon weary of any soil in which I may be temporarily deposited" (*Passages from the French and Italian Notebooks* 2:193). Here the author expresses his fatigue with travel and yearns for more permanent habitation. Hawthorne continues to use the vernacular of vegetation in framing his departure from ancestral stock: "Doubtless, however, either of these stern and black-browed Puritans would have thought it quite a sufficient retribution for his sins, that, after so long a lapse of years, the old trunk of the family tree, with so much venerable moss upon it, should have borne, as its top-most bough, an idler like myself" (*Scarlet Letter* 12).

Uprooting

Just as Hawthorne assails the fruit of his family tree, privileging the individual independent of the customs of family, church, and state, so, too, does Lahiri. Throughout *Unaccustomed Earth,* the author explores the disruption of customs, and the uprooting of characters from places, relationships, and institutions. The author's invocation of Hawthorne illuminates characters' navigations of the tensions between the individual and the collective, between the transcendentalists' ideas of self-reliance, and familial tradition. As Brodhead argues about the absence of custom in *The Scarlet Letter,* "Placed outside the bounds of the Puritan community, Hester is also placed where the Puritans' codes cease to structure her thought" (192). She must create a new "daily custom" for herself as soon as she exits the prison (*Scarlet Letter* 55). Lahiri recreates both "The Custom-House" narrator's misanthropic tendencies and Hester Prynne's singular customs in Ruma, her female protagonist, dissociating her from familial and cultural heritage. She, her husband, Adam, and their son, Akash, move across the country to Seattle, departing from East Coast family and friends. When examining the friendships Ruma leaves behind on the Brooklyn playground, Lahiri invokes Hawthorne's horticultural language: "For all the time she'd spent with these women the roots did not go deep, and these days, after reading their e-mails, Ruma was seldom inspired to write back" (35). Her mother has died, her husband is absent from home because of work, and she has left her work as an attorney, preferring to stay at home with her child. "Growing up, her mother's example—moving to a foreign place for the sake of marriage, caring exclusively for children and a household—had served as a warning, a path to avoid. Yet this was Ruma's life now" (11). The distinction, however, is that Ruma does not preserve Bengali customs in her home; she remembers little of the language and resists cooking Bengali food. Sacvan Bercovitch characterizes Hawthorne's relationship with the Salem community as a "paradox of dissent," in that Hawthorne simultaneously affirmed and repudiated an engagement with his birthplace.[7] Many of Lahiri's characters exhibit similar subversive or rebellious relationships with Bengali customs.

While Ruma is relatively rootless by choice, she is also cognizant of her increasing isolation. "Though she was growing familiar with the roads, with the exits and the mountains and the quality of the light, she felt no connection to any of it, or to anyone" (34). *The Scarlet Letter* features a clear geographic center; the scaffold and Market-Place are central to the town's activities, both punitive and heraldic. As Lawrence Buell notes, "To study the cult of the New England village is to study the most distinctively New Englandish contribution to the American social ideal" (305). Lahiri renders Ruma alien, without any native territory or adopted home. This sense of alienation is not limited to "Accustomed Earth." In the story "Only Goodness," Sudha's parents find "the rituals of small town New England . . . confounding" (138). All Indian American characters in the text feel, whether because of constant travel or expatriate existence, a sense of displacement. While this is the antithesis of Hawthorne's connection to Salem's people and streets, there is a parallel between Ruma and Hester as they exist, to the extent possible, outside social customs, preferring to chart domestic lives with their child. As Brodhead notes, "The whole form of Hester's experience forces her . . . into an uncharted ethical *terra incognita,* a place where known imperatives lose their authority and essential questions come open again. On such a ground the ethical world both can and must be newly constructed" (192). Yet Hester's questions are not necessarily ethical but existential, like Ruma's. In domestic quietude, Ruma sets aside modern expectations of participation in various communities, professional and social.

The author propagates Hawthorne's musings about transplantation and migration throughout *Unaccustomed Earth.* The title story revolves around the garden's evolution, to which her father dedicates his trip. "It was a modest planting, some slow-growing myrtle and phlox under the trees, two azalea bushes, a row of hostas, a clematis to climb one of the posts of the porch, and in honor of his wife, a small hydrangea" (49). His greatest pride at his former home in Pennsylvania was his garden harvest, with "guests marveling that the potatoes were from their own backyard, taking away bagfuls at the evening's end" (49). A skilled gardener, he models techniques as he models parenting. However, when Ruma's father teaches the next generation, his grandson Akash buries only plastic. "Into the soil went a pink rubber ball, a few pieces of Lego stuck together, a wooden block etched with a star" (44). Planting things that cannot grow, Lahiri seems to imply that the next generation and harvest are uncertain. The reader may be reminded of the remnants of the past that Hawthorne finds on the grounds of the Old Manse: Revolutionary War–era timbers and

gravestone, Native American arrowheads and implements. The site is identified by the spear and arrowheads, the chisels and other implements of
war, labor, and the hunt, which the plough turns up from the soil. Of these
discoveries, Hawthorne tells us, "Thoreau, who has a strange faculty of
finding what the Indians have left behind them, first set me on the search;
and I afterwards enriched myself with some very perfect specimens. There
is an exquisite delight, too, in picking up, for one's self, an arrow-head
that was dropt centuries ago, and has never been handled since, and which
we thus receive directly from the hand of the red hunter, who purposed
to shoot it at his game, or at an enemy. Such an incident builds up again
the Indian village, amid its encircling forest, and recalls to life the painted
chiefs and warriors, the squaws at their household toil, and the children
sporting among the wigwams; while the little wind-rocked papoose swings
from the branch of a tree" (*Mosses from an Old Manse* 20). With these artifacts, Hawthorne imagines the extinct Indian village brought back to life.

Ultimately, the most pervasive and injurious uprooting is Ruma's mother's death. "Where had her mother gone, when life persisted, when Ruma
still needed her to explain so many things?" (59) Lahiri poses this question
after Ruma finds a postcard her father leaves behind at her house, one he
wrote to his romantic interest. Penned as it is in Bengali, Ruma is unable to
decipher it but grasps its import. In the last sentence of the story, she pre-
pares the postcard for the mail, affixing a stamp to it and brushing off dirt.
Throughout the story, dirt coats objects and individuals as if they have
just been exhumed; it is with a character's excavation of the postcard that
Lahiri recreates "The Custom-House" most explicitly. Ruma discovers an
illicit letter—not a storied, frayed initial but a postcard—signifying a love
affair. Mailing the letter is an act of unburdening, equivalent to Hester
removing the scarlet letter from her chest. Both women unburden themselves. Ruma's act of mailing the postcard is the act of telling the story
and disseminating it, much like the premise behind "The Custom-House."[8]

The postcard, whose seemingly inscrutable meaning Ruma grasps
immediately, points to another Hawthorne-Lahiri parallel: semiology.
Enigmas and auguries resound in *The Scarlet Letter;* as Millicent Bell writes,
"The very title of the book is a sign, the smallest of literary units. . . . Reading will be given the broadest meaning in this novel. It will become a trope
for the decipherment of the world as a text. *The Scarlet Letter,* then, is, as
much as any work of fiction can be, an essay in semiology. Its theme is

the obliquity or indeterminacy of signs" (452). Similarly, Ruma attempts to infer meaning from the signs around her: her father's drying teabag near the stove, the clean bowl and cup on the drainboard, the objects that Akash attempts to plant, the hydrangea that will yield either pink or blue flowers, and, most importantly, the postcard in Bengali. But as in *The Scarlet Letter,* the most challenging signs are not material but psychological and ethereal, concerning human nature. Ruma contemplates the ponderous impact of her mother's death, recognizing that one effect is the loss of her cryptographer, as she realizes that "there were sentences her mother would have absorbed in an instant, sentences that proved, with more force than the funeral, more force than all the days since then, that her mother no longer existed" (59). While Hawthorne's signs often relate to the tension between the individual and the larger structures (church, state) in which they exist, Lahiri's signs in "Unaccustomed Earth" concern the diasporic tension between generations of immigrants. The incremental losses of language and tradition render some signs indecipherable to the next generation.

The absent father and matriarchal structure of *The Scarlet Letter* find resonance in Lahiri's text.[9] Lahiri notes Adam's absenteeism through the double entendre of husbandry. When Ruma's father visits her new home, he appraises the garden:

> "Adam planted all this?" her father asked, taking in the garden that was visible through the kitchen window, mentioning Adam for the first time.
> "No. It was all here." (16)

The unaltered landscape reflects the absence of Ruma's husband and implies that the marriage is not fertile. For his wife, Ruma's father "had toiled in unfriendly soil, coaxing such things from the ground" (16). The father is a provider in ways that Ruma's husband is not. He is present to help Ruma with Akash, bathing and dressing him, helping him eat, reading to him, and teaching him how to garden. His postgardening cleansing ritual is one he repeats with his grandson, "scrubbing the caked-on dirt from his elbows and knees" in the bath (48). Ruma's husband, Adam, is peeved that his father-in-law is planting a garden, and asks whether he will be around to take care of it. Through the dissociation of the inhabitants of a house from their property, Lahiri underscores that transplantation can effect more shallow roots. When Ruma's father informs her that he will avail himself of the neighborhood's nursery, she misconstrues the word to refer to school for Akash. The hydrangea he plants—pink or blue, depending on the soil—is a monument to his wife, and the horticultural metaphor for Ruma's future child. On departing from the house in Seattle, Ruma's father tells her, "Let me know how the garden comes along," before acknowledging her belly and adding, "I am waiting for the good news" (56). Toward the conclusion of the story, Lahiri returns to Hawthorne's metaphor of plantings and generations. ("Childless men," Hawthorne writes in "Mosses," "if they would know something of the bliss of paternity, should plant a seed—be it squash, bean, Indian corn, or perhaps a mere flower, or worthless weed—should plant it with their own hands, and nurse it from infancy to maturity, altogether by their own care" [16].)

Though Ruma's father savors his newfound freedom from obligation, he also mourns his rootlessness. "He missed working outside, the solid feeling of dirt under his knees, getting into his nails, the smell of it lingering on his skin even after he'd scrubbed himself in the shower" (49). Lahiri thus complicates the notion that transplantation necessarily strengthens cultivation. Srikanth argues that "the rootedness that Hawthorne's narrator is determined to avoid and the different or unaccustomed earth he is moved to explore can hardly be construed as analogous to the forces that extricate individuals and groups from one location and cast them in unimaginably unaccustomed ground" (56). Lahiri's characters, who emigrate in search of economic and educational opportunity, represent a different relationship with rootedness.

Immigrant Customs

Both "The Custom-House" and *Unaccustomed Earth* deal in import and export. Lahiri's final three stories, in Part 2 of the collection, are devoted to two characters, Hema and Kaushik, who are teenagers when we meet them, and middle-aged or deceased at the end of the trilogy. The first story, "Once in a Lifetime," takes place in the 1970s and chronicles Hema's family's relationship with the Choudhuris, Kaushik's family, who reside in Cambridge, Massachusetts, choose to return to India, and then emigrate once more back to Massachusetts. Hema contemplates the similarities and differences between the two families, and learns of Kaushik's mother's breast cancer. The subsequent story, "Year's End," chronicles a college-age Kaushik's mourning for his mother, as well as his feelings of revulsion toward his father's new wife and stepdaughters. The last story in the trilogy, "Going Ashore," features Hema and Kaushik as adults. Hema, now a Latin professor at Wellesley, is on sabbatical in Rome before entering into an arranged marriage with a man recommended by her parents. She meets Kaushik, now a nomadic war photographer, and the two have an affair before separating to pursue the next stages in their lives: marriage and pregnancy for Hema, a job in Hong Kong for Kaushik. Their separation is rendered even more definite when Kaushik dies tragically while on vacation in Thailand, in the 2004 tsunami. Ambreen Hai writes, "But the structure of *Unaccustomed Earth* does not just enact variations on the same theme, nor is the collection structured on linear principles to privilege the ending as a site of resolution or (dis)closure. Instead, the stories are arranged to produce a prismatic effect of reseeing a central problematic as it rotates through different refractions, different angles, with unexpected twists and surprises" (188). In other words, the collection functions as a self-reflective whole.

Hema is Hester's contemporary equivalent in many ways. She becomes a college professor at Wellesley, spends her sabbatical abroad in Rome, living independently; and immerses herself in an affair with Kaushik before succumbing to tradition and accepting an arranged marriage with Kevin. Hema, like Hester, is rebellious and wise, navigating a life perched between the individual and the collective, between proud independence and the Bengali community. Considering Hawthorne and literary influence, David Greven suggests, "We might imagine influence facilitating Hawthorne's stated hope of achieving 'intercourse with the world,'" an act of community building that took place, could only take place, on the page" (7). As Lahiri interrogates the tensions between individual and communal identity, she participates in a literary community and tradition.[10] Hema shares this self-reliance with other strong female protagonists of *Unaccustomed Earth,* including Ruma of the title story and Sudha of "Only Goodness." Though both women marry, they exist, like Hester, with husbands largely absent from the narrative. All three women must unburden themselves of the weight of history and tradition, whether religious or ethnic. In this way the characters function much as their authors do, reconciling past literary and linguistic traditions.

If Hema, like Ruma, is Hester's descendant, Kaushik, a war photographer and detached observer, recalls Hawthorne himself. He is the most transient character in the collection, a citizen of somewhere else. Steeped in melancholy after the loss of his mother, he considers himself without a home; as an adult, he makes his temporary residence wherever there is international conflict, and rarely returns to the United States. This rootlessness is a function not only of geography but also of psychology; he is a casualty of too many transplantations. Like Hawthorne, who, as Edwin Haviland Miller argues, "ventured farther than any of his predecessors or contemporaries in America into the labyrinths of the unconscious or the inner landscape" (283), Lahiri employs both internal and physical landscapes to map iterations of citizenship and belonging.

Along with the reconciliation of identity that results from transplantation or displacement, Lahiri is interested in existential inquiry. How do we pursue not only truth and knowledge but also tranquility and stability in a life defined by movement or relocation? Lahiri's most striking images in the collection capture the paradoxical moments in life when joy, beauty, and their transience are sharpest: Hema trying on bras with Kaushik's mother, who is dying of breast cancer, in the story "Once in a Lifetime"; the narrator's mother, Aparna, pinning her sari and dousing herself with gasoline, about to self-immolate before a neighbor greets her in the afternoon light in the story "Hell-Heaven"; Kaushik letting go of the boat and trusting the calm sea just before the onslaught of the tsunami in the story "Going Ashore." In *Septimius Felton, or, the Elixir of Life,* Hawthorne's unfinished, posthumously published romance (1872), the author's discussion of these issues is familiar. Describing a character's contemplation of his love interest, Hawthorne writes, "In short, it was such a moment as I suppose all men feel (at least, I can answer for one), when the real scene and picture of life swims, jars, shakes, seems about to be broken up and dispersed, like the picture in a smooth pond, when we disturb its tranquil mirror by throwing in a stone; and though the scene soon settles itself, and looks as real as before, a haunting doubt keeps close at hand, as long as we live, asking, 'Is it stable? Am I sure of it? Am I certainly not dreaming? See, it trembles again, ready to dissolve.'" In Hawthorne's characterization and Lahiri's illustrations of this idea, both reality and stasis are questioned. Lahiri shares Hawthorne's interest in epistemology but reframes it in the context of diaspora.[11] It is striking that Hawthorne uses aquatic imagery to explore the idea of transient calm: the picture in the smooth pond swims and shakes in response to the stone's arrival.

Lahiri uses similar water imagery in *Unaccustomed Earth*. In "Once in a Lifetime," Hema narrates Kaushik's family's real estate search, in which water is paramount. "They sought an in-ground pool, or space to build one; your mother missed swimming at her club in Bombay. 'Water views, that's what we should look for,' your mother said, while reading the classified section of the *Globe* one afternoon, and this limited the search even further. We drove out to Swampscott and Duxbury to see properties overlooking the ocean, and to houses in the woods with views of private lakes" (244). Later, a grieving Kaushik remembers his mother's appreciation of her daily laps, as long as her body is capable. He yearns for her swimming prowess. In "Year's End," Kaushik escapes an uncomfortable domestic dynamic with his father, stepmother, and stepsisters by driving north along the New England coast until he reaches Maine. Traversing the coastal towns, the summer tourists long gone, he recognizes that "the water was the most unforgiving thing, nearly black at times, cold enough, I knew, to kill me, violent enough to break me apart. The waves were immense, battering rocky beaches without sand" (289). The encounter with the sinister Atlantic foreshadows his death in a benign tropical sea, "as warm and as welcoming as a bath" (331), off the coast of Thailand. Another bath scene takes place in "Only Goodness," when the female protagonist, Sudha, and her husband entrust their son to Sudha's alcoholic brother, Rahul. "She found Neel in the tub, filling his sippy cup with water and pouring it out. He was sitting without the plastic ring they normally put him in so that he wouldn't tip over. He was trembling but otherwise happy, intent on his task, the water up to the middle of his chest, the mere sight of him sitting there, unattended, causing Sudha to emit a series of spontaneous cries and a volt of fear to seize her haunches. The water was no longer warm" (170). Sudha meets her husband, Roger, at the National Gallery, where he begins explicating Jan van Eyck's 1434 painting *The Arnolfini Portrait*. The painting depicts the Italian merchant Giovanni di Nicolao Arnolfini and his wife, likely engaged in a betrothal or legal ceremony, in the interior of their Flemish home in Bruges. The painting is noteworthy for, among other attributes, its masterly use of perspective; the mirror behind the couple reflects two men, witnesses to the ceremony but not immediately evident to the viewer. Sudha has a flashback to the image in the mirror at her wedding, recalling "the small mirror . . . revealing more than the room at first appeared to contain" (157). Sudha sees the parameters of Rahul's existence in this mirror; Lahiri implies that problematic familial networks and contexts are inevitable, the roots running farther and wider than those that may be visible.

Both Hawthorne and Lahiri interrogate the possibility of death caused by a substance vital to life and crucial to early immigration, whether it is to be found in a bathtub, a swimming pool, or an ocean. Just as in *The Scarlet Letter*, whose last chapters remind the reader of the presence of the port by mentioning the Spanish shipmaster, the ship sailing to Bristol, and Pearl's eventual residence abroad, the last chapter of *Unaccustomed Earth* invokes the sea. Hawthorne emphasizes the gathering strength of humanity after Dimmesdale delivers the Election Sermon: "There were human beings enough, and enough of highly wrought and symphonious feeling, to produce that more impressive sound than the organ-tones of the blast, or the thunder, or the roar of the sea; even that mighty swell of many voices, blended into one great voice by the universal impulse which makes likewise one vast heart out of the many" (158).

In contrast, Lahiri's invocation of the sea at the end of *Unaccustomed Earth* only reasserts the brutal power of nature and the vulnerability of man. In the final story in the collection, "Going Ashore," Kaushik's photographs, published in major newspapers, "wash up on his father's doorstep" (306) in repeated migrations of their own. Kaushik drowns in the 2004 tsunami as Hema proceeds with her arranged marriage and becomes pregnant, feeling "the ground once more underfoot" (333).[12] "He wanted to swim to the cove as Henrik had, to show his mother he was not afraid. . . . He held on to the edge of the boat, swinging his legs over the side, lowering himself. . . . His feet touched the bottom, and so he let go" (331). This is simultaneously a joyous and freeing yet dark and tragic turn in the collection. Samuel Chase Coale notes the "darkness that overtook Hawthorne's later romances" (20), which reflected the "dualistic antagonisms" of a "very Manichean world [Hawthorne] had attempted to surmount. "This irony," he argues, "embodies the great American theme of escape from and submission to that world of fact that appears again and again in the fantastic, overwrought romances of great American writers" (21). Lahiri confronts a similar polarity in the transient bliss of Hema and Kaushik's romance and Kaushik's subsequent demise at sea.

Whereas the majority of the stories are domestic in scale, "Going Ashore" broadens its scope to be global. Heidi Elisabeth Bollinger observes, "Lahiri's characters evince a penetrating awareness of life's dreadful possibilities—a quietly fatalistic understanding that at any moment, something could go terribly wrong. . . . [They] recognize the tenuousness of their future plans, and yet the disasters that they anticipate, in a state of paranoid daydreaming, never materialize. The true disaster is defined by its unexpectedness" (497). Bollinger's observations about Lahiri's fiction pertain more broadly to life; tragedy is more often than not unexpected. In a 2008 interview, Lahiri addressed the role of the tsunami in *Unaccustomed Earth:* "The real event just sort of caught my character in there. . . . I don't like to read about something—an event, a cataclysm—in fiction for the sake of reading it. . . . I think that the fact there is a major global event in this book—I don't know if it was okay or not" (qtd. in Kachka).[13] Lahiri's words are interesting to read in the context of her reverence for Hawthorne, who blended history with fiction in *The Scarlet Letter* and appropriated the experience of his own ancestors. But the tragedy that Lahiri invokes arises out of missed opportunity and a lack of communication. That Hema and Kaushik choose to separate is somewhat inexplicable; as with many instances in life, the severe consequences of this separation seem avoidable but are finite.

The title of the last story suggests the end of travel for the protagonists; it also recalls the first landing of the Puritans in the Massachusetts Bay Colony, in addition to Hawthorne's words near the end of "The Custom-House." One also thinks of the current migrant crisis and refugees going ashore only to continue their journeys: the idea of home as a fallacy, continuous migration, destinations never reached. Of Salem, the narrator opines, "Henceforth, it ceases to be a reality of my life. I am a citizen of somewhere else" (35). Despite this earnest claim and the family's departure from Salem, several years later Hawthorne penned *The House of the Seven Gables* (1851), another text firmly rooted in Salem's earth. There too, he attempted his Salem leave-taking, concluding with a rejection of the locale.

Immigrant Fiction

In her *New York Times* review of *Unaccustomed Earth,* Michiko Kakutani notes that Lahiri "shows how haunted [the characters] remain by the burden of their families' dreams and their awareness of their role in the generational process of Americanization." Kakutani could easily be speaking about Hawthorne's texts here; her observation applies not just to familial relations but to literary genealogies as well. Robert Milder notes that in Italy, where Hawthorne wrote *The Marble Faun,* he "was challenged, like James's Americans abroad, by the obliquities of an older, denser civilization morally and culturally distinct from his own" (ix). A parallel exists for contemporary writers, especially those wrongly cast in a separate immigrant or ethnic tradition. In a 2017 *New York Times* interview with Michiko Kakutani about his reading proclivities, President Obama mentioned his admiration for the work of Lahiri and Junot Díaz, intuiting that their texts "speak to a very particular contemporary immigration experience. But also this combination of—that I think is universal—longing for this better place, but also feeling displaced and looking backwards at the same time. I think in that sense, their novels are directly connected to a lot of American literature."[14] All American literature descends from this narrative.

Critics have mistakenly segregated twentieth-and twenty-first-century literature by immigrants into a separate category. Lahiri herself addressed this problem in an interview, after being asked to name influential "immigrant fiction." She responded,

> I don't know what to make of the term "immigrant fiction." Writers have always tended to write about the worlds they come from. And it just so happens that many writers originate from different parts of the world than the ones they end up living in, either by choice or by necessity or by circumstance, and therefore, write about those experiences. If certain books are to be termed immigrant fiction, what do we call the rest? Native fiction? Puritan fiction? This distinction doesn't agree with me. Given the history of the United States, all American fiction could be classified as immigrant fiction. Hawthorne writes about immigrants. So does Willa Cather. From the beginnings of literature, poets and writers have based their narratives on crossing borders, on wandering, on exile, on encounters beyond the familiar. ("Jhumpa Lahiri")

That Hawthorne and Lahiri address the nature of citizenship and migration so many generations apart suggests that these questions are never settled. What is domestic, foreign, national, transnational? Examining this literary symbiosis, to use David Cowart's term, illuminates how Lahiri's text can in turn affect our understanding of Hawthorne's text as an immigrant narrative.

In an effort to enliven a "Custom-House" class discussion, I cobbled together a version of the storied package from tea-bathed parchment and an embroidered felt A. A student with whom I was in cahoots then made the dramatic discovery of the package in the corner of the classroom. Though we were far from Salem's shore, the exercise provided a useful microcosm of Lahiri's reenactment of the narrator's activity in "The Custom-House," recovering a remnant of the past and appropriating it to tell a story. Much of American literature today concerns archaeology, recovery, and retelling. Lahiri's return to Hawthorne is both a pilgrimage to the past and an investment in the future of American literature. Her invocation of *The Scarlet Letter* is an act of putting down roots, claiming American literature as her soil. Describing her own roots, Lahiri laments, "My upbringing, an amalgam of two hemispheres, was heterodox and complicated; I wanted it to be conventional and contained. I wanted to be anonymous and ordinary, to look like other people, to behave as others did. . . . For much of my life, I wanted to belong to a place, either the one my parents came from or to America, spread out before us. When I became a writer my desk became home; there was no need for another" ("Trading Stories"). She is in good company. In the custom house, overlooking Salem's harbor, a desk sits empty, its erstwhile surveyor having long since traded his customs desk for a writing one, having become "a citizen of somewhere else" (*Scarlet Letter* 35).

3

Short Happy Palimpsest

Ernest Hemingway's "The Short Happy Life
of Francis Macomber" and Junot Díaz's
The Brief Wondrous Life of Oscar Wao

They say it came first from Africa, carried in the screams
of the enslaved; that it was the death bane of the Taínos,
uttered just as one world perished and another began;
that it was a demon drawn into Creation through the
nightmare door that was cracked open in the Antilles.
Fukú americanus, or more colloquially, fukú—generally
a curse or doom of some kind; specifically the Curse and
the Doom of the New World. . . . No matter what its name
or provenance, it is believed that the arrival of Europeans
on Hispaniola unleashed fukú on the world, and we've all
been in the shit ever since. Santo Domingo might be fukú's
Kilometer Zero, its port of entry, but we are all of us its
children, whether we know it or not.

—Junot Díaz, *The Brief Wondrous Life of Oscar Wao* (2007)

"THEY SAY IT CAME first from Africa." The opening words of Junot Díaz's
novel *The Brief Wondrous Life of Oscar Wao* speak to the colonial origin of

the fukú curse that dooms Dominican characters in the book, but also hint at the literary genealogy of the narrative: Ernest Hemingway's "The Short Happy Life of Francis Macomber" (1936). Díaz has claimed that although Hemingway's short story "helped shape some of the early bones" of the novel, he was "never a huge fan of Hemingway's work in general" (Johnson, "Rethinking Hemingway"). This is an intriguing claim, given the novel's apparent allusion to Hemingway's short story. Yet as Kirk Curnutt observes in an illuminating essay that contextualizes Hemingway's associations with his contemporaries, "Affiliations and feuds among authors are often as entertaining as the literature they produce. The benefits of the former seem obvious enough. By aligning with each other, writers enhance their cultural visibility by forming cliques, launching movements, and promoting coterie aesthetics" (163). Simultaneously invoking Hemingway's oeuvre and dismissing it, Díaz attracts readers but maintains the autonomy of his work.[1] Yet, he acknowledges, "Even someone like me who didn't operate consciously under Hemingway's shadow was still somewhat touched by Hemingway's shadow. He had an enormous influence on male writing in America, and his echoes, I suspect, are to be found almost everywhere" (Johnson, "Rethinking Hemingway"). Read in light of the first sentences of *Oscar Wao,* the language Díaz uses to introduce the curse and the language he employs to acknowledge literary influence are strikingly similar. Both speak to the impact of influence, whether or not we are cognizant of it. Within the respective scopes of the New World and American literature, both speak to the vast territory of colonization, literal and figurative, with which Díaz engages in his work. Finally, and perhaps most important, both speak to the "children" inheriting specters of generations past: national, familial, and literary.

Perhaps anticipating the reader's question of how to escape such potentially paralytic trauma, Díaz suggests the only method of liberation just a few pages later:

> Anytime a fukú reared its many heads there was only one way to prevent disaster from coiling around you, only one surefire counterspell that would keep you and your family safe. Not surprisingly, it was a word. A simple word (followed usually by a vigorous crossing of index fingers).
> Zafa . . .
> Even now as I write these words I wonder if this book ain't a zafa of sorts. My very own counterspell. (*Oscar Wao* 7)

Díaz thereby lends authority to his own narrative and to the power of writing, whose strength he posits in the face of oppression. Jennifer Harford Vargas and others cast the zafa as Yunior speaking back to Trujillo. As Harford Vargas writes, "The novel thus stages a conflict between the fukú and the zafa, between domination and resistance. The two underlying symbolic organizing principles embody the dual signification of dictating as dominating (the fukú) and dictating as recounting or writing back (the zafa)" (10). This can be applied to intertextual relationships as well, in the form of the later text resisting the predecessor.

Written over the faint remnant of "The Short Happy Life of Francis Macomber," *Oscar Wao* is, ultimately, a palimpsest. Here I propose a new category of intertextuality: literary colonialism, in which an author responds not to geographic occupation but to canonical occupation, and seeks to reclaim this space. Díaz's text counters hegemony in a new dialogic language encompassing countless codes and registers. *Oscar Wao* is a postmodern herald of an American literature that is constituted by countless genres, places, languages, and ethnicities, as well as the story of a man whom a certain literary predecessor might have deemed a loser.

Francis and Oscar

When *Oscar Wao* was published in 2007, several reviewers noted the title's allusion to Hemingway's story, first published in the September 1936 issue of *Cosmopolitan* magazine, but assessments of parallels ended there. Díaz's nod to Hemingway is fairly overt: two adjectives, without the intercession of a comma, precede a life and a name. The biographical subjects of both works experience joy only briefly, and rather desperately, before meeting their respective ends. In Hemingway's short story, Francis Macomber and his wife, Margot, accompanied by expert hunter Robert Wilson, pursue game while on safari in Africa. After Macomber exhibits fear in an encounter with a lion, his wife skewers his cowardice and flaunts a brazen tryst with Wilson. When Macomber successfully slays a buffalo the following day, he regains his pride. Pursuing the last wounded buffalo into the bush, Macomber kills it just as he is about to be gored, but is himself simultaneously killed by Margot's shot from the car. The idea is that in his final successful hunt, Macomber frees himself from a woman who could be the female descendant of Rip Van Winkle's termagant wife, who emasculates and provokes the dolorous need for liberation. Francis Macomber is dead at thirty-five; the reader knows that before this gruesome end, the protagonist made money, married a beautiful but cruel woman, and booked a safari. Hemingway is less interested in providing the ancillary information that rounds out a life, preferring instead to focus on a few days' time, from which the reader is to infer past grievances, and a problematic gender dynamic having unfurled over the course of many years or, in a broader sense, centuries.[2]

In Díaz's novel, the narrator, Yunior, Oscar's college friend and his sister's erstwhile lover, offers the reader a more extensive life portrait of about twenty years, introducing Oscar De León as a child, ending with the cessation of his life in his late twenties. Though he does not make it as far into adulthood as Macomber, Oscar's dimensions are far more defined. A resident of Patterson, New Jersey, Oscar is a bookish, depressed Dominican American with a fraught family life. Committed to science fiction, fantasy, and magical realism, obsessed with successive unrequited love interests, he is too intelligent for his surroundings and too sensitive for the cruelties the world visits upon people, both nationally, in the form of corruption and serial human rights abuses, and personally, in the form of frat boys and shallow women. As the opening reference to the fukú indicates, the narrative of Oscar's life seems written without his input. Oscar ultimately escapes the mediocrity of his environment through the pursuit of a woman rather than an animal, a venture just as dangerous. He resolutely declares his love for Ybón, a prostitute in the Dominican Republic, despite threats from her police captain boyfriend, whose thugs eventually kill Oscar. The narrative is far more complicated than Oscar's quest to lose his virginity, however, as Díaz interweaves the national history of the corrupt dictator Rafael Trujillo with the familial history of the De Leóns.

The Masculine Ropes

Díaz's twenty-first-century riff on "Macomber" reconfigures the crisis of masculine identity in transnational contexts. Díaz has a particular concern with Dominican masculinity, which he underscores through the contrast of

Oscar and Yunior. From the beginning of the novel, the narrator emphasizes Oscar's bad luck with women—or, rather, girls—after the age of seven,
lamenting his impotence as a Dominican male. What begins as humor evolves
into tragedy as Oscar's adult relationship with a woman causes his death. As
Paul Jay writes, "Oscar's inability to live up to what seems at the outset of the
book to be a thoroughly trite form of Latin machismo is used to weave a complex transnational meditation on the relationship between masculinity, voice,
storytelling, and performance . . . leading to forms of brutality that flow out
of Trujillo's world into Oscar, Lola, and Yunior's America" (182). Díaz connects
Yunior's promiscuity with Trujillo's reputation with women, thus indicating
the malignancy of such masculine ideals. Regarding the grandfather Abelard's
attempt to protect his daughter from Trujillo, Díaz writes, "If you think the
average Dominican guy's bad, Trujillo was 5000 times worse. . . . If the pro-
curement of ass had been any more central to the Trujillato the regime would
have been the world's first culocracy (and maybe, in fact, it was)" (217).

Oscar represents a departure from this regime. His love interests during high school and college are both perspicacious women prone to friendship with Oscar and abusive relationships with their boyfriends, who are
also Dominican. One of the most humorous scenes in the novel arrives
when Oscar's crush, Ana, informs him of her boyfriend Manny's anatomi-
cal gift. Oscar then imagines protecting Ana from nuclear apocalypse while
Manny leaves a "half-literate" suicide note, "*I koona taek it*" and Oscar com-
forts Ana, "He was too weak for this Hard New World" (43). Oscar's lack
of experience with women leads to his nickname, Oscar Wilde. Yunior
asserts one Halloween, "I couldn't believe how much he looked like that
fat homo . . . and I told him so" (180). Their friends hear Wilde as Wao, and
the nickname sticks, in a confused, homophobic mockery of masculinity.
In Edwidge Danticat's interview of Díaz, published in *BOMB*, Díaz comments, "But more than people, fake or real, I tried to stuff as many books
as I could into Oscar Wao. I mean, shit, even the title refers to Oscar Wilde
and 'The Short Happy Life of Francis Macomber' simultaneously." Danticat replies, "Damn, how could I have missed that?" Compounding these
associations is Oscar's interest in fantasy fiction. When Oscar informs one
tough guy that he's "into the more speculative genres" (43), the reader may
recall Wilson's derision of Macomber, "Now what in hell were you going to
do about a man who talked like that" (8).[3]

While Yunior and assorted other characters represent the hypermasculine Dominican male, Díaz is sure to critique this prowess. As Elena Machado Sáez contends, "So while Díaz's novel aims to represent the linguistic
diversity of the Dominican diaspora, it does so by following the nation's
logic of consolidation, specifically demarcating the borders of a representative diasporic subject in terms of masculinity and sexuality" (523).
A weightlifter, womanizer, and serial philanderer, Yunior is Wilson to
Oscar's Macomber: a hunter of prey, the man who seems to get all the girls,
morality and honor notwithstanding. But Yunior does not, ultimately, get
the girl; Lola, Oscar's sister, finally leaves him.[4] Díaz thus troubles what
Hemingway seems to present so simply in "Macomber," the matter-of-fact
offering of gimlet, gun, and conquest. Sharing his own familiarity with
this construct in the interview with Danticat, Díaz remarks: "The thing
with me was that I was a nerd embedded in a dictatorial military family
where the boys had to fight all the time, where we were smacked around
regularly by our father (to toughen us up), where we shot guns every week-
end (just in case anything should happen), where you were only a human
being if you were an aggressive violent hombre."

Though masculinity is often aligned with physical aggression, an idea
Hemingway explores in "Macomber," Díaz undermines this idea in several ways. The book's title also invokes *A Brief Account of the Destruction of
the Indies* (1552) by the Spanish Dominican friar Bartolomé de las Casas.
Las Casas chronicled the Spanish abuses of the indigenous peoples of the
Greater Antilles, particularly Hispaniola. Las Casas's text led to the passage
of the New Laws of the Indies for the Good Treatment and Preservation
of the Indians, which prohibited the enslavement of indigenous people. In
Díaz's short story collections *Drown* (1996) and *This Is How You Lose Her*
(2012), Yunior and Rafa's last name is "de las Casas," interrogating notions
of nativity and diaspora. The adjective "brief," in both *The Brief Wondrous
Life of Oscar Wao* and *A Brief Account of the Destruction of the Indies,* belies
the enduring and expansive nature of each work. Deploying the adjective
in his own work, Díaz pays homage to a man who bore witness to and pro-
tested against colonial violence.

The title of the novel implies that Oscar is a contemporary corollary to
Macomber's character. Hemingway provides ample illustration of Francis
Macomber's dubious masculinity; aside from the safari during which he is

cuckolded, the bit of biography is not flattering. Beyond his weakness and obsession with the failed hunt, Hemingway catalogs Macomber's expertise as follows: motorcycles, motor cars, duck shooting, fishing (trout, salmon, and big-sea), and "sex in books, many books, too many books" (18). Oscar, too, knows about masculinity from books (and video games). As the narrator explains, "It wasn't just that he didn't have no kind of father to show him the masculine ropes, he simply lacked all aggressive and martial tendencies" (15). Yet Hemingway qualifies the importance of sexual experience when Wilson praises Macomber's hunting triumph. "He'd seen it in the war work the same way. More of a change than any loss of virginity. Fear gone like an operation. Something else grew in its place. Main thing a man had. Made him into a man" (36). *Oscar Wao* seems to be Díaz's response to this assertion, privileging love over violence in the making of a man.

Like Macomber, Oscar finds redemption in the minutes before he is shot, having made the deliberate decision to return to the Dominican Republic despite the threat of violence, in addition to having experienced love and sexual fulfillment. After the successful hunt, Macomber declares, "You know something did happen to me. . . . I feel absolutely different" (25). Wilson attempts to educate Macomber that speech is inferior to action: "Doesn't do to talk too much about all this. Talk the whole thing away. No pleasure in anything if you mouth it up too much" (26). In contrast, it is clear that Oscar's courageous speech in the face of death ushers him into manhood:

> This time Oscar didn't cry when they drove him back to the cane fields. . . .
> He told them that what they were doing was wrong, that they were going to
> take a great love out of the world. . . . He told them that it was only because
> of her love that he'd been able to do the thing that he had done . . . told them
> if they killed him they would probably feel nothing and their children would
> probably feel nothing either, not until they were old and weak or about to be
> struck by a car and then they would sense him waiting for them on the other
> side and over there he wouldn't be no fatboy or dork or kid no girl had ever
> loved; over there he'd be a hero, an avenger. (321–22)

It is his final speech act, rather than an act of violence or sex, that masculinizes him. Oscar's delivery adheres to what Kenneth Johnston defines as the "Hemingway code: a personal code of conduct, self-imposed, characterized by courage, stoicism, dignity, and honor. . . . The code permits a character to retrieve a victory, usually moral, as he goes down to what the uninitiated would call defeat" (rpt. in Flora 175).

Yet Macomber is not necessarily Oscar's progenitor, an ambiguity that relates to Díaz's emphasis on the dialogic rather than the dialectic. Díaz introduces the protagonist, whose last name is De León, by telling us he does not live up to his name: "Our hero was not one of those Dominican cats everybody's always going on about" (11). Lest we forget the lion, per Margot's sardonic assertion, Díaz returns to the trope throughout the novel. When Beli, Oscar's mother, is beaten by the Trujillo family's henchmen, the musicians who find her describe her emergence from the fields of sugar cane as "something lion-like in the gloom" (150). The driver subsequently suggests that Beli was attacked by a lion. "Let the lion finish her," the driver urges, trying to avoid trouble (151). The De Leóns constitute both the lion and the lion's prey. In "Macomber," the lion casts a pall over the story from the beginning; the reader is aware of it in the same way the reader of Oscar Wao is aware of the fukú, the curse that vanquishes the De León family. Oscar's defiant speech in the cane fields before he is shot mirrors the lion's last stand. "All of him, pain, sickness, hatred and all of his remaining strength, was tightening into an absolute concentration for a rush. He could hear the men talking and he waited, gathering all of himself into this preparation for a charge as soon as the men would come into the grass" (16). It is the lion's final charge that colors the entire narrative. Similarly, even after death, Oscar's voice persists, in the form of manuscripts and letters, mailed before his death and received many months later.

Wilson and Yunior are hypermasculine foils to the title characters of each text. Wilson's observation of Macomber's growth—"he had seen men come of age before and it always moved him. It was not a matter of their twenty-first birthday" (25)—parallels Yunior's elation that Oscar finally consummates a relationship, though this revelation is posthumous.

> Anyway, the package that did arrive had some amazing news. . . . He reported that he'd liked it . . . but what really got him was not the bam-bam-bam of sex—it was the little intimacies that he'd never in his whole life anticipated, like combing her hair or getting her underwear off a line or watching her walk naked to the bathroom. . . . The intimacies like listening to her tell him

about being a little girl and him telling her that he'd been a virgin all his life. He wrote that he couldn't believe he'd had to wait for this so goddamn long. (Ybón was the one who suggested calling the wait something else. . . . Maybe, she said, you could call it life.) (334–35)

Ybón's redefinition of the wait is in turn a redefinition of the masculine ideal that Hemingway sketches.

Sentiment and sympathy play integral roles in both stories in relation to masculinity, as do historical distinctions between traditions of male and female writing. Hemingway incorporates sentimentalism in "Macomber" despite its modernism, while Díaz appropriates the structure of the sentimental novel as part of the text's polyphony. Sentimental texts traditionally feature an emphasis on emotion, through both characters' interactions and readers' responses to the text. Eighteenth-century sentimentalism led to nineteenth-century domestic fiction, in which protagonists experienced significant personal hardship, often without a stable familial structure, before achieving salvation through Christianity or marriage or both. In Hemingway's story, in the absence of Margot's emotional investment in her husband's happiness, Macomber attracts sympathy from Wilson:

"Then it's going to be just like the lion," said Margot, full of anticipation.

"It's not going to be a damned bit like the lion," Wilson told her. "Did you want another drink, Macomber?" (24)

It is not until Macomber is shot that Margot exhibits emotion, "crying hysterically" (27) and departing from modernism's resistance to the sentimental. As Michael T. Wilson observes, if Hemingway's fiction "blurred the lines of his own often-pronounced standards of writing—standards paralleling modernism's focus on those 'typically masculine virtues of emotional restraint'—it often did so in ways that actually heightened its emotional effect on his reading audience—then and now" (106). Hemingway's shifting narrative focalization in "Macomber" offers the reader different viewpoints, including that of the lion, which means that the animal is another potential recipient of sympathy in the story.[5] "Macomber did not know how the lion had felt before he started his rush. . . . Wilson knew something about it and only expressed it by saying, 'Damned fine lion,' but Macomber did not know how Wilson felt about things either. He did not know how his wife felt except that she was through with him" (18).

The Steinian repetition of feeling, knowing or not knowing how others feel, affirms subjectivity. It is worth noting that Hemingway himself later sympathized with the hunted; Michael Reynolds writes in his biography of Hemingway that during the author's second safari in Africa in 1953, he "preferred to drive around and look at the animals" and "had already begun to identify metaphorically with old trophy animals" (268).

Díaz consciously appropriates the tradition of sentimental fiction by titling the chapter that concerns Oscar's time at Rutgers University "Sentimental Education (1988–1992)," alluding to Flaubert's 1869 novel. Oscar lacks a father, has few friends, and cries regularly, in this way resembling delicate sentimental heroines. "His affection—that gravitational mass of love, fear, longing, desire, and lust that he directed at any and every girl in his vicinity without regard to looks, age, or availability—broke his heart each and every day. . . . He cried often for his love of some girl or another. Cried in the bathroom, where nobody could hear him" (23–24). He becomes severely depressed when rejected and goes so far as to attempt suicide. The fundamental distinction between the two works is that *Oscar Wao* is elegiac, whereas "Macomber" is ambiguous, even ambivalent, about the loss of the title character.

Hemingway's Shadows

Before Díaz, John Cheever took up the "Macomber" mantle in "O Youth and Beauty!," a short story first printed in the *New Yorker* (1953).[6] In the text, Cheever reframes the story of the African safari in suburban Shady Hill, USA. There are dinner parties in lieu of hunting parties, hurdle races in lieu of lion pursuits. Cash Bentley, a former track star reliving the glory days of his youth, is the domesticated Macomber, leaping over living room furniture at the close of dinner parties. The monotony of suburban existence, financial pressures, and quotidian responsibilities overwhelms the Bentleys, who routinely quarrel and make up. One evening, Cash fails to clear the living room hurdles at a neighborhood party, breaking his leg. This physical rapprochement, of course, symbolizes his aging, even decaying body (he is forty!), and causes him to contemplate the passage of time: "He does not understand what separates him from these children in the garden next door. He has been a young man. He has been a hero. He has been adored and happy and full of animal spirits, and now he stands in a dark kitchen, deprived of his athletic prowess, his impetuousness, his good looks—everything that means anything to him" (25). Cash stands alone in the house, just as Macomber lay alone in his dark tent, emasculated. Ultimately, when Cash attempts the hurdles one more time, his wife Louise shoots him inadvertently with what is supposed to be a starter pistol but is a real gun. Cheever is careful to invoke the same degree of ambiguity and intentionality as Hemingway, who commented on his own creation: "No, I don't know whether she shot him on purpose any more than you do. . . . The only hint I could give you is that it is my belief that the incidence of husbands shot accidentally by wives who are bitches and really work at it is very low" (135).

Many writers have noted Hemingway's impact on American literature and notions of masculinity. In "Blows to the Spirit," a dialog between Ken Kesey and Robert Stone in *Esquire* (June 1986), the writers discuss injuries to the psyche of the American male, including Hemingway's death:

> *Kesey:* To writers, Hemingway's suicide meant that for all that he claimed, and for all the toughness of his writing, he couldn't make it. This was a real blow to man's intellectual spirit.
> *Stone:* Hemingway had everything an American man desired. Glamour. Glamorous women. Adventure. He was a great fisherman. He was famous and skilled. He stood for a whole way of approaching life, and, when the guy who is proclaiming it can't do it, a lot of other people gave up, too.
> *Kesey:* He tricked us into following his mode, and then he conked out and shot himself.
> *Stone:* Leaving us holding the bag.
> *Kesey:* Holding this bag of dead Hemingway bones. (268)

Kesey and Stone's exchange explores inherited notions of masculinity in America: sport, physical strength, money, mobility, the company of beautiful women. Ironically, the criticisms of Hemingway's suicide participate in this ideology by implying that he was weak. Kesey's last statement about Hemingway's remains also pertains to the remnants of literary structure. One recalls Díaz's claim that Hemingway "helped shape some of the early bones of the novel," as well as the Latin phrase that Oscar's grandfather Abelard's daughter, Jacquelyn, writes on paper every morning, *"Tarde venientibus ossa* (To the latecomers are left the bones)" (219). In addition, Hemingway's "Papa" moniker is relevant here: the writers characterize his death as tantamount to a father abandoning his children.[7] Of course, *Oscar Wao* deals with many absent fathers, whether the absence is caused by elective abandonment or political violence. Díaz himself spoke to this desire for a figure of authority in both literature and life in an April 2008 *Slate* interview with Megan O'Rourke: "We all dream dreams of unity, of purity; we all dream that there's an authentic voice out there that will explain things, including ourselves. If it wasn't for our longing for these things, I doubt the novel or the short story would exist in its current form. Just remember: in dictatorships, only one person is really allowed to speak. And when I write a book or a story, I too am the only one speaking, no matter how I hide behind my characters." Here Díaz acknowledges the problem inherent in the hope for an omniscient figure, as well as the over-reliance on a single voice.

Being Antillean

One of the crucial questions that David Cowart poses in *Literary Symbiosis: The Reconfigured Text in Twentieth-Century Writing* addresses the efficacy of intentional intertextuality. "The important consideration," he writes, "at least for one interested in the genuinely problematic examples of literary symbiosis, would seem to lie in whether or not the 'guest' invites a comparison with the 'host.' Does the guest text, that is, manage to cast a new light on the original—the way Eliot says that the individual talent at once inherits and *modifies* the tradition?" (9). The most significant way in which Díaz accomplishes this relates to the primacy of race. Díaz revisions Hemingway's exploration of gender with additional considerations of cultural, national, and transnational belonging and citizenship.[8] "Macomber" begins with the description of the assembly of African boys in servitude to the white hunter and tourists. Wilson threatens to whip Macomber's personal servant, mitigating the racial import by telling Macomber, "We all take a beating every day, you know, one way or another" (7). Race is not a focus of the story but became an integral part of the story's afterlife.[9] As Nghana Tamu Lewis has rightly observed, "Hemingway's writings about Africa and African people raise questions

about historic conditions of oppression, resistance, and renewal that are
vital to understanding configurations of hegemonic power and counter-
hegemonic struggle that defined continental Africa throughout the
twentieth century" (316). In *Oscar Wao*, Díaz invokes both colonial history, beginning the novel with allusions to Christopher Columbus and
the invasion of Hispaniola, and the history of racial allegory in American
literature. In "Macomber," Wilson describes American women, and by
extension Margot, as "the hardest in the world; the hardest, the cruel-
est, the most predatory and the most attractive and their men have soft-
ened or gone to pieces nervously as they have hardened" (9). Hemingway's
characterization of Margot as predatory becomes racialized in Díaz's
iteration. When Oscar's mother, Beli, described as the darkest girl in her
school, pursues a boy with a light complexion, he is described as prey. The
narrator, as if suddenly reporting from the deck of the *Pequod*, queries,
"And of all these things the albino boy was the symbol. Wonder ye then
at the fiery hunt?" (95), casting Beli as Ahab, replacing *Moby-Dick*'s white
whale with the privilege of light skin.

Race is not only treated with characterization, but also framed through
setting. The respective locations of the protagonists' deaths, in the African bush and the Dominican sugar cane fields, are indexes of colonial
trade history, corruption, and subjugation by the United States. Trujillo's
operatives beat Beli "like she was a slave" (147) in the cane fields, the setting in which her future son will lose his life. By killing Oscar in the cane
fields, Díaz indicts not only the corruption in the Dominican Republic
but also the complicity of the United States, which, according to the U.S.
Department of Agriculture, imports more than 200,000 tons of sugar
from the Dominican Republic annually. It is impossible to invoke sugar
cane fields without implicating the history of sugar importation. Attention to this history has recently increased, with major museum exhibits
describing Hispaniola's history of slavery and rebellion, as well as the role
of trade. Kara Walker's 2014 installation at the Domino Sugar Factory in
Brooklyn, titled *A Subtlety, or the Marvelous Sugar Baby, an Homage to the
unpaid and overworked Artisans who have refined our Sweet tastes from the
cane fields to the Kitchens of the New World on the Occasion of the demolition of the Domino Sugar Refining Plant*, featured a thirty-five-foot-high figure, positioned like a sphinx, sculpted from four tons of sugar. The figure
was a hybrid of a stereotypical submissive Mammy figure and a sexual,

dominant woman. As Díaz's fellow novelist and friend Edwidge Danticat underscores in "The Price of Sugar," an article that discusses contemporary sugar plantations alongside related migration and citizenship concerns, this history remains very present today for both Dominicans and Haitians. Decrying the working conditions of the sugar industry in the Dominican Republic, Danticat notes that during the cane harvest season, or *zafra,* that Díaz references in his novel, harvesters are often treated like slaves, providing uncompensated or barely compensated forced labor, with their official identity papers confiscated by overseers. Danticat was one of a cohort of artists and writers responding to Kara Walker's exhibition. A year earlier, in a joint letter to the *New York Times* regarding the Dominican Republic's 2013 ruling (decreed retroactive to 1929) that children born to undocumented parents would have their citizenship revoked, Danticat, Díaz, Julia Alvarez, and Mark Kurlansky wrote, "Such appalling racism is a continuation of a history of constant abuse, including the infamous Dominican massacre, under the dictator Rafael Trujillo, of an estimated 20,000 Haitians in five days in October 1937. One of the important lessons of the Holocaust is that the first step to genocide is to strip a people of their right to citizenship."

Just as Jean Rhys's *Wide Sargasso Sea* gives voice to *Jane Eyre*'s Bertha, imagining the colonial subordination that preceded her torching of Thornfield, *Oscar Wao* is tantamount to "Macomber" rewritten from the perspective of the "native boys," with the narrative half in English and half in Swahili. In an allusion to the destructive history of colonialism, Díaz replaces Kurtz's last words in Joseph Conrad's *Heart of Darkness* (1899), "The horror! The horror!," with Oscar's exclamation, "The beauty! The beauty!" (335). The novel's epigraph is an excerpt from Derek Walcott's "The Schooner Flight," a poem narrated by a West Caribbean sailor navigating the aftermath of multiple colonizations: "I had a sound colonial education, / I have Dutch, nigger, and English in me, / and either I'm nobody, or I'm a nation" (lines 41–43). In his conversation with Danticat, Díaz acknowledges, "There are, as you and I well know, certain kinds of people that no one wants to build the image of a nation around. Even if these people are in fact the nation itself. Poor dark people are not usually central to a nation's self-conception (except perhaps as a tourist attraction)." Whether Oscar is a native boy, Macomber, or the lion, he is both nobody and a nation.

Ramón Saldívar proposes four parameters of the postrace aesthetic: first, that postrace and postmodern aesthetics are in dialogic relation; second, that the history of genre, in addition to a variety of generic forms, informs postrace aesthetics; third, that postrace aesthetics blends different iterations of realism (among them naturalism, social realism, and magical realism), the end product of which is speculative realism; and fourth, that postrace aesthetics is, seemingly paradoxically, about race (4–5). Saldívar specifically mentions Díaz's oeuvre with regard to the first and third characteristics, but the entire framework is useful for understanding race, genre, and literary history in *Oscar Wao*. Saldívar poses critical questions: "Why has postmodernism and the study of contemporary narrative, with very few exceptions, been so unconcerned with minority literature? Or, put differently, why have minority writers, again with a few exceptions, found postmodernism such an inhospitable domain for their representations of contemporary social conditions?" (4) This is, at its core, a canon segregation issue. Díaz connects Oscar's interest in genre to his ethnic background:

> Where this outsized love of genre jumped off from no one quite seems to know. It might have been a consequence of his being Antillean (who more sci-fi than us?) or of living in the DR for the first couple of years of his life and then abruptly wrenchingly relocating to New Jersey—a single green card shifting not only worlds (from Third to First) but centuries (from almost no TV or electricity to plenty of both). After a transition like that I'm guessing only the most extreme scenarios could have satisfied. (22)

The novel's dialogic bent, with multiple genres and literary movements, invites contextualization within a larger canon, one that combats the segregation of immigrant writing or contemporary ethnic American writing.[10] Díaz intentionally dabbles in many different forms: the novel is part memoir, with biographical pretense, and part fiction, with elements of postmodernism, postcolonialism, sentimentalism, and magical realism. The author moves in and out of various literary forms and audiences—for example, characterizing the police captain as "one of those very bad men who not even postmodernism can explain away" (294).

The dialogic relationship that Saldívar proposes, with obvious Bakhtinian roots, extends beyond genre and literary movement to multivalent language and culture, high and low. The assumed readership of *Oscar*

Wao encompasses academics, Dominicans and other Spanish speakers, New Jersey residents, Rutgers students, New Yorkers, science fiction fans, Dungeons and Dragons fans, and voracious canonical readers. He unites these different subcultures through characters' desires to escape or superannuate the monotony of the everyday. "[Belicia], like her yet to be born daughter, would come to exhibit a particularly Jersey malaise— the inextinguishable longing for elsewheres," the narrator tells us (77). In *The Dialogic Imagination* (1981), Mikhail Bakhtin argues that the novel encompasses a variety of forms and registers in a given language, which he defines as heteroglossia. Díaz's novel is a veritable epitome of Bakhtin's notion of heteroglossia, entailing coexisting, potentially conflicting voices, discursive styles, and points of view.

Like "Macomber," *Oscar Wao* is a story about dislocation. Oscar does not feel at home in New Jersey or the Dominican Republic. In the chapter that chronicles Oscar's months in the Dominican Republic, "Oscar Goes Native," the narrator tells us that Oscar "refuse[s] to succumb to that whisper that all long-term immigrants carry inside themselves, the whisper that says *You do not belong*" (276). From surviving photographs of the trip, Yunior discerns "You can tell he's trying too. He's smiling a lot, despite the bafflement in his eyes" (275). In *Toward the Geopolitical Novel*, Caren Irr writes, "Díaz tackles a prototypically American narrative that celebrates the revelatory powers of travel. . . . Like Hemingway's hunter, Díaz's narrator becomes importantly complicit in the story he conveys— a simultaneously American and Dominican narrative of displacement" (35). This sense of displacement, albeit in the context of heteronormativity, haunts Macomber, too. It is humorous to consider that "Macomber" appeared in *Cosmopolitan*'s special vacation issue, with a cover that featured a female bathing beauty in full makeup, about to lob a beach ball.[11] Readers acquainted with Hemingway's story might read Díaz's title and assume a return to Africa. That the story begins in Patterson, with the quotidian disappointments of domestic pressures (Belicia urging Oscar to play outside with other children rather than read at home), sets the stage for the potential departure from this existence.

The shifting narrative focalizations in each text contribute to the sense of displacement for the reader. Regarding the lion's narrative turn, Hemingway explained, "That's all there is to ["Macomber"] except maybe the lion when he is hit and I am thinking inside of him really; not faked. I can think inside of a lion; really. It's hard to believe and it is perfectly okay with me if you don't believe it. Perfectly" (rpt. in Flora 135). While Hemingway shifts between Macomber, Wilson, and the lion, as if gazing through a hunter's scope, Díaz shifts between different generations of the De León family in eponymous chapters. The narrative is also divided between the Dominican Republic and New Jersey, underscoring a hyphenated identity. As Paul Jay contends, "The effect of this shuttling back and forth is to locate the reader not in New Jersey or the Dominican Republic, but in a kind of virtual space in which the two locations intersect and combine into a single fluid space" (178). This fluidity defines more recent transnational American literature. It is also worthwhile to examine how Díaz connects place with generation: most of the Dominican narratives concern Abelard, La Inca, and Belicia, the older generations, while the chapters in the United States concern generations 1.5 and 2.0, Yunior, Oscar, and Lola. While *Oscar Wao* is purportedly narrated by Yunior, who weaves together Oscar's manuscript, journal entries, oral history, conversations with family, and personal interactions, the end product contains knowledge extending beyond a third party's capability to know. As a result, the text is really a third-person omniscient narration. The narrative threads that Díaz provides result in a sympathetic portrait of Oscar but also the expectation of doom; in addition to the ominous note of the title, Díaz reminds the reader of the curse, and Trujillo's atrocities, throughout the narrative.[12]

Canon and Category

Many critics have written about the seemingly disparate registers of *Oscar Wao*. Díaz's breadth means that the average reader is unlikely to comprehend all the references. Rune Graulund characterizes this as "revolv[ing] around translatability and intelligibility. How far do we have to veer from register Y into register Z before it becomes unintelligible to a speaker of register Y?" (33). Graulund theorizes X and Y: "The academic jargon of an English professor at Columbia may be unintelligible to a street-speaking Dominican teenager in Washington Heights, and vice versa" (32). Part of Díaz's project and, I would argue, part of the project of contemporary multiethnic U.S. literatures is to confound these binaries and divisions. If an author named Junot Díaz can craft a novel in this many registers, then one can infer that Oscar De Leóns exist—and in terms of readership, the plausibility of the Columbia English professor as the Dominican teenager grown up: one person, one reader. When I taught the novel at my home institution, New York City College of Technology (CUNY), my students provided helpful glosses for many Dungeons and Dragons, science fiction, comics, and Dominican references, among other categories, for the uninitiated. At one point, Yunior implores the reader to suspend belief: "I know I've thrown a lot of fantasy and sci-fi in the mix . . . but this is supposed to be a true account of the Brief Wondrous Life of Oscar Wao. Can't we believe that Ybón can exist and that a brother like Oscar might be due a little luck after twenty-three years?" (285). After all, even the narrative's science fiction elements are sometimes not so far removed from reality. Abelard, whose torture Díaz compares to a dissertation defense, and his grandson Oscar in some ways stand in for Jesús de Galíndez Suárez, the Basque nationalist writer who was last seen at a midtown Manhattan subway station in 1956, allegedly kidnapped and murdered by Trujillo's henchmen after Galíndez refused to surrender his book manuscript about Trujillo's dictatorship. *La era de Trujillo: Un estudio casuístico de dictadura hispanoamericana* was ultimately published in 1956, after Galindez disappeared; Oscar's final manuscript, written before he is kidnapped by the Capitan's henchmen, never materializes.

In the postmodern tradition, one way Díaz accomplishes multiple registers is through his use of footnotes to directly address the reader. Hemingway's terse prose is replaced by a novel whose footnotes alone likely exceed the length of "Macomber." The content of the footnotes, in the intertwining histories of the Dominican Republic and the De León family, is far-ranging. When the family deems Oscar the neighborhood parigüayo, a helpful footnote explains, "The pejorative parigüayo, Watchers agree, is a corruption of the English neologism 'party watcher.' The word came into common usage during the First American Occupation of the DR, which ran from 1916–1924. (You didn't know we were occupied twice in the twentieth century? Don't worry, when you have kids they won't know the U.S. occupied Iraq either)" (19).[13] In their explication of etymological and political histories that have been (or perhaps will be) lost, the footnotes participate in narrative recovery.

Díaz's departure from Hemingway's style extends to syntax. Hemingway notoriously rejected adjectives, believing that they distracted from
the core meaning of a sentence. Díaz takes particular delight in the adjectives populating Oscar's vocabulary: adamantine, orchidaceous, vertigi-
nous. However, it is worth noting that Díaz's earlier prose style in *Drown*
garnered comparisons with Hemingway's minimalist language. Writing
about Díaz's first collection of stories, Cowart observes, "Like a Hemingway of the barrio, Díaz contrives to convey a sense of strong emotion that
has been contained, channeled into a rhetoric of understatement easily
misunderstood as ghetto sangfroid (or *only* ghetto sangfroid)" (*Trailing
Clouds* 195). (This comparison is problematic as it relegates Díaz's work to
a particular class and ethnic demographics.) The different registers and
paratextual matter also speak to the complexity of a single person's story,
encompassing familial, social, fantastical, educational, geographic, and
ethnic networks. The networks, Díaz implies, multiply for an individual
navigating two countries and multiple threads of identity. The dialogic
nature of Díaz's work is central to understanding the vast territory he
metaphorically claims for contemporary immigrant writing in an act of
manifest destiny, erasing boundaries of canon and category. That much
of the literary criticism of the novel features claims about how Díaz's use
of multiple registers and code-switching intentionally befuddles readers
reveals more about the state of the academy than it does about Díaz's
authorial agenda.

Oscar's story is not one of coming to voice or choosing between divergent national identities, common themes in earlier ethnic American
literature. The novel is ultimately polyphonic, as Díaz engages in a dialogic rather than dialectic process, an ongoing conversation rather than
a discourse seeking resolution or central truth. What results is not only
a commentary on the ethnic subject as a dialogic self navigating multiple
external relationships but also a metanarrative on the state of contemporary ethnic fiction, resisting definition. The author Bharati Mukherjee
has challenged scholars to forge a new theory reflecting the many facets
of—or, really, catalysts for—immigrant literature:

> In the United States, we now have a sufficient body of "Literature of New
> Arrival" to distinguish it from traditional—canonical—U.S. immigrant
> literature. In the past, scholars have not recognized "literature of the

immigrant experience" as distinct in its aims, scope, and linguistic dexterity from postcolonial literature, literature of globalization, or diasporic literature, and have misapplied literary theories that are relevant to literatures of colonial damage, nation-building, dispersal, exile, voluntary expatriation, and cultural and economic globalization but are inappropriate templates for a literature that centers on the nuanced process of *rehousement* after the trauma of forced or voluntary *unhousement*. I urge scholars to come up with a new literary theory that provides a more complete, more insightful entry into the "literature of the immigrant experience," and enables a fuller understanding of this emerging sub-genre. ("Immigrant Writing" 683)

Returning to *Oscar Wao,* a text that begins with the conscious appropriation of the colonization of Hispaniola reflects its own kind of "literature of new arrival." While Mukherjee is correct in problematizing all immigrant literature as a single category, it is not clear that treating the "literature of new arrival" en masse would be productive. This seems to replicate the lack of distinction between different types of ethnic American writing about which Mukherjee expresses concern. If we adopt such a subgenre, we risk reverting to the problem of structuralist semiotics, treating texts as impermeable, discrete objects, whole unto themselves. Yet even as we acknowledge that texts are in conversation with prior texts, we must not concede authorship: the unique contributions of writers straddling cultures, languages, and geographies perhaps most directly underscore the legitimacy of the individual author.[14]

Cyrus Patell employs Raymond Williams's ideas about cultural materialism, including the residual and the emergent, to frame an understanding of contemporary immigrant narratives. Patell argues that Williams's definition of the emergent, a cultural site where new relationships are created,

offers a way of conceptualizing the projects of the literatures produced by Asian Americans, gay and lesbian Americans, Hispanic Americans, and Native Americans after 1968. Inspired by a dominant 'American' literary tradition that seems to exclude them and their writings, these writers find themselves with one foot inside and one foot outside of the U.S. literary mainstream. . . . The negotiations that take place between marginalized U.S. literature and whatever canon of literature occupies the center always invoke not only questions of literary influence among writers, but also other factors that previous literary historians might have considered to be extrinsic to literary studies. (5, 8)

Patell's use of Williams's framework is useful, as it provides another way to think about the ethnic American literary project in the context of dominant cultures. Today the bodies of literature that once occupied the margins have moved to the center, with ethnic American writers defining the literary zeitgeist. This means, curiously, that authors like Díaz write simultaneously in the residual and the emergent veins. It is crucial to note that this is not the only conversation in which Díaz engages.

We Are All of Us Its Children

When Yunior speculates about the catalyst for Oscar's love of genre, he initially attributes it to Antillean extraction, subsequently to the disorienting process of immigration. The narrator ultimately wonders whether it is because of "something deeper, something ancestral," but concludes, "Who can say?" (22). Definitive answers remain elusive; as Oscar writes to Lola in his final letter, received eight months after his death, "This [the second package] contains everything I've written on this journey. Everything I think you will need. You'll understand when you read my conclusions. (It's the cure to what ails us, he scribbled in the margins. The Cosmo DNA)" (333). Of course, the second package never arrives, and the antidote to the fukú is never shared. Diaz's resistance to resolution in turn speaks to the absence of a completely elucidated relationship between the novel and its short story predecessor. This supports Cowart's contention that "literary symbiosis is the expression of a resistance to closure; if it is also, at times, the vehicle of anxiety about the past and its parental artists, it very seldom seems the product of pathologies of emulation but rather of the common neuroses—and these it tends healthily to resolve" (24). Oscar's letter, written in the days before his death, implies his knowledge that he will never return to New Jersey. Silence and blankness are pervasive threats throughout the novel. Yunior dreams too late of a departure from this paradigm in his relationship with Lola: "I'd finally try to say the words that could have saved us" (327).

Ultimately, perhaps Díaz's most dramatic science fiction experiment is his use of interpolation, which functions as a centripetal force pulling together myriad individuals, fictional and real, texts, places, cultures, and generations into the single spatial, temporal zone of the novel, replacing absence and void with overpopulation and simultaneity. This is Díaz's response to literary colonialism, his zafa. The technique inverts diaspora, uniting people who were once dispersed, melding heretofore distinct national, political, literary, familial, and historical traditions, critiquing the fallacy of categorization and underscoring the elusivity of influence. Hemingway, looming large in the history of American letters, was only one of the text's many parents. As Lola tells us, "If these years have taught me anything it is this: you can never run away. Not ever. The only way out is in. And that's what I guess these stories are all about" (209).

4

New York Unearthed

Excavating the Works of Washington Irving,
Walt Whitman, and F. Scott Fitzgerald in
Colum McCann's *Let the Great World Spin*
and Joseph O'Neill's *Netherland*

IN 2010, WORKERS EXCAVATING Ground Zero discovered a thirty-two-foot wooden ship twenty feet below street level. Tests on the oak tree rings of the wooden hull revealed that the ship was constructed in 1773. In the early nineteenth century, the ship had been used in the landfill extending the shores of lower Manhattan. In the years between this expansion of lower Manhattan and the World Trade Center's construction, Greek Revival homes and nineteenth-century brownstones occupied the site. The eighteenth-century ship serves as a reminder of the city as a repository for artifacts; indeed, an archaeological museum, New York Unearthed, once existed to house, study, and exhibit what lay beneath. New York contains innumerable strata of past inhabitants—the Lenape, the Dutch, the British—and past identities as the world port, the immigrant conglomerate, the financial capital, and, recently, the site of terrorist attacks.

As she walks uptown and glimpses apartment interiors, Gloria, a character in Colum McCann's novel *Let the Great World Spin* (2009), asserts, "It had never occurred to me before but everything in New York is built upon another thing, nothing is entirely by itself, each thing as strange as the last, and connected" (307). Her words apply not only to the city but also to the American literary tradition, and to New York literature in particular. This chapter examines the ways in which McCann's *Let the Great World Spin* and Joseph O'Neill's *Netherland* (2008) unearth New York cultural and literary strata as a way to come to terms with the tragedy of the events of September 11, 2001. *Let the Great World Spin* pays homage to the poetry of Walt Whitman and the prose of F. Scott Fitzgerald's *The Great Gatsby* (1925), whereas *Netherland* takes up the legacy of Washington Irving's *A History of New York* (1809) and revisions *Gatsby* with multiethnic characters and a transnational plot. The contemporary novels summon up the ghosts of New York past both to nostalgize and to offer counternarratives to recent trauma.

Writing "in the shadow of no towers," to invoke Art Spiegelman's response to 9/11, authors have represented the tragedy from a variety of perspectives. In addition to Spiegelman's 2004 text, Don DeLillo's *Falling Man* (2007) and Jonathan Safran Foer's *Extremely Loud and Incredibly Close* (2005) place 9/11 in a context of historical fiction, imagining characters who are both witnesses to and severely affected by the attacks. Other writers have addressed 9/11 less directly: Jennifer Egan's postmodern *A Visit from the Goon Squad* (2010) speaks to the fractured unknowns of life after that fateful day, while Colson Whitehead's *Zone One* (2011) imagines a postapocalyptic New York. Though these novels do not focus exclusively on 9/11, the events of that day loom implicitly or explicitly over the narratives. *Poems from Guantánamo: The Detainees Speak* (2007), edited by Marc Falkoff, a lawyer for some of the prisoners, constitutes a unique contribution to the field, mourning the violation of human rights within a very different framework.[1] One could argue that all American fiction after the terrorist attack is fundamentally post-9/11 work as the violence gave birth to new genres and considerations for writers. In many cases, the uncertainty regarding how to treat the event resulted in indirect representation rather than direct narrativization of the tragedy. As Keith Wilhite writes in his introduction to *The City since 9/11,* "The chronotype of post-9/11 urban texts is a paradoxical space of permanence and vulnerability—a convergence point for anxieties about globalization, economic inequality, imperial history, postmodern virtuality, and future terror" (2–3). Katherine V. Snyder in "Gatsby's Ghost" observes, "The 'post-' in 'post-traumatic' signifies that a subject remains in a complex, ongoing relation with what has come before, that the past is far from over but remains present, albeit in ghostly or palimpsestic form. This 'post-' doesn't so much raise the question of whether or not it is possible to move on but asks what moving on might look like" (485). In this vein, both *Let the Great World Spin* and *Netherland* participate in an ongoing dialog with the past in order to reconcile contemporary trauma.

The Archaeology of Grief: Whitman, Fitzgerald, and McCann

McCann's *Let the Great World Spin* tells the intertwining stories of several New Yorkers: Irish immigrant brothers, bereaved mothers who lost their sons in Vietnam, prostitutes living in the South Bronx, and careless bourgeois artists. The author unites these purportedly discordant characters and structures his narrative around a few days in August 1974, when New York witnessed Philippe Petit's walk across a wire between the World Trade Center towers. Through the tribute to Petit's wondrous act, McCann pays tribute to the towers themselves; in this way, *Let the Great World Spin*, despite its 1974 setting, enters the pantheon of post-9/11 fiction. The novel is an elegy not only for the towers but also for the victims of 9/11, relayed through the stories of characters representing a spectrum of New York experience.

Solomon Soderberg, the judge in the novel who sentences Petit, thinks to himself, "The Twin Towers. Of all places. So brash. So glassy. So forward-looking" (248). If the towers looked forward, McCann looks backward to underscore that the buildings, like humans, were penetrable and ultimately fell to dust, and demonstrates that the high density—highest, of course, in buildings that were 110 stories tall—of the urban condition is a centripetal force that guarantees a spectrum of people will be affected by any single given event. Through Petit's high-wire walk, McCann replaces a horrific event with one that seems to conjure immortality rather than the precariousness of the human condition. This chapter examines McCann's narrative strategy of replacement—his use of history to discuss contemporary trauma, and his invocation of canonical New York literature—to unearth New York's usable past.[2]

A Counterhistory

Let the Great World Spin mines the strata of New York's history, literature, and residents. New York in the 1970s, the setting for most of the novel, suffered under a cycle of poverty, crime, anger, and despair, social ills that were perhaps more comprehensible, more local, and, ultimately, more accessible than any act of terrorism. Chronicling Petit's high-wire walk is a way for McCann to narrativize the towers in positive language even while connoting loss. However, setting the story in 1970s New York, during the era of the Bronx burning, Watergate, Nixon's resignation, and the fallout from U.S. engagement in Vietnam, along with IRA bombings in Dublin, makes Petit's miraculous walk seem an anomaly in a decidedly unsentimental time.[3]

McCann's choice to render many of the novel's scenes domestic offers a sense of protection to the reader, relief from the heightened state of emergency that could have dominated the narrative.[4] The novel opens in Ireland, with pleasant descriptions of the Sandymount Strand (recalling *Ulysses*) and the domestic safety offered by Ciaran and Corrigan's mother. While McCann colors Dublin as a city struggling with homelessness and alcoholism, the boys' house offers respite from the roughness, with the brothers' bunk beds and the wrapped replacement blanket their mother presents to Corrigan after he has given away his blanket to the needy providing warm domestic details. Corrigan is selfless in his outreach to others and, in the context of 9/11, recalls Father Mychal Judge, who was a Catholic priest and chaplain to the New York City Fire Department. Father Judge went immediately to the towers on 9/11 and was one of the first victims of the attacks. An iconic photograph shows policemen, firemen, and an office worker carrying Father Judge out of the chaos and debris. Corrigan later offers the same charity to prostitutes in the Bronx: his apartment serves as a refuge from the dangers of the street, supplying clean bathroom facilities and a hot cup of tea. When Ciaran objects to what he perceives as his brother's naïve charity, Corrigan removes the apartment door locks so the community can enter at will. On the Upper East Side, Claire's apartment shelters Gloria after she is mugged: "The doorman buzzed her and she ran down the stairs, came right out and paid the cab driver. She glanced down at my feet—a little barrier of blood had

bubbled over the edge of my heel, and the pocket of my dress was torn—
and something turned in her, some key, her face grew soft. . . . Her arm
went around me and she took me straight up in the elevator" (208). The
"key" that turns is maternal, communicated through Claire's hospitality
to Gloria. She is given first aid and slippers for her blistered feet, along
with a drink to calm her frayed nerves.

The tragedies that punctuate the novel, including the deaths of Corrigan and Jazzlyn in a car accident and the death of Claire and Solomon's
son Joshua in Vietnam, concern a loss of control. McCann counters the
feelings of powerlessness with incidents of agency. When Claire drives
Gloria home and they witness Jazzlyn's daughters being led out of the
projects, Gloria, in turn, offers people shelter.

> I stepped off the pavement and onto the road. I was still in Claire's slippers.
> "Hold on," I shouted.
> I used to think it had all ended sometime long ago, that everything was
> wrapped up and gone. But nothing ends. If I live to be a hundred I'll still be
> on that street.
> "Hold on." (322)

This is a fateful scene that occurs only because of the timing and particu-
larity of events that precede it: Gloria's decision to walk home, her subsequent mugging, her return to Claire's apartment, her ride home with
Claire's driver. On 9/11 there were many stories, both of survival and of
loss, that concerned individuals' timing: the employee who was saved from
annihilation because he was late getting to work after dropping off his
daughter at school; the employee who happened to be in the restroom
instead of her office at the time of the plane's impact, thus saving her
life; the Chicago resident in one of the towers for a meeting; the delivery
person or computer technician fulfilling quotidian duties. Gloria's pivotal
response, "Hold on," seems to stop time and the world's spin, disrupting
the bleak trajectory and ensuring that the girls will now have a home.
McCann's interest in timing is part and parcel of his interest in networks,
evident in the inclusion of the ARPANET as a metaphor for multifaceted
connection and interdependence: "This is America. You hit the frontier.
You can go anywhere. It's about being connected, access, gateways, like a
whispering game where if you get one thing wrong you've got to go all the
way back to the beginning" (197).

At the conclusion of the novel, McCann steps back from New York to include other places, and hardships, in the world. As an adult, Jaslyn, one of Jazzlyn's daughters taken in by Gloria, helps others without homes, working for a foundation that assists individuals displaced by disasters, including Hurricanes Katrina and Rita. She remembers the names of affected communities: "Sabine Pass and Johnson's Bayou, Beauregard and Vermilion, Acadia and New Iberia" (332). The novel ends with her visiting Ciaran and Lara in Dublin and, later, Claire in New York. The final scene occurs in the interior of Claire's apartment, with Jaslyn as Claire's caretaker. McCann's omniscient narrator returns: "The world spins. We stumble on. It is enough" (349). Numerous forms of human outreach throughout the novel relieve profound loss.

Literary Artifacts

In addition to unearthing the New York of 1974 to counter some of the darkness overtaking the New York of 2001, McCann excavates New York literature. *Let the Great World Spin* is a New York novel not only in its setting but also in its excavation of the belletristic ghosts of New York past. In "Mannahatta," Walt Whitman writes of "high growths of iron, slender, strong, light, splendidly uprising toward clear skies" (line 7). In *Let the Great World Spin*, McCann describes spectators trying to get a glimpse of the wire walker through the construction of the city, "to get a view unobstructed by cornicework, gargoyles, balustrades, roof edges" (4). Whitman's words take on new connotations when applied to buildings that were architectural marvels, known for the strength of steel beams that flexed in high wind and were supposed to withstand intense heat or explosion. McCann's homage to Whitman in the stunning opening of the book extends to the use of catalogs, one of the poet's signature devices embracing humanity. The preface is deceptive as it purports to be about the wire walk but is in fact about the regular New Yorkers who experienced the event. The author offers a catalog of streets ("Those who saw him hushed. On Church Street. Liberty. Cortlandt. West Street. Fulton. Vesey"); occupations ("Lawyers. Elevator operators. Doctors. Cleaners. Prep chefs. Diamond merchants. Fish sellers. Sad-jeaned whores. All of them reassured by the presence of one another. Stenographers. Traders. Delivery boys.

Sandwichboard men. Cardsharks"); businesses, from the local to the global (Charlie's Audio, Sam's barbershop, Con Ed, Ma Bell, Wall Street); sounds ("Car horns. Garbage trucks. Ferry whistles. The thrum of the subway"); transportation (subway, bus, limousine); and movement, including the arrival of the M22 bus, the settling of a chocolate wrapper, briefcases rubbing against trousers, revolving doors (3). The reader is reminded of the diverse occupations Whitman heralds in "Mannahatta," "Song of Myself," and "I Hear America Singing." Invoking Whitman along with the spectrum of New York witnesses, McCann signals to readers his interest in the streets of the city and the people on the ground.

Yet the beginning of the novel also provokes a sense of foreboding in its similarities to the morning hours of September 11, 2001. People's regular routines were disrupted, as the shock of the event seemed to cancel out all else. McCann writes about the 1974 witnesses, "Whatever else it was there would be no chance they could pull away now, no morning coffee, no conference room cigarette, no nonchalant carpet shuffle" (7). The people on the ground crane their necks, yearning to catch a glimpse of the goings-on in the sky a quarter mile above them. People from neighboring buildings, cars, the Staten Island Ferry, and a weather helicopter are witnesses to the walk between the towers. The multiple lenses of the spectacle expose the attempts to understand whether it is a suicide mission or a prank: "Swear words went between [perfect strangers], and whispers that there'd been a botched robbery, that he was some sort of cat burglar, that he'd taken hostages, he was an Arab, a Jew, a Cypriot, an IRA man, that he was really just a publicity stunt, a corporate scam, Drink more Coca-Cola, Eat more Fritos, Smoke more Parliaments, Spray more Lysol, Love more Jesus" (5). This speculation and unknowingness recall the dire, more serious confusion and horror of 9/11, when onlookers—whether watching from surrounding buildings in Lower Manhattan or watching events unfold on television halfway across the world—struggled to fathom what they were seeing. There was a gap between the act and the understanding of it. Similarly, Petit noted the confusion that arose after his feat. More than any other question, he was asked why he walked between the towers. "There is no why," he told reporters.[5] In the prologue, McCann also plays with images of falling objects. In this context, it is a shirt rather than bodies, but the prospect is just as frightening. "Some blessed themselves. Closed their eyes. Waited for the thump. The body twirled and caught and flipped, thrown around by the wind. Then a shout sounded across the watchers, a woman's voice: God, oh God, it's a shirt, it's just a shirt" (7). The gargantuan, inhuman scale of the buildings is juxtaposed with human mortality, the sense of relief of the onlookers' discovery mitigated by the knowledge contemporary readers have of victims who fell to their deaths.

In a companion piece to *Let the Great World Spin,* McCann writes about his father-in-law walking down fifty-nine flights of stairs and then uptown to his daughter's apartment. He changes his clothes and shoes after his granddaughter tells him he smells as if he is burning. If Whitman asks us in "Song of Myself" to look for him under our boot-soles, we can look for McCann in close proximity to his father-in-law's shoes, material reminders of hope in the midst of the terrible day. In an addendum to the novel, McCann writes of the sound of the firefighters' boots going up the World Trade Center stairs: "He still hears their boots on the stairs as he walks out into that white storm. . . . His own shoes sit in the box over my shoulder as I write—the suede is slightly crumpled, some of the dirt has fallen into the box, and the laces are slightly open as if waiting to speak" ("Walking an Inch Off the Ground" 358, 360).

In another intertextual homage to a New York story, McCann channels *The Great Gatsby*'s Tom and Daisy Buchanan through Lara and Blaine, who are driving a gold-colored car from the 1920s and listening to jazz when they cause the accident on the FDR Drive. Lara explains, "We developed our idea to live in the twenties, a Scott and Zelda going clean. We kept our antique car, even got it refurbished, the seats re-upholstered, the dashboard buffed. I cut my hair flapper-style" (126). The gold car may remind readers of another from 1925, one that flung Myrtle Wilson into the air. Of course, this is Gatsby's automobile, but Daisy is at the wheel. Nick Carraway concludes, "It was all very careless and confused. They were careless people, Tom and Daisy—they smashed up things and creatures and then retreated back into their money or their vast carelessness, or whatever it was that kept them together, and let other people clean up the mess they had made" (179). Nick Carraway's famous assertion about his peers initially applies to McCann's twenty-first century counterparts.

Yet if McCann summons up Fitzgerald's *Gatsby,* he also dismisses it. In *Let the Great World Spin,* Lara may be Daisy's anamnesis, but the would-be flapper has a conscience. She laments leaving the scene of the accident and journeys to the hospital seeking information about the victims, then attends Jazzlyn's funeral. McCann recreates the aftermath of the accident from *The Great Gatsby*, when Tom realizes it is Gatsby's car that killed Myrtle, yet rewrites the story to include Daisy's admission of guilt to Wilson. After the funeral, Lara walks with Ciaran to the car. "I suppose he knew it the minute he saw the Pontiac. It was parked with its front facing us. One wheel was up on the curb. The smashed headlight was apparent and the fender dented. . . . This is the car, isn't it?" Ciaran asks her (150). Ultimately, she not only admits her participation in the accident but also claims that she was driving in an effort to take even more responsibility than warranted. McCann thus inverts the Daisy/Gatsby death car scenario in which Gatsby takes the blame. The effect of the rewriting is to mitigate the tragedy and provide a catharsis of sorts, within *Let the Great World Spin* but beyond it as well, as it involves one of the haunting central plot devices of *The Great Gatsby*.

Recovered Portraits of Grief

While *The Great Gatsby* focuses on the undemocratic state of the American dream, *Let the Great World Spin* is democratic in its portrayals of a range of characters peopling New York. The narrative structure of McCann's novel replicates the "Portraits of Grief" series of victim biographies, published in the *New York Times* in September through December 2001. The brief biographies situated the victims in domestic contexts, which allowed ordinary people to identify with the victims and afforded them dignity as the deceased's lives, rather than the manner in which they died, were honored. Nancy K. Miller notes, "As in a high school yearbook, everyone memorialized was given equal space and equal treatment" (114). In its portraits of lives interrupted, the series is similar to the lives profiled in *Let the Great World Spin*. In her discussion of the "Portraits of Grief" series, Miller queries, "How could readers be made to care daily about the individual dead who, unlike the subjects of traditional *New York Times* obituaries, were neither eminent nor glamorous?" (114). In fact, the windows into the lives of average citizens were inordinately compelling: regardless of the prestige of the victims, "Portraits of Grief" offered a collection of anecdotes from people on the ground, just as McCann does. The anecdotes are part of narrative recovery, rebuilding and reconstructing a life through the remembrance of things past. One widow described her husband this way: "He was my plumber, my electrician, my seamstress. My everything, really," recalling Whitman's celebration of the everyman. McCann's novel is a portrait of grief, structured the same way, featuring people from all walks of life who all witnessed a single event—Philippe Petit's high-wire walk between the World Trade Center towers. They are brought together not only by the act of witnessing but also through the intersecting paths they took in a city as simultaneously enormous and small as New York.

In September 2011, ten years after the attacks, the *New York Times* published "Portraits Redrawn: Living with Loss," updates on the families profiled in the original "Portraits of Grief." The end of McCann's book could be titled similarly, as it makes oblique reference to the terrorist attacks not through Petit's walk but through a scene in airport security in 2006. He fast-forwards to the near present to recognize how much has changed in the wake of 9/11, as well as other calamities that have transpired since: Hurricane Katrina, the wars in Afghanistan and Iraq. Like the novel's discussion of the ARPANET during the Vietnam War, a technological metaphor for connection in a seemingly disconnected world, there is the acknowledgment of imbrication and narrative continuity. Solomon and Claire's deceased son Joshua Soderberg's Death Hack computer programming project in Vietnam is another, darker manifestation of this concept. "He had to go through the fields, key all the names in, add the men up as numbers. Group them, stamp them, file them, code them, write them. The problem was not even so much the dying as the overlap in the deaths. The ones who had the same names—the Smiths and the Rodriguezes and the Sullivans and the Johnsons" (88). This calls to mind the names of 9/11 victims, memorialized in Billy Collins's poem "The Names" (2002), democratic in its roll call. Collins makes the intentional choice of names that reflect the spectrum of ethnicity and the power of metonym, individuals representative of the whole.[6] McCann's Vietnam roll call, in the context of the networked community of the ARPANET, functions similarly.

Quotidian Artifacts

McCann's interest in the significance of objects is particularly evident in the novel's crash scene, when Corrigan's Bible and Jazzlyn's stiletto are thrown together in an odd coupling.[7] The author knows that the material possessions that make a life are as varied as their owners. This is reflected in the 9/11 Family Room at One Liberty Plaza, a private underground shrine at Ground Zero whose contents, left by mourners, were recently moved to the New York State Museum in Albany. A pair of spectacles, a red bandana, a birthday card with the picture of a frog on it—these and other mementos reflected the individual personalities of the victims. Material objects often survive trauma that humans do not, becoming imbued with cultural memory. The seemingly incongruent Bible and stiletto, *objets trouvé*, recall the minutes and hours after the attacks on 9/11, when residents of Brooklyn Heights, across the East River from the towers, found their yards littered with detritus, random objects that had been blown across the river by the wind when the buildings collapsed. Papers from someone's desk, whether mundane or pivotal, were now in another borough. There were also the tens of thousands of items that rescue workers sifted through in an attempt to give family members pieces of their loved ones. Credit cards, grocery shopping cards, plastic that survived when the people did not. Don DeLillo reflects on this phenomenon in "In the Ruins of the Future" (2001) as well: "The cell phones, the lost shoes, the handkerchiefs mashing in the faces of running men and women. . . . The paper that came streaming out of the towers and drifted across the river to Brooklyn back yards: status reports, resumes, insurance forms. Sheets of paper driven into concrete, according to witnesses." The recovery of these items contributed to narrative recovery, as it does for Lara when she examines the box of Corrigan's possessions. "The only things I could really jigsaw together was that John A. Corrigan, born January 15, 1943, five foot ten, 156 pounds, blue eyes, was probably the father of two young black children in the Bronx. Perhaps he had been married to the girl who was thrown through the windshield" (137). Lara attempts to reconstruct Corrigan and Jazzlyn's stories from the artifacts.

This challenge of narrative reconstruction is reflected in McCann's syntax. He renders the car crash, narrated from Ciaran's perspective, in one meandering sentence that travels from the highway to eternity.

> Yet the plain fact of the matter is that it happened and there was nothing we
> could do to stop it—Corrigan at the wheel of the van, having spent all day
> down in the Tombs and the courtrooms of lower Manhattan, driving north

up along the FDR, with Jazzlyn beside him in the passenger seat, her yellow high heels and her neon swimsuit, her choker tight around her neck, and Tillie had been locked away on a robbery charge, she had taken the rap, and my brother was giving Jazzlyn a lift back to her kids, who were more than keyrings, more than a flip in the air, and they were going fast along the East River, hemmed in by the buildings and the shadows, when Corrigan went to change lanes, maybe he hit the indicator, maybe he didn't, maybe he was dizzy or tired or out of sorts, maybe he'd gotten some medicine that slowed him or fogged his vision, maybe he tapped the brake, maybe he cut it too hard. . . . (169)

Exceeding the length of a full page, the run-on sentence continues long after this excerpt, with successive numerous clauses containing suppositions mixed with facts. McCann makes it clear that the Earth's rotation, and therefore, the progression of time, is inevitable; while parts of the novel speak to this as reassuring, there is also the reality that this movement is beyond our control. Whitman resurfaces in McCann's description of the accident: the sunlight on the water and swift currents Whitman alludes to in "Mannahatta" and "City of Ships," among other poems, are repurposed. Lara describes the wake of the accident, pulling over on the FDR: "The dapple of light on the water. The surging currents, their spinning motions" (117). The currents are those of the East River, but also those of life. The accident itself causes the literal spin of Corrigan and Jazzlyn's car; the spin also pertains to the Earth's rotation and the passage of time.

Film Archive

Like the novel, the documentary film *Man on Wire* (2008), which chronicles Philippe Petit's miraculous high-wire walk between the towers of the World Trade Center, pays tribute to the towers in Whitmanian fashion. Whereas McCann chooses to reference 9/11 toward the end of his narrative, the film's director, James Marsh, trusts the poignancy of the construction of the towers and Petit's fascination with them to connote loss. There is the wonder of their height, the feat of construction, the impressive workers, the mammoth steel beams being hoisted (rather than dismantled or destroyed). Annie, Petit's girlfriend at the time, tells viewers: "He could no longer continue living without trying to at least conquer those towers." The towers were a formidable foe rather than a capitalist target. In split frame, the filmmaker juxtaposes the construction of the World Trade Center towers with Petit as a child, with the point of codevelopment, almost symbiosis, leading toward eventual meeting of man and building. Petit's successful walk predated 9/11 in the annals of World Trade Center history. As with 9/11, questions arise regarding the possibility of a different history. What if the terrorist attack had been foiled? What if Petit had fallen? What would have had to change to alter the eventual outcome—to save people's lives?[8]

In paying homage to the architectural marvels of New York, Petit himself pays homage to Whitman, whether intentionally or unintentionally, in the *Man on Wire* documentary. "I heard the crowd, I saw the crowd, I heard the murmur," Petit recalls his time on the wire. Watching the documentary with my literature class at New York City College of Technology, part of the City University of New York, I saw my students visibly perk up at the NYPD officer's story of entreating Petit to leave the wire and come back to the building. After hearing the spectrum of accents and languages (mostly French) of those interviewed for the film, the New York accent and street talk represented the familiar, even if it transpired forty years earlier. Here again is the everyman. Marsh's film, like McCann's novel, does not privilege any particular perspective or voice. As McCann told Nathan Englander in an interview, "I wanted it to be a Whitmanesque song of the city, with everything in there—high and low, rich and poor, black, white, and Hispanic. Hungry, exhausted, filthy, vivacious, everything this lovely city is. I wanted to catch some of that music and slap it down on the page so that even those who have never been to New York can be temporarily transported there" ("Conversation" 368). Even Petit's version of events is not privileged over those of his colleagues. The multiple voices and stories represent Whitman's democratic vision and parallel McCann's attention to the citizens on the ground.

Neither the former triumph nor the latter tragedy of this scale is supposed to happen very frequently. As Petit's friend notes in the film, "So there will not be any more stories like that." Petit tells the camera, "The fact that wirewalking is framed by death is very interesting—it means you have to take it seriously." Petit's unlikely act provides a counternarrative to the tragedy of 9/11, when humanity fell to its death. McCann's invented narrative of interconnected New Yorkers, all witness to something miraculous instead of horrific, offers a salve to a city suffering from the terror of 9/11 and an attempt to historicize the now hallowed ground of the World Trade Center positively. Alluding to Petit's wire walk, Judge Soderberg asserts, "Every now and then the city . . . assailed you with an image, or a day, or a crime, or a terror, or a beauty so difficult to wrap your mind around that you had to shake your head in disbelief. . . . It happened, and re-happened, because it was a city uninterested in history" (*Let the Great World Spin* 247). The claim has merit. In 2005 the New York Unearthed Museum was forced to close and its entire staff was let go because of a lack of funding from the city. The museum's contents were shipped upstate, awaiting a time when chronology can be continuous rather than fragmented, when the remnants of a ship from 1773, a steel beam from the towers, and the wire that stretched between them can share contiguous space, along with a single, admittedly difficult story.

Recovered Myths of Old New York: Irving, Fitzgerald, and O'Neill

While *Let the Great World Spin* borrows characters and plot points (a careless, privileged couple, a fatal car accident) from *The Great Gatsby,* Joseph O'Neill's 2008 *Netherland* recreates elements of Fitzgerald's novel (an ambivalent, passive narrator, a beguiling gangster whose corpse is recovered from a body of water, a Jewish frontman) with a twenty-first-century cricket-playing, multiethnic immigrant and expatriate cast. *Netherland* also borrows from Washington Irving's *A History of New York,* in which the fictional historian Diedrich Knickerbocker offers a Dutch history of the area and its denizens, including the three Dutch governors of New Amsterdam. *Netherland* begins with the protagonist, Hans van den Broek, a Dutch financial analyst living in London with his British wife, Rachel, and their son, receiving a phone call informing him of the death of his former friend in New York, Chuck Ramkissoon. Chuck's murder provokes Hans to reflect on the time he spent in New York City in the years after 9/11. During this period, he simultaneously coped with personal loss, in the dissolution of his marriage, and collective loss, in a city reeling from the terrorist attack. Life felt precarious and uncertain. After his wife and son left New York, and Hans, to return to England, Hans took up cricket for community and company. At the Staten Island Cricket Club, he meets Chuck, a Trinidadian immigrant, and other teammates of West Indian descent. Chuck's (American) dream is to spread the gospel of cricket in the United States, thereby making the nation more civilized. His purchase of land to convert into a cricket field is only one of several moneymaking schemes; it becomes apparent that he is involved in various illegal activities, ultimately alienating Hans before the latter's return to London. The novel addresses the recovery and loss of the American dream as told through the tradition of the making (and breaking) of New York and New Yorkers.

Critics, perhaps hungry for multicultural uplift and unity in the wake of 9/11, celebrated *Netherland*'s ode to the ethnically diverse city. Writing in the *New Yorker,* James Wood lamented that *Netherland* is "consistently misread as a 9/11 novel, which stints what is most remarkable about it: that it is a postcolonial re-writing of *The Great Gatsby*." O'Neill has characterized *Netherland* as a leave-taking of *Gatsby,* "Saying goodbye to it perhaps, and to some of the notions associated with that wonderful book. This is by way of explanation of the fact that I actually see the book as a post-American novel" ("All over America"). This chapter examines the ways in which "some of the notions associated with" *Gatsby* live on in *Netherland.* The legacies of colonialism and colonization that Irving and Fitzgerald explore in *A History of New York* and *The Great Gatsby,* respectively, find metatextual manifestation in O'Neill's twenty-first-century considerations of ethnicity, nationality, displacement, and exile.

Excavating New Netherland

In its nostalgia for periods of discovery and colonization, *A History of New York* offers O'Neill an especially useful prototype for *Netherland.*[9] Irving begins with the claim of recovery: "TO THE PUBLIC: To rescue from oblivion the memory of former incidents, and to render a just tribute of renown to the many great and wonderful transactions of our Dutch progenitors, Diedrich Knickerbocker, native of the city of New York, produces this historical essay" (xix).[10] Irving historicizes the periods of exploration and colonization as a sort of antidote to the unrest of postrevolutionary America. Through Knickerbocker, a fictional Dutch historian, the author poses important questions about colonization, civilization, and citizenship. "What right," he asks, do "the first discoverers of America" have to "take possession of a country, without first gaining the consent of its inhabitants, or yielding them an adequate compensation for their territory?—a question which . . . until it be totally vanquished, and put to rest, the worthy people of America can by no means enjoy the soil they inhabit, with clear right and title, and quiet, unsullied conscience" (63). Irving poses a question that Knickerbocker discounts as he touts the many advantages of Dutch colonization. Whereas Irving treats the theft of land and the extinction of the native population with candor, Knickerbocker, in his satirical response, reasons that the acts of discovery, agricultural cultivation, and imposition of the Christian faith, among other introductions (alcohol, a dubious asset to the Native Americans, is noted), entail rights to possession. During an anxious time—the formation of a national identity in the wake of a declaration of independence from Britain—Irving returns to the illustrious history of Dutch forefathers. Knickerbocker's descriptions of privileged New Amsterdammers allows readers to escape to a seemingly simpler era and bask in the nostalgia of yesteryear.[11] At the same time, as Jerome McGann notes, "Knickerbocker's fantastical history of the seventeenth-century Dutch colony supports the book's running historical reflections on post-Revolutionary United States" (353). O'Neill employs a similar approach in *Netherland*: in resurrecting the Dutch history of colonization, he considers the melting pot of twenty-first-century New York.

Both *The Great Gatsby* and *Netherland* feature subjective historian-narrators like Knickerbocker. *Netherland*'s protagonist, Hans, spent his childhood in The Hague; it is not a stretch for the reader to imagine him in the role of Dutch explorer. A Dutchman who comes to New York by way of London, he travels a route reminiscent of that of another explorer, Henry Hudson, whose jaunts on behalf of the Dutch East India Company are invoked in *Netherland*. *Netherland* was published in 2008, a year before the quadricentennial celebration of Henry Hudson's voyage. Hans is the Dutch sailor two hundred years after *Gatsby* and three hundred years after the rise of New Amsterdam. In an interview with Katie Bacon, published in the *Atlantic* in May 2008, O'Neill observed, "To have a Dutch narrator in the context of an American novel is almost to have the original American narrator, because of course the Dutch were the first people here in New York." In *The Great Gatsby*, Nick's famous assessment of Tom and Daisy feels similar to Knickerbocker's consideration of the Dutch displacement, and eventual extermination of the native population: "They were careless people, Tom and Daisy—they smashed up things and creatures and then retreated back into their money or their vast carelessness, or whatever it was that kept them together, and let other people clean up the mess they had made" (179). These are Nick's observations of twentieth-century colonialism.

The nostalgia that suffuses *A History of New York* rings familiar to readers of *The Great Gatsby* and *Netherland*. Nick Carraway and Hans van den Broek's forebear, Diedrich Knickerbocker, walks around the Battery, gazes out at New York Bay, and muses: "The capacious bay still presented the same expansive sheet of water, studded with islands, sprinkled with fishing boats, and bounded by shores of picturesque beauty. But the dark forests which once clothed those shores had been violated by the savage hand of cultivation, and their tangled mazes and impenetrable thickets had degenerated into teeming orchards, and waving fields of grain" (182). The passage anticipates Nick Carraway's lamentation about civilization at the conclusion of *The Great Gatsby*. Irony assists Irving in subverting what is savage and what is civilized, as Knickerbocker applauds the "savage hand of cultivation" and all that has been wrought out of the land.[12] These are only passing thoughts, after all, before the narrator reaches optimistic conclusions about history and the present: "For some time did I indulge in a pensive train of thought, contrasting in sober sadness the present day with the hallowed years behind the mountains, lamenting the melancholy progress of improvement, and praising the zeal with which our worthy burghers endeavor to preserve the wrecks of venerable customs, prejudices, and errors, from the overwhelming tide of modern innovation; when, by degrees, my ideas took a different turn, and I insensibly awakened to an enjoyment of the beauties around me" (182). There are layers of obfuscation here, as the reader sifts through an invented Dutch historian's perspective. But Irving is clearly trying to decipher, rather early, questions of modernity and marginalization.

Fitzgerald, too, invoked the vernacular of colonization. When Nick is able to offer directions to a man looking for West Egg Village, our narrator notes, "I told him. And as I walked on I was lonely no longer. I was a guide, a pathfinder, an original settler" (4). Tom Buchanan informs us that the Nordics "produced all the things that go to make civilization— oh, science and art, and all that. Do you see?" (13). In a passage that recalls

Diedrich Knickerbocker's Battery musings, Nick Carraway lies on the beach and observes, "And as the moon rose higher the inessential houses began to melt away until gradually I became aware of the old island here that flowered once for Dutch sailors' eyes—a fresh, green breast of the new world" (180). Like Irving before him, Fitzgerald invokes the history of Dutch colonization and flashes back to a landscape as yet unspoiled by human destruction.

Through his Dutch narrator, the West Indian Gatsby, and the minor characters of cricket players all from nations with colonial pasts, O'Neill invokes the history of colonialism. Chuck is a Trinidadian Gatsby, possessed of a magnetic presence, grandiose and illegal schemes, and infectious energy and optimism. He is also an ardent patriot bent on transforming America. Chuck's cricket field, along with his theory that he will bring civilization to Americans with the sport, inverts the colonial relationship of the past. Cricket: "NOT AN IMMIGRANT SPORT," Chuck declares in one of many unsolicited public relations emails (101). Claiming cricket as the first national sport, Chuck, like Knickerbocker, acts to define a national history that is part personal invention. (The reader may recall that cricket makes an appearance in *Gatsby;* his Oxford photograph shows him holding a cricket bat.) Hans acknowledges the ludicrousness of Chuck's dream for a cricket empire but admits, "I had troubles of my own, and Chuck's companionship functioned as an asylum" and a "taking of his shelter" (135), characterizing their friendship as an occupation. Gatsby's green light across the sound and the green breast of the new world are replaced by the green of cricket fields. As Karolina Golimowska notes, *Netherland* "uses the game of cricket as a metaphorical framework to address immigrant communities, postcolonial legacies and the need for re-mapping of a wounded and paranoid city" (230). Just as the sport of cricket replaces baseball, Chuck Ramkissoon's number-running schemes with Abelsky stand in for the arrangements of Gatsby and Meyer Wolfsheim, the revolting Jewish gangster reprising his role.

The original title of the novel was *The Brooklyn Dream Game,* which brings to mind baseball—more specifically Ebbetts Field, the Brooklyn Dodgers and Jackie Robinson, and the destruction of the color barrier. *Netherland* instead offers us the converse: descriptions of cricket matches played by an immigrant underclass, with Hans as the only white player. An all but abandoned Floyd Bennett Field replaces Ebbetts Field. The white narrator possesses a mobility that other characters of color lack, navigating between the world of the Chelsea Hotel, the cricket fields on Staten Island and Brooklyn, and the financial worlds of New York and London, to which he ultimately returns.

After Hans leaves New York, technology aids his colonial reflections. He uses Google Earth to keep an eye on Brooklyn after he moves back to London. "I go to Google Maps. It is preset to a satellite image of Europe. I rocket westward, over the dark blue ocean, to America." Hans mimics the path of the explorers in his digital colonization. He continues:

> There is Long Island. . . . I veer away into Brooklyn, over houses, parks, grave-yards, and halt at olive-green coastal water. I track the shore. Gravesend and Gerritsen slide by, and there is Floyd Bennett Field's geometric sprawl of runways. . . . There's Chuck's field. It is brown—the grass has burned—but it is still there. . . . From up here, though, a human's movement is a barely intelligible thing. Where would he move to, and for what? There is no sign of nations, no sense of the work of man. (252)

The burned grass of the cricket field is a grave: the valley of ashes, a testament to vanquished dreams. Rendering borders and territories indiscernible from a distance, O'Neill zooms out from the traumatic histories of colonization and immigration. The novel ends with the literal and metaphorical act of seeing from a distance, as Hans, Rachel, and their son board the London Eye, a clever stand-in for T. J. Eckleburg. O'Neill describes the individual cars as eggs, harking back to the Long Island peninsulas. All these scenes feature witnesses to destruction.

What Lies Beneath

Progenitors Irving and Fitzgerald are especially evident in O'Neill's interrogation of Dutch colonial history. In A History of New York, Diedrich Knickerbocker walks around lower Manhattan and considers the natural history that preceded European arrival. In The Great Gatsby, Nick Carraway lies on a Long Island beach and begins to see the world through Dutch sailors' eyes. In Netherland, Hans encounters myriad reminders of Dutch heritage, regional and personal. As he travels north of the city through the Hudson Valley, O'Neill recreates Diedrich Knickerbocker's and Nick Carraway's passages backward in time. Hans thinks about the Dutch origin names of the towns, along with their inhabitants of yesteryear. He accompanies Chuck to a Brooklyn cemetery containing seventeenth-century Dutch gravestones and "practically hear[s] clogs ringing on the flagstone" (154). Yet he is unsure how to process this ancestry. "But then what? What was one supposed to do with such information?," he asks while standing before the Dutch names in the cemetery. Another cemetery visit, to Green-Wood, yields a grave with a single word, "DAISY." Even if Hans cannot decipher the signs around him or process the "obligation of remembrance" (154), O'Neill asks the reader to contemplate the dual legacies of the colonial and literary past. Describing a tryst with an Anglo-Jamaican woman, Hans observes their reflection in the windows of the Chelsea Hotel: "I was not shocked by what I saw—a pale white hitting a pale black. . . . I recall, also, trying to shrug off a sharp new sadness . . . produced when the mirroring world no longer offers a surface in which one may recognize one's true likeness" (115). The scene captures Hans's vague identification with colonial power.

Chuck Ramkissoon, the Trinidadian Gatsby who hails from a country colonized by the British, who warred with the Dutch for New Netherland, defers to this history. He courts Hans with colonial flattery: "Dear Hans," he writes to him, "You know that you are a member of the first tribe of New York, excepting of course the Red Indians. Here is something you might like" (58). He includes a copy of *Dutch Nursery Rhymes in Colonial Times,* a reprint of the 1889 original by Mary Ferris, already trafficking in colonial nostalgia. Hans reads the compilation with curiosity, as he knows "next to nothing about the ancient Dutch presence in America" (61). One of the poems rhymes slaves with Indian braves in a scene that takes place under a Christmas moon in Rensselaerwyck, New Netherland: "Down to the riverbank, Mijnheer, his guests, and all the slaves / went trooping, while a war whoop came from all the Indian braves" (61). There are abundant reminders of America's sins, even if Hans does not fully understand the connotations.

Like *A History of New York* and *The Great Gatsby,* O'Neill's *Netherland* includes a discussion of the colonizers and the colonized. The title invokes New Netherland, New York's first colony. In *Knickerbocker: The Myth behind New York,* Elizabeth Bradley points out, "The book's title strongly hints at the Dutch historian's unabashed agenda: to reclaim New York City and all

New Yorkers for Holland. This repatriation takes place not through any outright subversion of historical fact . . . but by Knickerbocker's success at mapping the forgotten colony for contemporary New Yorkers. He does so through a constant litany of familiar, enduring city names and landmarks, reminiscences, and pointed anecdotes, all calculated to reveal the Dutch origins of a variety of 'authentic' New York features" (3). Chuck performs this function for Hans in *Netherland* as he schools him in Dutch colonial history. He also "map[s] the forgotten colon[ies]" of Brooklyn when he introduces Hans to the West Indian and Caribbean neighborhoods of Brooklyn. With Hans behind the wheel, Chuck plays navigator through the "nether regions" (164) of the borough: Midwood, East Flatbush, Little Pakistan, Brighton Beach, Chinatown. He acquaints Hans with the diverse ethnic citizenry that has replaced the more monolithic past.

Signs of Dutch ancestry, contemporary pluralism: it is all foreign to Hans. His continuous marvel recalls the bewilderment of a character in another Knickerbocker tale, "Rip Van Winkle" (1819). Having slept through the American Revolution, Rip struggles to understand the signs around him: a tavern named General Washington, and "instead of the great tree that used to shelter the quiet little Dutch inn of yore, there now was reared a tall naked pole . . . fluttering a flag, on which was a singular assemblage of stars and stripes—all this was strange and incomprehensible." Irving invokes the Dutch and British colonial history of New York as a meditation on the evolution of American identity.

"Can't Repeat the Past? Why, of Course You Can!"

That O'Neill, who grew up in the Netherlands, can raise some of Irving's questions regarding colonization two centuries later suggests that the specters (headless horsemen) remain. Despite the depictions of people of all stripes, colonizer and colonized, mingling on the cricket fields, O'Neill does not shy away from illustrating ethnic stereotypes and prejudices. In an interview with the *Sunday Times,* he asserts that the novel is "a farewell to *Gatsby.* Because the premise of *Gatsby* is that America is this exclusive, privileged land of opportunity. And that is not the case anymore. In the globalized economy, the great narrative of the American dream has been dissipated".[13] In language reminiscent of colonization, O'Neill claims narrative territory and broaches the idea of replacing Fitzgerald's story with a more contemporary one. In doing so, he reminds us that not only characters, plots, and ideas but also texts themselves become embroiled in power relations. Mary Orr reads texts as possessing colonizing potential and notes that even texts that purport to counter or displace urtexts can replicate or even worsen the original set of problems (60). *Netherland,* in its echoes of *The Great Gatsby,* does not seem to dispatch Fitzgerald's narrative. O'Neill's farewell contention would seem more accurate, perhaps, if Gatsby's twenty-first-century equivalent were white, Meyer Wolfsheim's counterpart were Protestant, and Nick's character were Puerto Rican, Jamaican, or Pakistani. Class and ethnic differences in the novel, along with the alignment of particular religions and ethnicities with nefarious activity, underscores that the world Fitzgerald portrayed is not so distant.

Even if his narrator feels perpetually alien, O'Neill is sure to ground his work in the history of American letters. In the last pages of the novel Hans thinks back to a childhood trip he took with his mother to New York. He remembers their glorious ride on the Staten Island Ferry, at sundown. "I can state that I wasn't the only person on that ferry who'd seen a pink watery sunset in his time" (255). His language recalls Whitman's words from the ninth strophe of "Crossing Brooklyn Ferry," originally titled "Sun-Down Poem": "Flow on, river! flow with the flood-tide, and ebb with the ebb-tide! / Frolic on, crested and scallop-edg'd waves! / Gorgeous clouds of the sunset! drench with your splendor me, or the men and women generations after me! / Cross from shore to shore, countless crowds of passengers!" (lines 101–4) As Hans's childhood memory predates the destruction of the twin towers, the novel ends with nostalgia for youth, for the city, and for the literary past.

Fitzgerald's final words about his protagonist—"Gatsby believed in the green light, the orgastic future that year by year recedes before us. It eluded us then, but that's no matter—to-morrow we will run faster, stretch out our arms farther. . . . And one fine morning . . ." (180)—not only reflect the failure of Gatsby's dream, but also reveal the fallacy of the broader American narrative, a series of myths promulgated throughout each period of American history. In her review of *Netherland* in the *New York Times,* Michiko Kakutani wrote, "Most memorably, he gives us New York as a place where the unlikeliest of people can become friends and change one another's lives, a place where immigrants like Chuck can nurture—and potentially lose—their dreams, and where others like Hans can find the promise of renewal." Kakutani's curiously romantic assessment was typical of contemporary reviews: no matter that Chuck's body is found in Brooklyn's Gowanus Canal, a site so toxic that it could have ended his life without any nefarious human activity. O'Neill may offer a counternarrative to the bleakness of post-9/11 New York, but at the same time he illuminates still-problematic narratives concerning ethnicity.[14]

Critics eager to define new literary movements have called *Netherland* a postnational novel, a term that may be bandied about in the arts but is not grounded in quotidian American experience. In all three texts, *A History of New York, The Great Gatsby,* and *Netherland,* New York stands in for America, telling the story of discovery, settlement, revolution, and the American dream. It also reveals the story of destruction, colonization, violence, loss, and trauma, a history that was reflected in the tragedy of 9/11.[15] O'Neill contends with all these stories and strata, sometimes with an oblivious narrator's lack of historical knowledge, sometimes with comforting anecdotes about individuals of all backgrounds on a cricket field, sometimes with regressive anecdotes about ethnic and class difference. The story of those disenfranchised, whether because of religion, class, ethnicity, or gender, continues, borne back ceaselessly into the past. The story of subjugation is older than the fresh green breast of the new world that the Dutch sailors glimpsed and as nascent as today's news. Through invoking and mythologizing local American history, these texts continue to build an American literature that is recursive and self-reflexive.

Resurrecting the ghosts of New York past, *Let the Great World Spin* and *Netherland* offer readers escape from a traumatic present. As Kathleen Brogan writes, "The ghosts haunting contemporary American literature lead us to the heart of our nation's discourse about multiculturalism and ethnic identity. When summoned for close examination, they reveal much about the dynamics of social and literary revisionism in response to crosscultural encounters" (4). Even Knickerbocker was aware that "the people of this country had a *variety of fathers,* which, as it may not be thought much to their credit by the common run of readers, the less we say on the subject the better" (61). The "variety of fathers" concept is one McCann and O'Neill try to impart to their own readers through unfurling the literary past. Engaging with the work of Irving, Whitman, and Fitzgerald, integral to the folklore of New York, McCann and O'Neill locate their novels in the American literary tradition and proffer counternarratives and commemorations to a city grappling with loss and destruction. *Let the Great World Spin* examines unity as a response to tragedy, whereas *Netherland* explores diaspora. *Let the Great World Spin* invokes earlier New York literature in order to provide solutions to past fictional and national grievances and celebrate the city's stories. *Netherland*'s invocations remind the reader of the long history of displacement and destruction in New York, and of dreams deferred. Arguing for the importance of both temporal narrative (people living in the same time, across geography) and spatial narrative (the history of a single space, through time), both authors use cultural and literary history, at a safe remove, to address contemporary wounds.[16] Yet each narrative's chronicle of a bygone era, whether seventeenth-century, nineteenth-century, or early twentieth-century New York, acts as a palliative that may alleviate pain but cannot treat the cause of the condition.

5

Black Boys and White Whales

Ta-Nehisi Coates's Conversations with Herman Melville, Richard Wright, and James Baldwin

He'd call me down to the basement and assign another book, another history that traced our days from the Nile Valley to the Zulus' last stand. When I turned the pages, I could feel the Something More, like a smoldering fire across the room. Days later Dad would ask for a report. But try as I might, I could only half remember what I'd read, and what I remembered I could not really recite. My dad's response—a sudden shining in his eyes at the sound of certain words or at my stuttering approximation of some crucial idea— suggested to me that even the little I retained had gold in it. But none of it made sense. I was young and could not see the weaponry my ancestors had left for me, the shield in the tall brown grass, the ax lying right next to the tree.

—Ta-Nehisi Coates, *The Beautiful Struggle* (2008)

AS A CHILD, TA-NEHISI COATES attempted to grasp seemingly disparate literary and historical traditions in order to piece together a coherent narrative and find his own place within it. As an adult, Coates is a writer acutely attuned to influence and ancestral "weaponry." In his memoir *The Beautiful Struggle* (2008), he explores personal and communal identity, in the process mapping familial and literary ancestry. Reaching forward rather than back, Coates's subsequent memoir, *Between the World and Me* (2015), is a letter to his son, Samori, concerning race in America. As the author nears forty and his son fifteen, he feels the pressing need, perhaps inherited from his father, to educate the next generation about, and attempt to protect it from, the intrinsic peril of being a black man in the United States. His impetus arises from both his own life experience and from the murder of Prince Jones, his classmate at Howard University. In 2000, in Prince George's County, Maryland, Prince Jones was mistaken for a criminal, followed in his car by an undercover police officer, then shot and killed, without witnesses.

Between the World and Me resurrects several forebears. Coates's memoir is named for a Richard Wright poem of the same name, an excerpt from which Coates employs as one epigraph. In a second epigraph and in its epistolary form, the book pays homage to James Baldwin's "Letter to My Nephew on the One Hundredth Anniversary of Emancipation," originally published in 1962.[1] While the Wright and Baldwin ancestry is more explicit, *Between the World and Me* engages with the ideas of other antecedents, including a seemingly improbable text from 1851, *Moby-Dick*. In December 2016, Coates tweeted, "Was reading Melville aloud to the kid and he says 'He sounds like you.' Was like, Uh, reverse that. I learned sentences from this dude."[2] This succinct revelation of intellectual influence alludes to the broader issue of filiation, both literal and literary. This chapter discusses the rich intertextuality of *Between the World and Me* to examine how Coates redeploys earlier texts to plumb issues of race, masculinity, paternity, and inheritance.

Between Coates and Melville

In a May 2011 article for the *Atlantic,* Ta-Nehisi Coates wrote that the opening lines of *Moby-Dick* constituted "the greatest paragraph in any work of fiction, at any point, in all of history." Coates returned to this passage in December 2016 on Twitter when he provided a rationale for his appreciation of Melville: "Kid just asked me 'why' I loved Moby-Dick. I just looked at him like 'Come on, now.' In rapid succession, he rattles off sentences as evidence: 'With a philosophical flourish Cato throws himself upon his sword; I quietly take to the ship.' Tell em how you feel, son . . . / 'This is my substitute for pistol and ball.' Come on now." Modern technology offers Coates a format for casual conversation with Melville. It also inspires reflection on more profound similarities in the authors' texts. Beyond the humorous fellowship evinced here, across generations and across ethnicity, his praise makes sense for numerous reasons.

Both *Moby-Dick* and *Between the World and Me* can be categorized as literature of the quest. They are variations on the bildungsroman, with male protagonists who embark on a search for meaning and fellowship and come of age through exposure to the world. Ishmael traverses the seaport streets, lamenting their landlocked limitations. When he describes the water-gazers dotting the "insular city of the Manhattoes," he directs the reader to "circumambulate the city of a dreamy Sabbath afternoon. Go from Corlears Hook to Coenties Slip, and from thence, by Whitehall, northward" to find "mortal men fixed in ocean reveries" (*Moby-Dick* 18). We are not given the reason for Ishmael's hypos, but Melville immediately associates the condition with mortality. Coates is clearer about the factors that induced his need for escape. As a sixth-grader in Baltimore, he stood in the parking lot of a 7-Eleven after school, watching a crew of older boys taunt another boy his age, until one of the group brandished a gun. The gun was tucked away before physical violence occurred, but the psychological damage remained. Even as a child, Coates realized that his West Baltimore neighborhood, along with the north side of Philadelphia and the South Side of Chicago, neighborhoods where family members and friends resided, were places where death could arise on a random afternoon and where fear supplanted safety. "What was the exact problem here? Who could know?" Coates queries (*Between the World and Me* 19). What he did know was that he had to free himself from the prison of the streets, "unshackle [his] body and achieve velocity of escape" (21). This is not the hypos getting the best of him but the terrifying lack of ownership over one's body and surroundings. Ishmael's circumambulation of the city is not possible for him; as Coates explains, "I have never believed the brothers who claim to 'run,' much less 'own,' the city. We did not design the streets. We do not fund them. We do not preserve them. But I was there, nevertheless, charged like all the others with the protection of my body" (22). By contrasting the protagonists' respective relationships with the surrounding geography in each text, the reader glimpses the relative freedom Ishmael possesses even inland, whereas Coates had to navigate "the array of lethal puzzles and strange perils that seem to rise up from the asphalt itself" (21). The stark distinction between their departures speaks to matters of mobility and privilege.

If a whaleship is Ishmael's Harvard or Yale, Howard University served as Coates's equivalent experience. We are familiar with the diversity of the *Pequod*'s crew, whose first mates hail from the Vineyard, Cape Cod, and Nantucket; whose harpooners hail from the South Seas; whose cook hails from Roanoke County. Melville engages the potential of American democracy in the "Anacharsis Clootz deputation from all the isles of the sea, and all the ends of the earth, accompanying Old Ahab in the *Pequod*" (107). The deputation is akin to the spectrum of black life Coates encounters in college. Howard is "the Mecca," "the crossroads of the black diaspora" (40). In the Yard, where students gather, he espies AME preachers, recent converts to Islam, Russian speakers, budding anthropologists, Christian cultists, the children of Nigerian aristocrats, math geniuses. He writes, "It was like listening to a hundred different renditions of 'Redemption Song,' each in a different color and key" (41). His classmates, combined with Howard's illustrious history, offer innumerable iterations of the self. But this is different from Ellison's presentation of the problematic divisions of black life in *Invisible Man;* Coates is not pressured to join any particular faction.

Setting up camp in the Moorland-Springarn Library days on end, he realizes that the diversity he witnesses in the Yard extends beyond the social, to intellectual tradition.

> The trouble came almost immediately. I did not find a coherent tradition marching lockstep but instead factions, and factions within factions. Hurston battled Hughes, Du Bois warred with Garvey. . . . I felt myself at the bridge of a great ship that I could not control because C.L.R. James was a great wave and Basil Davidson was a swirling eddy, tossing me about. . . . By my second year, it was natural for me to spend a typical day mediating between Frederick Douglass's integration into America and Martin Delany's escape into nationalism. Perhaps they were somehow both right. I had come looking for a parade, for a military review of champions marching in ranks. Instead I was left with a brawl of ancestors, a herd of dissenters, sometimes marching together but just as often marching away from each other. (47)

Here Coates employs Melville's maritime vernacular to discuss grappling with his own intellectual evolution. More than any classroom, the library offers him freedom and growth.

Once ensconced in their new surroundings, both Melville's narrator and Coates delight in initially foreign bedfellows who offer them enormous comfort. At the Spouter Inn, Ishmael overcomes any squeamishness about sharing a bed with the likes of a pagan harpooneer hawking embalmed heads to revel in the warmth of Queequeg's companionship. Their nighttime scene of ceremonial exchange and confabulation relates to one Coates shares with his readers. While still in college, Coates falls ill at his job and is rescued from the floor of a stockroom by an enigmatic female classmate. She assists him to the street, hails a cab, holds him as he vomits, then tucks him into her bed, leaving behind water and a bucket. He marvels at the care and protection she provides him, declaring, "I grew up in a house drawn between love and fear. There was no room for softness. But this girl with the dreads revealed something else—that love could be soft and understanding; that, soft or hard, love was an act of heroism" (61). Ishmael is of course fictional, but Melville and Coates both capture positive exposure to different lives. In this difference, their respective protagonists find the value of insulation from a cruel world that does not otherwise offer nurture.

Relatedly, each author is captivated by orphans, surrogate families, and the search for a father. One figure Melville turned to was Hawthorne. As Edwin Haviland Miller writes of Sophia Hawthorne's observations, "She intuited that the relationship was that of father and son, without knowing that Hawthorne was in the flesh an answer to Melville's preoccupation with a son in search of either a father or an elder brother such as Whitman speaks of. The desire—actually a hunger, like Bartleby's—haunted him from his earliest published essay, a banal little piece in an Albany newspaper in 1839, to the story of Billy Budd which he left unfinished at his death in 1891" (316). In *Moby-Dick,* Melville's orphan narrator conveys the significance of paternity in the story. We also encounter a crew of men separated from their families: Starbuck yearns for his wife and child, and Pip, already separated from any familial structure, is left alone in the water while the *Pequod* pursues a whale. Stubb informs him, "We can't afford to lose whales by the likes of you; a whale would sell for thirty times what you would, Pip, in Alabama" (321). Pip is rendered "another lonely

castaway" before finally being rescued by the *Pequod* after he has been forever altered. And of course the captain of the *Rachel* attempts to enlist
Ahab's assistance in looking for his sons, mistakenly appealing to Ahab
as a fellow father.[3] "For you too have a boy, Captain Ahab—though but a
child, and nestling safely at home now" (398). Ultimately, "the devious-
cruising Rachel . . . in her retracing search after her missing children, only
[finds] another orphan" (427). The paternal preoccupation that Sophia
Hawthorne observes is evident throughout *Moby-Dick*.[4]

Coates's discussion of fatherhood focuses on its relationship with blackness and masculinity. Ahab's monomaniacal pursuit of the white whale is
not so far removed from Paul Coates's relentless study of black identity;
both figures inflict these quests on those they expect to empathize: crew
and children, respectively. Coates underscores paternity as multivalent;
only one page into the book he connects its lexicon to race. "Race is the
child of racism, not the father," he argues. "And the process of naming 'the
people' has never been a matter of genealogy and physiognomy so much
as one of hierarchy" (7). Actual and imagined father-son relationships are
a theme throughout his letter to his son; they are part of both personal
and national narratives. Coates's wife, Kenyatta, "had never known her
father, which put her in the company of the greater number of everyone I'd
known" (65). Prince Jones is a father whose daughter will grow up without
him. Among other victims of racial brutality, Coates brings up Eric Garner,
who was a father, and Trayvon Martin, a son (one is reminded of President Obama's comment at the time: "You know, if I had a son, he'd look
like Trayvon" (qtd. in *Washington Post*, March 23, 2012). Coates argues, "All
of them should have had fathers—even the ones who had fathers, even
you" (131), underscoring the literal and connotative weight he attributes
to paternity. For Coates, the search for a father is a search for both an
intellectual tradition and a personal one. It means studying the work of
black theorists and intellectuals in books his father gives him, at Howard's
Moorland-Springarn Library, and at public lectures in order to decipher
his own place within sometimes contradictory or conflicting narrative traditions. While he studies distinct cultures coming out of Africa, the Caribbean, the Americas, and the United States, his search for an intellectual
ancestry also means locating his work independent of race. After praising
Melville's prose, Coates, sounding like the author himself, instructs his
Atlantic readership in May 2011: "Do not come to me with your lectures

on the tyranny of Dead, Straight White Male Writers. They're great! I love them all! Even Henry James's boring-ass!!"

Color is a central consideration in both *Moby-Dick* and *Between the World and Me*. Melville's musings on whiteness speckle the story but, steeped in symbolism and allegory, remain "unpainted to the last" (218). "But not yet have we solved the incantation of this whiteness," he notes. "Or is it, that as in essence whiteness is not so much a color as the visible absence of color; and at the same time the concrete of all colors; is it for these reasons that there is such a dumb blankness, full of meaning, in a wide landscape of snows—a colorless, all-color of atheism from which we shrink?" (165). He considers the relationship between whiteness and blackness and is aware that one may be used to define the other. Coates opens his book with a similar meditation on the meaning of color but rejects the notion that any of it is an unknowable mystery or accident. He writes, "But the belief in the preeminence of hue and hair, the notion that these factors can correctly organize a society and that they signify deeper attributes, which are indelible—this is the new idea at the heart of these new people who have been brought up hopelessly, tragically, deceitfully, to believe that they are white" (7). Racism is not individual but institutional and systemic. Coates is interested in the deliberate promulgation of the color construct in the United States. He writes his narrative in part to address this monomaniacal pursuit, the system of white beliefs that demands the destruction of the black body. Melville's words in the chapter titled "The Whiteness of the Whale" apply here: "I know that, to the common apprehension, this phenomenon of whiteness is not confessed to be the prime agent in exaggerating the terror of objects otherwise terrible" (163). Coates corrects the record by evincing the clear guilt of the perpetrators. He discusses the "specious hope" (10) of the "most gorgeous dream" of whiteness by cataloging what he deems the accoutrements of white life: "Memorial Day cookouts, block associations, and driveways . . . treehouses and Cub Scouts. The Dream smells like peppermint but tastes like strawberry shortcake," and this "rests on the backs of black people" (11). While Ishmael professes that the Fates assigned him a bit part in a whaling voyage, Coates does not subscribe to providence, aware that the role he plays is not one of fate but of active construction of race. He cautions his son not to let the Dreamers define his quest, or destroy his body. "Here is what I would like for you to know: In America, it is traditional to destroy the black body—it is heritage" (*Between the World and Me* 102). The Dreamers render the black body black. Who renders the white whale white? Who bears responsibility for destruction?

Coates appreciates Melville's interrogation of predator and prey in the novel, observing that the white whale's refusal to occupy the singular role of the hunted results in the consternation of the hunters. When Stubbs accosts Fleece the cook for not cooking a whale steak to his liking, the older man exclaims, "Wish, by gor! Whale eat him, 'stead of him eat whale. I'm bressed if he ain't more of shark dan Massa Shark hisself" (243). Melville questions the identity of the aggressor here. There is also the scene with the injured senior whale, "horribly pitiable" for his old age, blind eyes, and one arm. The more humane Starbuck unsuccessfully attempts to prevent Flask from cruelly harpooning the whale an additional time and causing further suffering. Melville catalogs the whale's humanity and condemns the hunters.

In an April 26, 2011, *Atlantic* article, Coates discusses his process as a writer, noting his penchant for rereading an author he admires when struggling with writing. He highlights an extensive passage from *Moby-Dick*: "For, when swimming before his exulting pursuers, with every apparent symptom of alarm, he had several times been known to turn around suddenly, and, bearing down upon them, either stave their boats to splinters, or drive them back in consternation to their ship" (155). Coates intuits, "What drives the whalers crazy is the very fact that the whale, a creature which they have defined as prey, refuses to remain in that assigned box. And so the tactics of Moby Dick, who is essentially fighting for his life, are dubbed 'treacherous,' his will to claim, protect and direct his own life an 'intelligent malignity.'" As F. O. Matthiessen writes in *American Renaissance,* "[Melville's] theme of the White Whale was so ambivalent that as he probed into the meaning of good and evil he found their expected values shifting" (656). Coates is interested in Melville's inversion of the idea of prey, as well as in the devious intentions ascribed to the victim of the hunt. It is a language he recognizes from the claims about black men—deemed perpetrators—attempting to protect themselves from police brutality and government-sanctioned violence. Training his eye on other beings under threat, he writes to his son, "You have been cast into a race in which the wind is always at your face and the hounds are always at your heel," and we glimpse who is really hunted and haunted. We see unlikely parallels between the white whale and the black man as Coates considers an essential paradox: what it means to live in a body that is existentially threatened and, potentially perceived as threatening. He examines the violence that results from this paradox; the violence to the black body and the violence that occurs in attempting to protect the black body from violence. "Resent the people trying to entrap your body and it can be destroyed," he informs his son (*Between the World and Me* 9). To deny the legitimacy of this instinct is to deny the victim's subjectivity and very personhood.

In an April 2011 *Atlantic* post, Coates demonstrates his interest in the ways Melville's writing mechanics worked in concert with ideas in *Moby-Dick:*

> This sentence, in particular, is gloriously all over the place:
>
> > *But though similar disasters, however little bruited ashore, were by no means unusual in the fishery; yet, in most instances, such seemed the White Whale's infernal aforethought of ferocity, that every dismembering or death that he caused, was not wholly regarded as having been inflicted by an unintelligent agent.*
>
> The commas, the semicolons, the stops and starts, the double negatives, the qualifiers all add up to a kind of hedged chaos. . . . But in that chaos, in that lack of clear, explicit direction, I feel that I am in the mind of the whalers, I am as whirled about as they are. ("A Couple of Thoughts")

The contemporary author deconstructs Melville's language to expose how his narrative ambiguity reflects the sentient ambiguity of the prey and moral ambiguity of the predator. There is no clear subjectivity or separation between predator and prey in the sudden chaos of the hunt. While Coates does not explicitly reference Melville in *Between the World and Me*, his informal writing, in tweets and blog posts, testifies to influence. In a December 2016 Twitter post, Coates recorded a relevant interaction with his son: "I work with the boy on writing, and he says 'But you're always telling me to simplify my sentences, how can you like this?' / And I told him you gotta learn how to make the simple sentences first, then you can throw in the crazy commas and semicolons."

Both Melville and Coates are critical not only of the project of the United States but also of religion; their atheism and criticism of the nation go hand in hand. In a November 20, 1856, notebook entry, Hawthorne wrote of Melville, "He can neither believe, nor be comfortable in his unbelief; and he is too honest and courageous not to try to do one or the other. If he were a religious man, he would be truly one of the most truly religious and reverential; he has a very high and noble nature, and better worth immortality than most of us" (*English Notebooks* 2:163). Ishmael is skeptical of all the faiths he encounters, ranging from the religiosity he finds exhibited in an African American church to Father Mapple's sermon, from Quakerism to Christianity. He is open to Queequeg's paganism, which affords Melville several opportunities to question a Christian nation. Pip "saw God's foot upon the treadle of the loom, and spoke it; and therefore his shipmates called him mad. So man's insanity is heaven's sense; and wandering from all mortal reason, man comes at last to that celestial thought, which, to reason, is absurd and frantic; and weal or woe, feels then uncompromised, indifferent as his God" (322). Melville attributes the most religious sensibility to Pip and to Queequeg. Even Captain Bildad, Ishmael assumes, "very probably . . . had long since come to the sage and sensible conclusion that a man's religion is one thing, and this practical world quite another" (74). Yet Pip's awareness of God's foot upon the treadle is Melville's acknowledgment of larger forces at work. Though he survives his time in the ocean, he is forever changed, similar to Coates's transformation in the wake of Prince Jones's death.

At the church service for his murdered Howard University classmate, Prince Jones, Coates is aware that he cannot "retreat, as did so many, into church and its mysteries" (28). Believers around him ask for forgiveness for the officer who killed him, but Coates remains hardened against this idea. He explains his thought process: the story of Prince Jones did not concern one officer or one tragic episode but a national narrative of destruction: "And raised conscious, in rejection of a Christian God, I could see no higher purpose in Prince's death. . . . I sat there feeling myself a heretic, believing only in this one-shot life and the body. For the crime of destroying the body of Prince Jones, I did not believe in forgiveness. When the assembled mourners bowed their heads in prayer, I was divided from them because I believed that the void would not answer back" (79). One is reminded of Ishmael's foreign presence in both the black church he stumbles into and the Whaleman's Chapel with the cenotaphs. In fact, the critical reception of *Moby-Dick* in 1851 and that of *Between the World and Me* in 2015 share some resemblance, as their assertions about religion were considered blasphemous, their patriotism questioned by contemporaries.

Here it is relevant to invoke another lonely castaway, C. L. R. James, the Trinidadian theorist Coates references in his awakening at Howard University's Moorland-Springarn Library, and the author of *Mariners, Renegades, and Castaways: The Story of Herman Melville and the World We Live In* (1953).[5] James wrote the book on Ellis Island, where he awaited deportation from the United States and was surrounded by the renegades and castaways of his title, immigrant detainees he likened to the crew of the *Pequod.* In *Mariners,* James indicts not only Ahab but also Ishmael as the dominant voices of a totalitarian state, and gives voice to the crew, constructing what Donald Pease in his introduction to *Mariners* (2001) deems a "counter-hegemony" (xiv). About Ahab, James notes, "But there is a fatal flaw in his misery and his challenge and defiance. Never for a single moment does it cross his mind to question his relations with the people he works with. Those relations he accepts. His personality is suffering. *He* will defy his tormentor. *He* will find a way out. He has been trained in the school of individualism and an individualist he remains to the end" (11). The way in which James describes Ahab as a destructive force recalls Baldwin's characterization of the crime of his countrymen in "Letter to My Nephew." Their ignorance of the destruction of black lives, whether deliberate or unintentional, does not render them innocent. James's observations of Ahab also parallel Coates's point about the Dreamers and abdication of responsibility. There are serious consequences to Ahab's madness, which James connects to the twentieth century. "Mad he undoubtedly was by now, but that which was madness in a book one hundred years ago, today is the living madness of the age in which we live. It has cost our contemporary civilization untold blood and treasure. We shall conquer it or it will destroy us. Before we go further with Ahab, let us take a look at ourselves" (12). In the end, James tells us, "The whole point is the intimate, the close, the logical relation of the madness, to what the world has hitherto accepted as sane, reasonable, the values by which all good men have lived" (13). He excavates the bones of national constructs, and of social hierarchies accepted as truth.

While James rereads the story of the *Pequod* from the perspective of its crew, Coates considers the narrative from the perspective of another victim, the whale, and draws parallels between the hunt for Moby Dick and the shootings of unarmed black men. James devotes time to exploring the identities and motivations of the hunters and the hunted. "To get the full effect of this catastrophe," James writes, "we must understand not only the history of Ahab but the history of Moby Dick. Moby Dick is an extraordinarily large and powerful whale. What is striking about him is that he does not rush away from ships and whale-boats, but wherever they appear, chases and fights them. He fights with such ferocity and cunning that he has become a terror of the seas" (11). Both James and Coates employ Melville to plumb the ideas and structures girding these monomaniacal pursuits, the mythologies of the United States, and of the constructs of nation and color. James's book, like Coates's, is dedicated to his son and to the idea that the next generation should not have to face such heinous truths.

Yet another parallel exists between James and Coates: their work attracted criticism of their attitudes toward citizenship and patriotism. In the last chapter of *Mariners*, James includes a plea for citizenship. His more radical readers thought his plea undermined his critique of the state, and publishers excised this content from the book's first editions. For *Between the World and Me* and his criticism of law enforcement as an arm of the corrupt state, Coates was attacked by the Right as being antipatriotic and even treasonous. Coates is a Baltimore native rather than an immigrant like James, but as a black man, he does not enjoy the same rights of citizenship as his white compatriots, and questions the very legality of the state as long as it reinforces this inequality. Though the specific circumstances of the writers differ, they share a common thread in the reception to their work. Some readers were unable to reconcile their criticism of a country with their desire to belong to it, as if praise of, or indifference to, inequality and empire constituted patriotism.

The Drama's Done. Why Then Here Does Any One Step Forth? —Because One Did Survive the Wreck

Like *Moby-Dick*, *Between the World and Me* is simultaneously life-affirming and funereal. Coates explains the beauty he discovers in existence even as he mourns contemporary and historical, aggregate losses. A century and a half apart, Melville and Coates explore the tension between the story of the individual and the story of a nation in which individuals can be subsumed. How does a man negotiate the consequential hypos, and where does he go when they get the best of him? Sometimes no ship or university is an option for an escape route; and sometimes even the escape routes are doomed, which is why each narrative is suffused with a melancholic tone and memento mori. The marble cenotaphs Ishmael sees in the Whaleman's chapel in New Bedford ("Yes, Ishmael, the same fate may be thine" [43]) are the stories Coates knows about black men lost to the violence of the streets or the criminal justice system. Of course, centuries of African American loss—in education, labor, property, employment, and income—predate and inform what Coates sees before him.[6] In *Mourning, Gender, and Creativity in the Art of Herman Melville,* Neal Tolchin addresses how Melville's unresolved grief after the death of his father finds varying expression in his work, which is pervaded by a sense of loss. Tolchin writes of Melville, "From the outset of his career, his social consciousness is highly developed; however, as he writes more deeply into both himself and his time, his fiction shows an intensified recognition of the relationship between private griefs and social grievances" (xiii). The same can be said of Coates, whose title sums up his search for better understanding of the relationship between one's own story and the larger nexus. Starbuck cannot alter the course of the *Pequod;* Coates cannot bring back Prince Jones. After his talk with Mable Jones, he laments, "I thought of the loneliness that sent [Prince Jones] to The Mecca, and how The Mecca, how we, could not save him, how we ultimately cannot save ourselves" (146). Both stories concern a lack of control over bodies and lives. Fictional nineteenth-century narrator and actual twenty-first-century black man are witness to the destruction of life, a destruction deemed inevitable. But an inordinate distance, beyond era, exists between Ishmael and Coates. In the "Loomings" chapter, Ishmael interrogates the reader:

> What of it, if some old hunks of a sea-captain orders me to get a broom and sweep down the decks? . . . Who ain't a slave? Tell me that. Well, then, however the old sea-captains may order me about- however they may thump and punch me about, I have the satisfaction of knowing that it is all right; that everybody else is one way or other served in much the same way- either in a physical or metaphysical point of view, that is; and so the universal thump is passed round, and all hands should rub each other's shoulder-blades, and be content. (21)

We know that Melville did not subscribe to this notion of false equivalence, and neither does Coates, who takes pains to convey that this is not the truth underlying race relations in the twenty-first-century United States, that there is no universal thump.

Moby-Dick and *Between the World and Me* take their readers on tours of the places and people their respective narrators have encountered in their quest for belonging. Melville's narrator assures his reader, "I, Ishmael was one of that crew; my shouts went up with the rest" (152), and Coates assures his son, "I always had people" (88). But Melville's fictional protagonist and Coates are alone at the close of their books, left to tell their stories, cognizant that their lives, too, exist on a precipice. Ishmael, "floating on the margin of the ensuing scene," is "drawn towards the closing vortex" of the sunken ship, a vortex that subsides as he nears (427). Coates ends his story with his interview of Dr. Mable Jones, Prince's mother, after the loss of her son. His encounter with Dr. Jones continues his quest to see "the watery part of the world" and "drive off the spleen" (18)—in other words, to continue pursuing truth. Sitting in the car outside the house, he contemplates the dark narrative behind and before him. A lone black man behind the wheel, like Prince Jones before him, he drives past liquor stores, beauty salons, and derelict housing, and feels the old fear. In his final words to his son, he writes, "Through the windshield, I saw the rain coming down in sheets" (152). His drive away from the house is Coates clinging to the coffin life buoy in the vastness of the ocean. We understand that like Ishmael, Coates alone escaped to tell us.

Between Coates and Wright

The same interest in subjectivity that draws Coates to Melville also draws him to Richard Wright.[7] Coates takes the title of his memoir from the Richard Wright poem of the same name.[8] He repurposes the first stanza of Wright's "Between the World and Me," published in 1935, as his epigraph:

> And one morning while in the woods I stumbled suddenly upon the thing,
> Stumbled upon it in a grassy clearing guarded by scaly oaks and elms.
> And the sooty details of the scene rose, thrusting themselves between the
> world and me. (lines 1–3)

The speaker describes encountering the remnants of a lynching. In the following stanzas he is not witness to the charred aftermath but is the victim himself. Inhabiting the victim's body, he traces the sequence of events: an enraged, drunken mob, a flask of gin being passed around, a whore applying lipstick, his body tarred, set ablaze.[9] The poem concerns violence to the black body, a body whose ownership is constantly in question, destroyed by criminals and sinners in an America in which no one is responsible. The poem also concerns the destruction of subjectivity: of the selfhood and identity of the victim, but also the witness. Any division between the victim of the lynching and the speaker of the poem is lost.

While most of the poem is in past tense, Wright shifts to present tense in the last line: "Now I am dry bones and my face a stony skull staring in yellow surprise at the sun." The present tense renders the event more immediate to the reader. Diana Fuss in *Dying Modern* observes, "In spite of its disturbing ending, this poem draws its tremendous power not only from its ability to portray the radial dehumanization of the lynching victim but also from its simultaneous ability to rehumanize the dead through the agency of voice" (60). Wright gives voice to the victim instead of the mob witnesses. The poem ends without the speaker's exit from the identity of the victim, as if to suggest that after witnessing such a scene one never fully emerges from it. Jelani Cobb has connected the body in Wright's poem to the body of Michael Brown, whose corpse lay uncovered in the Ferguson street for several hours and was photographed by bystanders. Cobb states, "The idea, in both instances, is that, like Wright's narrator, any of us could be Martin, Brown, or one of the hundreds of others who have died under questionable circumstances" ("Between the World and Ferguson"). Wright's speaker "stumble[s] suddenly upon" the aftermath of extreme violence (line 1). Imparting all of his knowledge, willing Samori to vigilance and consciousness, Coates attempts to prevent his son from any sudden stumble.[10] But he knows there are contemporary examples of the spectacle of violence to the black body. Coates refers back to the killing of Michael Brown and his son's distraught reaction to the news that the officer will not be indicted. While Coates acknowledges the complications of the case, he also notes the spectacle of violence to the black body. By including Wright's poem, Coates invokes the history of violence and destruction visited on the black body as well as an African American author's response to it.

In the third stanza, the speaker briefly descends into apathy and distance from the victim. "And while I stood my mind was frozen within cold
pity for the life that was gone. / The ground gripped my feet and my heart
was circled by icy walls of fear" (lines 11–12). The result of this attempt at
distance is the victimhood of the speaker. The poem brings up the specter
of witness to challenge the reader's intersubjectivity: To what extent can
the reader, the witness to the scene, empathize with the victims? To what
extent can the reader remain detached? The poem also works as a metonym for the book, for Coates to tell his son what he has seen.

It is difficult to discuss Wright without also invoking his history with
Baldwin, whose essay "Everybody's Protest Novel," collected in *Notes of
a Native Son* (1955), indicted both Harriet Beecher Stowe's *Uncle Tom's
Cabin* and Richard Wright's *Native Son* for problematic portrayals of African American characters. Bigger Thomas, Baldwin argued, furthered a
grotesque caricature of the black man as an existential threat to whites.
He followed up on this concept of African American dehumanization in
another essay in *Notes*, "Many Thousands Gone":

> The premise of the book is, as I take it, clearly conveyed in these first pages:
> we are confronting a monster created by the American republic and we
> are, through being made to share his experience, to receive illumination as
> regards the manner of his life and to feel both pity and horror at his awful
> and inevitable doom. This is an arresting and potentially rich idea and we
> would be discussing a very different novel if Wright's execution had been
> more perceptive and if he had not attempted to redeem a symbolical mon-
> ster in social terms. (34)

In his assessment, Baldwin raises the issue not only of aesthetics but of
the broader implications (and burdens) of African American literature
contributing to or counteracting narratives of social progress.

The mixed legacy of Wright's work appears in Coates's first memoir, *The
Beautiful Struggle*, published in 2008. Detailing Paul Coates's burgeoning
literary interest, Coates recounts his father, in the midst of army training,
finding a copy of Wright's *Black Boy* left out, seemingly for him, in a common area. He absconds with the book, "mostly because he was touched but
also to keep the book from playing a part in any further racist slights" (72).
This is an interesting scene, as he protects both the book and himself, but
Coates expands Wright's impact further: "From Wright he learned that

there was an entire shadow canon, a tradition of writers who grabbed the pen, not out of leisure but to break the chain. . . . He went back to Baldwin, who posed the great paradox that would haunt him to the end: Who among us would integrate into a burning house?" (72–73). He mentions the turn toward Wright and Baldwin alongside the assassination of Malcolm X; all are figures who offer sustenance and relief to Paul Coates, who finds his own struggle in their pages. These writers and others sketch the parameters of Coates's father's existence, and thereby his son's: Paul Coates reads vociferously, earns a degree in library science, becomes a special collections librarian at Howard University's Moorland-Springarn Research Center, establishes Black Classic Press as a radical, once bare-bones publishing operation to resurrect lost black texts; and rather relentlessly assigns such texts and others to his son. *The Beautiful Struggle* is a window into its author's intellectual influences as much as it is a memoir of growing up. It is clear that Coates credits his father, along with literary ancestors such as Wright, Baldwin, and others, with his intellectual evolution.[11]

Between Coates and Baldwin

Much has been written about Coates inheriting Baldwin's mantle. Coates reread *The Fire Next Time* (1963) before writing *Between the World and Me*, and Toni Morrison's famous endorsement graces the back cover of the book.[12] "I've been wondering who might fill the intellectual void that plagued me after James Baldwin died. Clearly it is Ta-Nehisi Coates," the endorsement reads. The two essays that constitute *The Fire Next Time*, "Letter to My Nephew on the One Hundredth Anniversary of the Emancipation," which originally appeared December 1, 1962 in the *Progressive*, and "Letter from a Region in My Mind," which was published November 9, 1962, in the *New Yorker,* contain many elements that Coates revisits, though *Between the World and Me* is determinedly atheist.[13] But the texts share more than content or structure: they are both responses to racially motivated violence in America. Baldwin's essays were published a year before the assassination of Medgar Evers, the election of George Wallace as governor of Alabama, the March on Washington and Martin Luther King's "I Have a Dream" speech, and John F. Kennedy's assassination. Published in July 2015, *Between the World and Me* hit bookstands a month after the horrific mass shooting at Mother Emanuel AME Church in Charleston, South Carolina.[14] *Between* also emerged during the height of the Black Lives Matter movement: one year after the deaths of Eric Garner and Michael Brown, two years after the death of Trayvon Martin. Connecting these recent senseless deaths to the murder of Prince Jones, Coates writes, "Sell cigarettes without the proper authority and your body can be destroyed" (9), and considers his son's experience of these injustices. In his unfinished manuscript "Remember This House," Baldwin reported on the state of the nation through the lenses of three assassinated civil rights activists: Medgar Evers, Malcolm X, and Martin Luther King Jr.[15] He knew their widows, who joined forces, in the wake of their husbands' murders, to advocate for civil rights. Today, Mothers of the Movement, women whose sons were killed by police brutality or gun violence, speak as a group. Baldwin's "Letter to My Nephew" and Coates's *Between the World and Me* may be written 53 years apart, but they confront eerily similar national tragedies. As Baldwin wrote: "And I know, which is much worse, and this is the crime of which I accuse my country and my countrymen, and for which neither I nor time nor history will ever forgive them, that they have destroyed and are destroying hundreds of thousands of lives and do not know it and do not want to know it" (*The Fire Next Time* 5). The past is very present.

There are clear structural similarities between the two texts. In his missive to his son, Samori, Coates employs the same epistolary device Baldwin used for his letter to his nephew, James. Both letters are simultaneously private and public. Dana A. Williams in "Everybody's Protest Narrative" contends that the genre limits what Coates can achieve. The work "makes clear that we do need, still, to develop a faculty that reflects and considers the special imperatives of those distinctly black experiences in America that allow us to think and act otherwise. Finally, it reveals that the epistolary memoir as protest, because of its concern with identity politics and its attachment to individualism, cannot take us there" (182). Her criticism of the form seems to deny the importance of subjectivity and individual experience, both extremely significant to the history of African American literature. Cornel West also criticized Coates for his focus on the individual rather than the group. West's Facebook post, a mere paragraph, garnered enormous attention, despite several inaccuracies that revealed a lack of familiarity with Coates's work. On July 16, 2015, he wrote,

Coates's fear-driven self-absorption leads to individual escape and flight to safety—he is cowardly silent on the marvelous new militancy in Ferguson, Baltimore, New York, Oakland, Cleveland and other places. Coates can grow and mature, but without an analysis of capitalist wealth inequality, gender domination, homophobic degradation, Imperial occupation (all concrete forms of plunder) and collective fightback (not just personal struggle) Coates will remain a mere darling of White and Black Neo-liberals, paralyzed by their Obama worship and hence a distraction from the necessary courage and vision we need in our catastrophic times.

In the post titled "In Defense of James Baldwin—Why Toni Morrison (a literary genius) Is Wrong about Ta-Nehisi Coates," West went on to imply that the literary comparison between Baldwin and Coates is tantamount to an attack on Baldwin. West decried what he perceived to be Coates's lack of political engagement, calling him cowardly for avoiding a critique of President Obama (Coates had in fact criticized President Obama for his lectures to African American audiences on personal responsibility and for not advocating more vociferously for black policy) and deriding his lack of involvement in any larger movement. The post contrasted the two writers: "Baldwin was a great writer of profound courage who spoke truth to power. Coates is a clever wordsmith with journalistic talent who avoids any critique of the Black president in power. Baldwin's painful self-examination led to collective action and a focus on social movements." Jesse McCarthy concluded his own assessment of Coates's work on an antithetical note: "But like all those who have taken up the pen to strike at America's racial injustice, [Coates] is also the inheritor of a proud tradition that has relentlessly and defiantly believed that we have it in our means to break the spell of oppression, and that speaking truth to power is not an act of despair, but one of candescence" (22). West again attacked Coates's work in a December 2017 *Guardian* article, which ignited a feud between the two public intellectuals that in turn led Coates to quit Twitter. It is unfortunate to lose Coates's voice on Twitter as his posts contained germinating ideas, casual literary musings, and notes of the writing process often uncaptured in other rhetorical forms. Both West and Williams contend that Coates's choice of genre, the memoir, is inherently individualistic. To better understand this question of limitation, we can turn to Coates's reading of *Moby-Dick,* a novel that purports to be a memoir of a single man. Yet Ishmael's account of his experience with the *Pequod* is the story of a universal human struggle. Just as Melville drew on a plethora of sources and traditions—accounts of the whaleship *Essex,* the legacy of Mocha Dick, Shakespearean tragedy, nautical expertise, maritime lore— Coates, too, incorporates myriad voices in his text. These inclusions offer a rebuttal to the notion of memoir as exlusionary.

At the same time that Coates was critiqued for supposed narcissism, he was also asked for solutions to the larger social ills he chronicles. Michelle Alexander writes about searching in vain for Coates's proposed solutions to the problems of race he addresses. In an August 17, 2015, *New York Times* review, while lauding his journalism, Alexander deemed Coates's book "unfinished," with "critically important questions" "left unanswered." It is worth noting that some of the same criticism was leveled at James Baldwin for his fiction. In a 1979 *New York Times* review of *Just above My Head,* John Romano expressed disappointment that Baldwin, the essayist and author of *The Fire Next Time,* did not ground his latest novel in the politics of place or provide enough contemporary context of racial struggle. Romano noted, "His fiction has often been attacked, notably by younger black writers in the 1960's, as too personal, too patently a working-out of inner conflict at the price of distorting the realities of race and racial conflict in America." The presumption that Baldwin, Coates, or any individual could provide answers to problems plaguing the United States since before its inception is rather confounding. The notion that *Between the World and Me* is unfinished speaks to its participation in several ongoing literary traditions: protest literature, literature of mourning, black autobiography. None of these traditions necessarily offers consolation, nor should it. "Like Baldwin, I tend to think we must not ask whether it is possible for a human being or society to become just or moral [as Coates does]; we must believe it is possible. Believing in this possibility—no matter how slim— and dedicating oneself to playing a meaningful role in the struggle to make it a reality focuses one's energy and attention in an unusual way," Alexander continues in her *New York Times* review. Here she emphasizes the importance of optimism as well as social responsibility: we must believe in the possibility of reform and then, accordingly, take on the burden of reforming individuals and groups. She asks for a different narrative, as these are not Coates's concerns. Coates's only stipulation to Samori is to let his struggle be his own, avoiding reliance on others' progress.

Though Coates employs Baldwin's epistolary form as his architext, Coates's narrative is more autobiographical. He grounds his polemic in firsthand experience that no one can take away from him. He uses the framework of the dream, subverting the reader's expected connotation of the word (positive associations with Martin Luther King Jr. and Barack Obama). Instead, the dream is actually the false construct of race, the belief in difference and superiority based entirely on skin color. But Coates veers away from abstraction, sharing specific memories of encounters with race at the fore, both positive (Howard University, Paris) and negative (West Baltimore, Upper West Side). This is his rhetorical armor, pressed into use for a public argument that is also profoundly personal. Baldwin, on the other hand, prefers broader concepts and theories (your grandmother worked for whites but remains invisible; they do not know Harlem and you do) to specific anecdotes. Baldwin, whose brother's childhood fall down the cellar stairs is one of the few concrete stories related, shifts from more typical, universal concern for any child to awareness of extraordinary injury to the black body. He recalls comforting his brother after the fall, but also declares, "I know what the world has done to my brother and how narrowly he has survived it" (*The Fire Next Time* 5). Both Baldwin and Coates connect the ongoing threat of physical violence to the psyche. As McCarthy writes, "Perhaps one discomfiting lesson of Coates's book is that the work of living with a free mind has to be undertaken whether or not one can ever truly live in a free body" (14).

The epistolary form works to explicate accrued wisdom to the next generation but also to entreat readers to step outside their personal experience. In a January 1963 review of Baldwin's book, *New York Times* editor Sheldon Binn assesses this tactic: "The listener can be transformed, as far as words will take him, into the skin or the teller. Out of his own pain and despair and hope, Mr. Baldwin has fashioned such a transformation. . . . He has pictured white America as seen through the eyes of a Negro." Readers may be sympathetic—or resistant—to transformation. Baldwin anticipates this resistance and waves it aside: "I hear the chorus of the innocents screaming, 'No! This is not true! How *bitter* you are!'—but I am writing this letter to *you*, to try to tell you something about how to handle *them*, for most of them do not yet really know that you exist" (6). The epistle girds itself against readers ready to reject these truths.

The greatest difference between the two texts is one of tone. "Hope" is the word most often used to characterize the distinction between Baldwin and Coates. Though Baldwin warns his nephew of the perilous construct of race, he does not relinquish hope for progress: "It will be hard, James, but you come from sturdy, peasant stock, men who picked cotton and dammed rivers and built railroads, and, in the teeth of the most terrifying odds, achieved an unassailable and monumental dignity. You come from a long line of great poets, some of the greatest poets since Homer. One of them said, *The very time I thought I was lost, My dungeon shook and my chains fell off*" (10). Baldwin invokes literary ancestry here, citing a negro spiritual. He also reassures James of his own ability to counteract larger forces. Espousing a belief in future conversion, Baldwin asserts, "We cannot be free until they are free" (10).

In contrast, Coates declares loyalty to the struggle over any sort of external conversion. He concludes, "I do not believe we can stop them, Samori, because they must ultimately stop themselves. And still I urge you to struggle. Struggle for the memory of your ancestors. Struggle for wisdom. Struggle for the warmth of The Mecca. Struggle for your grandmother and grandfather, for your name. But do not struggle for the Dreamers. Hope for them. Pray for them, if you are so moved. But do not pin your struggle on their conversion" (150). Though critics of the book deemed this conclusion disempowering due to a perceived emphasis on lack of agency, Coates refutes this idea. Work for a greater purpose, he tells his son, independent of whether others join you or whether they possess the same consciousness. He is a writer, not a politician or lawmaker, and his work lies in drawing attention to these important issues rather than solving them.

Comparisons of Baldwin and Coates do not take into account the breadth of Baldwin's oeuvre or the profound despair he expresses in texts published both before and after 1963. Baldwin's literary influence on Coates extends beyond *The Fire Next Time* to several other works, including his essay collection *Notes of a Native Son* and the nonfiction book *No Name in the Street* (1972). Several essays in *Notes of a Native Son* pertain to Coates's project. Like *Between the World and Me, Notes of a Native Son* alternates between black autobiography and cultural criticism and is divided into three parts, though the essays making up each part are more distinct.

Part 1 critiques African American representation in literature and art. Part 2 examines the stories of African Americans in both the north (Harlem) and the south (Atlanta), along with Baldwin's relationship with his father and encounters with segregation.[16] In the essay "Notes of a Native Son," Baldwin explores the 1943 intersections of the death of his stepfather, his nineteenth birthday, and the Harlem race riots. Similar to Coates, Baldwin explores the issue of paternal influence. Whereas Coates is grateful for his father's intellectual interests and participation in family life when many other fathers are, in Coates's words, ghosts, Baldwin tries to reconcile his stepfather's anger, concluding that hatred destroys both its subject and object. Baldwin's conclusion that "this was his legacy: nothing is ever escaped" (602) recalls the ideas that Paul Coates imparts to his son in both *The Beautiful Struggle* and *Between the World and Me*. The writers' fathers warn their sons against becoming another statistic, whether on the Avenue in Harlem or in the Baltimore projects. The sons must reconcile the intellectual and existential struggle with how to live on a quotidian basis.

In Part 3 of *No Name in the Street*, Baldwin recounts his experiences in France and Switzerland in order to address the broader issue of how racial history informs contemporary race relations in the United States and Europe. In his essay "Encounter on the Seine: Blacks Meets Brown," Baldwin compares African Americans to those of African descent in France, realizing they possess distinct histories that separate them. "But the ghetto, anxiety, bitterness, and guilt continue to breed their indescribable complex of tensions" (90). He contends that only time will offer the chance for America and, concurrently, African Americans to decipher and be at peace with their identities. There are direct parallels with *Between the World and Me*, as Coates, too, considers the extent to which his identity shifts in Paris. There he chronicles a psychological liberation in Paris: what it means to live in a place unburdened by the history of slavery and brutality. The attraction begins with Kenyatta's photographs of Parisian doors, one of which is included in the book. Coates informs Samori,

> Your mother had taken many pictures, all through Paris, of doors, giant doors—deep blue, ebony, orange, turquoise, and burning red doors. I examined the pictures of these giant doors in our small Harlem apartment. I had never seen anything like them. It had never even occurred to me that such

giant doors could exist, could be so common in one part of the world and totally absent in another. And it occurred to me, listening to your mother, that France was not a thought experiment but an actual place filled with actual people whose traditions were different, whose lives really were different, whose sense of beauty was different. (119)

Kenyatta's documentation of the doors becomes a metaphor for Coates's sense of freedom. In a narrative full of restrictions, dead ends, and no exit, Paris, like the Mecca, offers new avenues to consider.

Coates anticipates and denies the reader's comparative instinct: "I arrived in Paris. I checked in to a hotel in the 6th arrondissement. . . . I did not think much about Baldwin or Wright" (122). Yet he draws many of the same conclusions as Baldwin: while both authors contemplate the idea of freedom outside the history of race relations in the United States, they posit that shackles remain. In his essay "Equal in Paris," Baldwin describes being jailed for using a bedsheet an acquaintance took from a hotel. He spends a week in prison, during which time he is denied legal representation for several days, becomes increasingly terrified by inexplicable protocol, and finds himself longing for the more predictable identity politics in America, however grim they may be. Though the case is finally dismissed amid jocular exchange in the courtroom, Baldwin is shaken by his sudden loss of control, along with the government's cavalier response to due process. He concludes, "This laughter is the laughter of those who consider themselves to be at a safe remove from all the wretched, for whom the pain of living is not real. . . . This laughter is universal and never can be stilled" (116). His liberation is ultimately set into motion not by living in a freer society but by accepting that this laughter exists everywhere. Like Baldwin, Coates stresses awareness of these structures, telling his son that despite his joy in Paris, "to be distanced, if only for a moment, from fear is not a passport out of the struggle. We will always be black, you and I, even if it means different things in different places" (127). France has its own dream, in its history of colonization.

In addition to *Notes of a Native Son,* Coates seems also to have been influenced by Baldwin's *No Name in the Street* (1972), in which he discusses his views of several African American civil rights leaders, along with the question of his own participation in the movement. Baldwin wrote about the catalyst, in 1957, to return to the United States from Paris and his expatriate existence. He tells of his guilt in reading from afar the newspaper accounts of school integration in Charlotte, North Carolina: of the angry mob hurling insults and saliva toward fifteen-year-old Dorothy Counts. "It made me furious," he reports. "It filled me with both hatred and pity, and it made me ashamed. Some one of us should have been there with her! . . . It was on that bright afternoon that I knew I was leaving France. . . . Everybody else was paying their dues, and it was time I went home and paid mine" (50). Baldwin attributes particular importance to witnessing and to bodily presence. This responsibility figures into the weight and obligation of the struggle, of initially attempting to live free of it or escape, but ultimately coming to face it. Coates, like Baldwin, seems to feel a responsibility to address the wrongs of our society, not only for his son, clearly, but for the public. For all of Baldwin's and Coates's notoriety, their criticisms of the nation come at a price, dismissed as angry, unpatriotic, even dangerous. Anointed as speakers for their respective generations' civil rights dialog, Baldwin and Coates carry heavy burdens, especially from listeners and readers who desire only hopeful messages. But their voices are not meant to reassure or assuage, as some critics wrongly seem to expect, but to inform and address. As Daryl Pinkney points out in his review of *Between,* "No author of a book on this subject can be filled with as much hopelessness as the black writer who no longer sees the point in anyone offering a polemic against racist America" (30). There is hope in the effort and the publication of the project.

Between Coates and Obama

Coates's work as a national correspondent writing about racial politics in America for the *Atlantic* provided ample preparation for his second memoir. Prior to *Between the World and Me,* he penned articles on African American engagement with the Civil War, the Trayvon Martin case and Florida's "stand your ground" law, African American integration of a white neighborhood outside Detroit, race and the Obama presidency, and reparations for African Americans.[17] At the conclusion of President Obama's second term, Coates wrote "My President Was Black" for the *Atlantic.* Penned a little more than a year after the publication of *Between the World and Me,* the series appraises the state of the country's race relations through the lens of the Obama presidency. Continuing to mine American literature, Coates employs Nick Carraway's parting words to Gatsby as the article's epigraph: "'They're a rotten crowd,' I shouted across the lawn. 'You're worth the whole damn bunch put together.'" When President Obama was elected, a flurry of articles welcomed the advent of a postracial America. Colson White-head, hailed as a postracial writer himself, mocked the idea in a November 2009 *New York Times* article, "The Year of Living Postracially." "One year ago today, we officially became a postracial society. Fifty-three percent of the voters opted for the candidate who would be the first president of African descent, and in doing so eradicated racism forever," he wrote. The article went on to explore what pop culture would look like if all defini-tively black stories were revised to be more white. Whitehead approaches the postracial idea with mirth; it does not seem insignificant that his novel *Sag Harbor* (2009), which chronicles the summertime Hamptons shenani-gans of upper-middle-class black teenagers, and *The Underground Railroad* (2016), which chronicles the brutality of slavery and a fugitive slave wom-an's escape, served as very distinct bookends to the Obama presidency. In "My President Was Black," Coates examines the role of race in President Obama's writing and presidency. Coates's literary sensibility suffuses his appraisal of Obama's identity politics as he locates the president's auto-biography, *Dreams from My Father: A Story of Race and Inheritance,* in the historical context of black memoir. In his own interrogation of literary influence, Coates invokes the autobiographies of Frederick Douglass, Har-riet Jacobs, and Malcolm X.[18] Yet Coates distinguishes the literary tradi-tion he sees as underlying his own work from that of President Obama. In the January–February 2017 issue of the *Atlantic,* he wrote, "Obama's DNC speech is the key. It does not belong to the literature of 'the struggle'; it belongs to the literature of prospective presidents—men (as it turns out) who speak not to gravity and reality, but to aspirations and dreams." Just as President Obama's vision, expanded upon in *The Audacity of Hope: Thoughts on Reclaiming the American Dream* (2006) conflicts with Coates's treatment of hope in *Between the World and Me,* "My President Was Black" serves as an illuminating conversation between two perspectives on twenty-first-century race relations. The work also serves as a final extratextual element to consider, a coda of sorts to Coates's letter to his son.

After an event celebrating the publication of *Between the World and Me*, attendee Karen Pearson stood in a line for Coates to sign her book, commenting, "I hope it provokes a really honest conversation" (qtd. in Schuessler). With *Between the World and Me*, Coates participates in many conversations: literary, national, racial, parental. Coates's conversations with Melville, Baldwin, Wright, Obama, and others concern the project of the United States, the problematic coexistence of its diverse inhabitants, and the premises on which the country was built. In the face of criticism of his work as isolationist, Coates has acknowledged his debt to tradition. In one of the last articles he penned for the *Atlantic* before announcing his departure, on May 7, 2018, Coates wrote about the deleterious effects of fame: "My sense of myself as part of a community of black writers disintegrated before me." Establishing Coates in dialog with a variety of voices, times, and traditions mirrors his experience sitting in the Moorland-Springarn Library, poring over infinite books, puzzling over the streams of dissent. Any single alignment of literary inheritance is reductionist and does not do justice to the mixed heritage of his work. Coates's conversations also concern the project of American literature and its criticism. Black boys, white whales, everybody's protest novel: these stories belong to the same canon.

Conclusion

PERRY MILLER'S CONTRIBUTIONS TO American literary scholarship spanned three decades that included World War II, the Cold War (during which *The Raven and the Whale* was published), and the civil rights movement. The author considered the legacy of early American literature, from the Puritans to the Transcendentalists, at a time when both international order and national identity were in question. These ideas were not only examined in his books; unlike some of his American studies compatriots, Miller believed passionately in U.S. intervention in World War II and left his teaching post at Harvard to serve in the Army from 1942 through the war's end. Both before and after the war, Miller turned to seventeenth- to nineteenth-century American literature for existential insight into the American self and national character. In the November 25, 1965, issue of the *New York Review of Books*, Alfred Kazin reviewed Miller's last work, *The Life of the Mind in America: From the Revolution to the Civil War* (1965), which was published posthumously and won the Pulitzer Prize. "His passion was for history," Kazin wrote, "precisely the history of American Society as experienced in ideas. Miller wanted to demonstrate, to bind up together in the pages of one mighty life-work, the structure and sources of the American mind. And he meant *American* and *mind* as only historians ever do—through the involvement of many minds—some by no means distinguished, but effective. In the end, the national mind is the national force." Miller understood the national mind, similar to his own, to be in a state of perpetual formation and reformation. In essays throughout the 1950s and 1960s, he returned again and again to Emerson's "American Scholar," evidently working through evolving notions of his own place in the pantheon of American intellectual history.[1]

Today, at a time when nationalism and its social, historical precepts are being brought to bear, one ponders Miller's interest in the forces and personalities surrounding the establishment of a national literature, as well as whose voices would be included in this construction. Once heralded, Miller's work fell out of favor during the late twentieth century, when the culture wars of the 1980s and 1990s brought about an expansion of the canon to include more diverse representation across race, class, gender, and geography. Scholars noted that New England, and the study of Puritanism, had inexplicably dominated the study of early American history and literature.[2] As the literary canon evolved to embrace the representation of a spectrum of voices, so too did American literary criticism. However, this important and long-overdue progressive shift led to the dismissal of the work of an entire generation of critics, and perhaps failed to sufficiently take into account some earlier scholars' extensive political engagement with questions of national identity. Miller's own words on Melville in *The Raven and the Whale* offer curious insight into the eventual resistance to his literary criticism:

> An artist can, once he has caught the ear of his people, abruptly discover himself cut off not because he thunders some clear sanctity against their insanity, but because he participates completely in their befuddlement. He accepts as the terms of his problem precisely the terms they propound to him, and can conceive no others; then he finds himself, despite the power of genius, no more capable of resolving the antinomies, or of making good the pretensions, than they are. If at the end of his exertions, no matter how titanic, he confronts the blank emptiness of defeat, if then he is relegated to the unreverberating solitude of failure, the tragedy is not so much his overreaching as an inescapable collapse of the structures his society provided him—indeed, imposed upon him, with no allowance for alternatives. (4)

Even as we continue the important cultural work of recovering neglected voices and further expanding the literary canon, it seems useful to contemplate the important foundations early critics laid, enabling later generations to build outward and upward. *Children of the Raven and the Whale* examines palimpsests: connections between contemporary texts and the historically canonical texts lying beneath. To examine these textual constellations is to acknowledge the mixed legacy of U.S. history and the privileging of some voices while others were muted. This study is an exercise in limitation and constraint: the historical limitations of the canon in turn reflected the historical—and current—limitations of U.S. society, in which many voices are still suppressed.

In other works that bracketed *The Raven and the Whale,* such as *The New England Mind: The Seventeenth Century* (1939) and *Errand into the Wilderness* (1956), among others, Miller focused on the seventeenth-century Puritan sermon, which typically condemned the sins of the community and exhorted congregants to atone by returning to the true faith. Sacvan Bercovitch took up this mantle in *The American Jeremiad* (1978), examining the ways in which U.S. writers engaged with the jeremiad's iterations post-Enlightenment. The Christian call to return to faith became a secular call to reclaim the promise of the United States by enacting the democratic ideals that underlay its founding. Bercovitch writes, "American writers have tended to see themselves as outcasts and isolates, prophets crying in the wilderness. So they have been, as a rule: American Jeremiahs, simultaneously lamenting a declension and celebrating a national dream" (180). In the background of this book is the concept of the jeremiad—a perpetual state of seeking, searching, and yearning for progress—and the exhortation to the United States to bridge the "distance between promise and fact" (23), to use Bercovitch's terminology. The contemporary writers discussed in this project remind us that the dream is ever elusive, and has perhaps never existed in any discernible form. Resisting ideas of American exceptionalism, and cohesion, the writers redefine the errand and remap notions of wilderness.

Ethnic American writers are often understood to be writing counter-histories that refute official or accepted accounts of cultural repression: among many examples, Sherman Alexie accomplishes this for the Spokane in *Reservation Blues* (1995), while Fae Myenne Ng fulfills this agenda in her novel *Bone* (1993), unearthing the immigrant strata of San Francisco's

Chinatown. In *Brother, I'm Dying* (2007), Edwidge Danticat offers a counternarrative to the U.S. government's report on her uncle's death, speaking for the dead as well as for those left behind. In her first short story collection, *Krik? Krak* (1995), Danticat utilized as her framework a form of traditional Haitian storytelling that entails call and response between the storyteller and the audience. The call to begin the story is also a call to recover it. In a larger sense, the intertextuality with which ethnic American writers engage is not so different; heeding such calls and seeking to emend the literary record parallels some of the politics involved in the American literary canon. What qualifies as American literary history? Whose testimony is most credible, and whose testimony circulates? Though the majority of intertextual relationships discussed in this book are not oppositional, they are deliberate conversations that might not occur without direct allusion. Coates's work in particular speaks to the potentially larger cultural function of these contemporary American counternarratives to extend beyond fiction to social justice. Yet I do not argue that fiction matters only if it inspires overt activist agendas. Rather, all these texts convey the importance of a plethora of voices authoring our understanding of history and humanity. Ultimately, it is important to understand not only how these intertextual relationships illuminate the study of U.S. literature but also the ways in which U.S. literature informs theories of intertextuality. The authors of the new American Renaissance traverse borders and eras to participate in age-old debates about the Constitution of the United States, each voice contributing a paragraph to the single, complicated, long-running story of one nation composed of many.

In November 2018, 168 years after Hawthorne and Melville ascended Monument Mountain and almost two decades after the *New Yorker* fiction issue gathered a team of trailblazing authors who were to change the landscape of American literature, the *New York Times* convened thirty-two black male authors for an article titled "Black Male Writers for Our Time," by Ayana Mathis. The photographs of the men, who had assembled in the library of the Brooklyn Historical Society, register immediate historical import. In light of the intellectual firepower assembled in a single space, how marvelous it would have been to traverse Pierrepont Street, where the Brooklyn Historical Society sits, and witness Ishmael Reed, Dinaw Mengestu, Rowan Ricardo Philips, and Cornelius Eady walking down a single street in Brooklyn Heights, one autumn day! "These 32 American men, and their peers, are producing literature that is essential to how we understand our country and its place in the world right now," the article's tag line declared. The gathering was important not because the talent was new but because it was so old, yet unheralded. It took more than one hundred years after the period Matthiessen deemed the first American Renaissance for voices like those of Harriet Jacobs and Frederick Douglass to be restored. Even as we celebrate the plural nature of American literature today, it is incumbent upon us to continue to restore the multiplicity of voices from earlier periods to our classrooms and the canon, and to remember that many more voices existed that never reached the printed and disseminated page. As long as the United States distributes rights unequally, there will be voices on the margins. As Mathis notes, "We must pay keen attention to who's in the moment and who's left out, and why." Any grouping, of course, including the cohort of authors whose work is taken up in this book, inevitably leaves out many other important voices. The same October day that the authors assembled, my American literature class at City Tech, City University of New York, was meeting less than half a mile away. Less than half a mile, but a great distance between the moneyed enclave of Brooklyn Heights and underfunded public education. Had I known about the gathering, my students and I would have walked over to Pierrepont Street and cheered for the writers en route. When we talk about the expansion of the canon and the plural voices of contemporary literature, we are not only talking about including more authors, but also including more readers. Expanding access to quality public education provides exposure to reading great work, and the inspiration to create great work. The next American Renaissance—the children's children—will likely emerge from this synergy of public education and individual experience.

Innumerable writers will inherit the mantle of American literature or build a wholly new one of their own, pen our contemporary jeremiads, and embark on errands into the new, old wilderness of the United States. At the conclusion of the *New York Times* article, Mathis pondered the unusual proliferation of literary talent that provoked the historic convention in Brooklyn. "I wonder if, in the annals of history," she wrote, "this extraordinary period of artistry will find a name, or a unifying sentiment that codifies it as a movement. Perhaps, or perhaps not." The writers of the new

American Renaissance illustrate that with each new generation, American literature, and indeed the American project, regenerates, moving ever closer to a receding democratic, humanist ideal.

> It eluded us then, but that's no matter—tomorrow we will run faster, stretch out our arms farther. . . . And then one fine morning—
>
> So we beat on, boats against the current, borne back ceaselessly into the past.

Notes

Introduction

1. While Lethem's *Motherless Brooklyn* does not explore Judaism, other works of his, including *Dissident Gardens*, discuss Jewish American cultural heritage, and his work has been situated in the Jewish American tradition. For more on this topic, see William Deresiewicz's essay "The Imaginary Jew."

2. On the fortieth anniversary of *MELUS: Multi-Ethnic Literature of the U.S.*, retiring editor Martha Cutter evaluated the influential role of the journal at the forefront of the field. In an editorial titled "Multi-Ethnic 'Literature' of the 'United States': Thinking beyond Borders," Cutter reflected on new developments in the field: debates over what constitutes U.S. literature, and whether forms of visual media qualify as literature worth consideration in the journal. A survey of *MELUS* scholarship in the last two decades reveals a growing body of cross-racial and cross-ethnic scholarship. In the Winter 2018 *MELUS*, "Twenty-First Century Perspectives on U.S. Ethnic Literatures," guest editors A. Yemisi Jimoh and Angelo Rich Robinson identified important future sites of study: intersectionality and multimedia and mixed-genre cultural work. Ronald Takaki's *A Different Mirror: A History of Multicultural America* was at the forefront of comparative multiethnic literary and historical study and remains a groundbreaking text.

3. The photographs are also poignant, as one of the authors, David Foster Wallace, is no longer with us.

4. I thank an anonymous reviewer for the University of Virginia Press for suggesting the inclusion of Jauss's work.

5. For a helpful overview of influence and intertextuality, see Eric Rothstein and Jay Clayton, editors, *Influence and Intertextuality in Literary History,* and David Cowart, *Literary Symbiosis: The Reconfigured Text in Twentieth-Century Writing.*

6. Several decades later, Bloom revised his ideas in *The Anatomy of Influence.* In this work, he returns to the subject on a more autobiographical note, and departs from the complicated Greek ratios and a focus on competitive struggle to look in particular at the storied legacies of Shakespeare and Whitman.

7. As David Cowart points out in *Literary Symbiosis,* "Though without doubt psychoanalysis must remain one of the instruments whereby the critic assesses the guest text and its author . . . there is more to symbiosis than the psychoanalytic myth permits the critic to grasp" (24).

8. See Mary Orr's *Intertextuality: Debates and Contexts* for a compelling defense of Kristeva's early (1969) formulation.

9. Roger Sale's *Literary Inheritance,* which examines seventeenth- to twentieth-century, mostly British literature in an effort to plot a continuum of literary tradition and the ways in which authors adhere to or depart from it, was an especially helpful model. Betina Entzminger's *Contemporary Reconfigurations of American Literary Classics* appears on its surface to be a similar study but employs cognitive psychology to argue that contemporary writers revise American origin myths in order to manage their own lived experiences.

10. Cowart includes an appendix that catalogs generations of American fiction writers by the decade of their birth, with the exception of a category titled "The Immigrants," who are listed together. The appendix illustrates the debates surrounding the segregation of immigrant and multiethnic writing from other American writing.

11. For various treatments of this topic, see William Cain, F. O. *Matthiessen and the Politics of Criticism;* Sacvan Bercovitch, editor, *Reconstructing American Literary History* (dedicated to Matthiessen and Miller); and Cyrus Patell, *Emergent U.S. Literatures.*

12. My conclusion here about American literature relates to a larger argument about globalization, which Paul Jay in *Global Matters* argues is "characterized by complex back-and-forth flows of people and cultural forms in which the appropriation and transformation of things—music, film, food, fashion—raise questions about the rigidity of the center-periphery model" (3).

1. "A Walker in the City"

1. See Tim Engles, "Visions of Me in the Whitest Raw Light," Daniel Kim, "Do I, Too, Sing America?," Liam Corley, "Just Another Ethnic Pol," David Cowart, *Trailing Clouds,* and Christian Moraru, "Speakers and Sleepers," for additional discussion of Whitman's presence in *Native Speaker.*

2. It is worth noting that despite the positive critical reception of Lethem's novel, there is little scholarship devoted to *Motherless Brooklyn.* The few existent treatments concern disability studies. For example, J. L. Fleissner writes in "Symptomatology and the Novel," "From a strictly neuropsychiatric perspective, the attribution of any kind of meaning to the tic would be an error" (390).

3. For a history of walking in New York literature, see Stephen Miller's *Walking New York: Reflections of American Writers from Walt Whitman to Teju Cole.*

4. In a 2003 interview with Lorin Stein in the *Paris Review,* Lethem described his writing process as "pedantic:" "I'm a tortoise, waking each day to plod out my page or two" ("Jonathan Lethem").

5. Lethem also establishes a map of downtown Brooklyn in his 2003 novel *Fortress of Solitude,* in which he addresses themes of gentrification and racial dissonance more explicitly.

6. Teju Cole's *Open City: A Novel* (2011) is a more recent literary exploration of mapping diaspora in New York's streets. Cole's novel features a Nigerian doctor as he meanders aimlessly throughout Manhattan.

7. See Liam Corley's "Just Another Ethnic Pol" for further discussion of the *Golden Venture.*

2. Literary Custom House

1. For works that treat Hawthorne's intertextuality with other authors, see Richard Kopley's discussion of Hawthorne's engagement with Poe, "Hawthorne's Transplanting and Transforming 'The Tell-Tale Heart,'" and James A. Schiff's discussion of Updike's response to Hawthorne, "Updike's *Scarlet Letter* Trilogy: Recasting an American Myth." Richard Brodhead's *The School of Hawthorne* is a more comprehensive look at the author's literary influence (he discusses Melville's, Howells's, James's, and Faulkner's uses of Hawthornian themes).

2. For further information on the importance of place in Hawthorne's writing, see Philip McFarland, *Hawthorne in Concord;* Michael Davitt Bell, *Hawthorne and the Historical Romance of New England;* Robert Milder, *Hawthorne's Habitations: A*

Literary Life; and Edwin Haviland Miller, *Salem Is My Dwelling Place: A Life of Nathaniel Hawthorne.*

3. Lahiri makes note of East India Company–related imports in Massachusetts. In "Hell-Heaven," Pranab Kaku "would take us to India Tea and Spices in Watertown" (66).

4. It is worth noting that before Lahiri reached back to Hawthorne, Hawthorne reached back to Washington Irving, who invented the persona of Dutch historian Diedrich Knickerbocker to narrate *A History of New York* (1809) and "Rip Van Winkle" (1819). In the same way that Hawthorne was conscious of Irving in the lexicon of American letters and foundational folktales, Lahiri is conscious of Hawthorne. Chapter 4 discusses Irving more extensively.

5. In *The Holder of the World* (1993), Indian-born American author Baharti Mukherjee retells *The Scarlet Letter* in three locations and two time periods: seventeenth-century India (during the reign of the British East India Company), seventeenth-century colonial America, and twentieth-century Boston. Mukherjee imagines Indian ancestry and events preceding Hester Prynne and her contemporaries in the Massachusetts Bay Colony.

6. Hawthorne describes Thoreau's vegetable garden in the preface to *Mosses.*

7. See Sacvan Bercovitch's *The Office of The Scarlet Letter* for an extended discussion of this idea, including Hawthorne's preface to the second edition of the novel.

8. Toward the end of the novel, Hawthorne expresses his wish to erase the profound imprint of the scarlet letter from his psyche, but, as Sacvan Bercovitch observes in an extended analysis of the letter's ambiguity, "even that wish for finality works to open (rather than resolve) questions about the letter's office" (113).

9. For a discussion of masculinity, law, and critical nationalism in Hawthorne's work, see Lauren Berlant's *The Anatomy of National Fantasy: Hawthorne, Utopia, and Everyday Life.*

10. Donald Pease argues that the act of writing *The Scarlet Letter* enabled Hawthorne to combat both his dismissal from the custom house and his feeling that he is "forgotten by his age." "Only his reactivation of an as yet incomplete communal process enabled him to feel sufficiently remembered by his culture" (*Visionary Compacts* 80). Pease's argument leans toward the abstract and completely theoretical, but the idea of community is important. Writing about a particular historical community enabled Hawthorne not only to reassert his authorial prowess at a time when his identity and purpose in life were under duress but also to participate in a community he was born into, even if he ultimately chose to reject it.

11. For a sustained consideration of Hawthorne and epistemology, see Zachary Turpin, "Hawthorne the Unreliabilist."

12. The separated lovers Hema and Kaushik thinking of each other, Kaushik's tragic death at sea, and Hema's lack of awareness ("All day I was oblivious" [331]) recall Edwidge Danticat's story "Children of the Sea," in her first short story collection, *Krik? Krak!* (1995).

13. Bollinger questions the ethics of employing an actual tragedy, the 2004 tsunami, in fiction. She writes, "Interestingly, Lahiri speaks as if the tsunami caught her, as well as her character, by surprise. She expresses doubts about the ability of *Unaccustomed Earth* to help readers understand the nature of disaster and its aftermath. Moreover, she implies that if it fails to do so, perhaps her choice to include this 'major global event' was unethical. Certainly, *Unaccustomed Earth* does not 'tackle' the event, for it does not offer an extended meditation on the cultural meaning and effects of a disaster, unlike the majority of post-9/11 fiction" (499).

14. Adopting a cynical view, Srikanth argues that Lahiri's works "enable white and other non–South Asian American readers to confer on themselves the self-congratulations of a multicultural and cosmopolitan sensibility" (51).

3. Short Happy Palimpsest

1. Díaz perhaps displays more equanimity than his predecessor, however. As Curnutt writes, "The list of modernist mentors and peers [Hemingway] publicly renounced is long, from Sherwood Anderson, Gertrude Stein, and Ford Madox Ford to F. Scott Fitzgerald and John Dos Passos" (163).

2. Hemingway wrote in "The Art of the Short Story," a piece masquerading as a lecture to college students, "A few things I have found to be true. If you leave out important things or events that you know about the story is strengthened. If you leave out or skip something because you do not know it, the story will be worthless" (qtd. in Flora 130). This was one formulation of his illustrious iceberg theory of writing.

3. For a discussion of Francis Macomber's genesis in F. Scott Fitzgerald, see Joseph Flora's *Ernest Hemingway: A Study of the Short Fiction*. Flora argues that Hemingway was dismayed by Fitzgerald's humble candor in "The Crack-Up," published in *Esquire* in February 1936.

4. Díaz treats this subject matter most directly in *This Is How You Lose Her* (2012).

5. In discussing the issue of lion hunting and sympathy, I would be remiss not to bring up the case of Cecil, a black-maned Zimbabwean lion that lived in the Hwange National Park and was killed by Walter Palmer, an American recreational game hunter (and dentist) in July 2015. Cecil's killing attracted widespread outrage from

animal conservationists, politicians, and celebrities, garnering far more attention than other contemporary calamities or human rights abuses. Hemingway's first safari (1933–1934) resulted in both "The Short Happy Life of Francis Macomber" and the hide of a black-maned lion, among other trophies.

6. I would like to thank my colleague Rebecca Mazumdar for mentioning the story in the course of a conversation on literary influence.

7. In an interview, Díaz described the experience of his own father's departure from the family: "It was terrible because you have this real masculine role model that you look up to, and then, 'Adios'" (Mason 2008).

8. Any discussion of Hemingway, Díaz, and gender is complicated. Both authors have been criticized for misogyny in their writing.

9. Kelli A. Larson argues that Hemingway's treatment of race changed after a second African safari in the 1950s. "When compared to the writings from his first safari, *Green Hills of Africa* (1935), 'The Snows of Kilimanjaro,' and 'The Short Happy Life of Francis Macomber,' these later posthumous works [*True at First Light* (1999) and *Under Kilimanjaro* (2005)] . . . reveal an evolution in the author's attitude toward the continent and its people and invite scholars to reassess the roles that Africa and race play in his writings" (330).

10. In *Toward the Geopolitical Novel: U.S. Fiction in the Twenty-First Century,* Caren Irr writes, "Authors such as Helon Habila, Amitav Ghosh, Junot Díaz, Daniel Alarcon, and Daniyal Mueenuddin may have spent time in MFA programs in the U.S. and their work may signal 'high cultural pluralism' to some readers. Nonetheless, their writing also engages with other traditions—such as Nigerian popular fiction, the Indian nationalist novel, and Latin American neorealism" (8). While it is an understatement to say that Díaz "engages with other traditions" outside "high cultural pluralism," it is worth sharing this debate because of the attempt to segregate forms of knowledge (ethnic, educational, etc.).

11. When *Oscar Wao* first appeared in short story form in the *New Yorker*'s December 25, 2000–January 1, 2001 issue, it was already presented in the context of American literary classics. The issue's cover featured a subway car recreated as a reading room at a library. One destination is listed as East Egg, while graffiti tags include "Fahrenheit 451" and "Catch-22."

12. For a fictional treatment of the story of the Mirabal sisters, see Julia Alvarez's acclaimed historical novel *In the Time of the Butterflies* (1994).

13. Díaz's footnotes are not unlike the glossary in *Death in the Afternoon* (1932), which Hemingway uses to define the many components of bullfighting and in the process, exhibits his knowledge of Spanish. In the case of both authors, however, the footnotes don't necessarily clarify readers' confusion, as the footnotes themselves are often complex.

14. Carine Mardorossian observes that many postcolonial writers now consider themselves migrant, rather than exiled, writers. She notes that Salman Rushdie and Mukherjee herself refer to their work as "(im)migrant," while other writers are also less concerned with thematizing exile in their work (15). She continues, "Writers might still be undeniably living 'in exile,' from their native land, but the shift from exile to migrant literature challenges literary criticism's traditional reliance on that experience as the 'basis' of explanation in literary analysis. Instead it makes us look at exile as a condition that itself requires explanation and ideological analysis" (16). The debate about terminology may shift again, however, as the current migrant crisis continues.

4. New York Unearthed

1. Regarding *Poems from Guantánamo,* Erin Trapp writes, "The uniqueness of the collection lies, then, in asking us how to read the writing of the enemy and in the challenge it thereby poses to received ideas about the testimonial function in both 9/11 and human rights literature." See Trapp, "The Enemy Combatant as Poet."
2. See Russell Reising, *The Unusable Past: Theory and the Study of American Literature.* Reising contends that through the late twentieth century, American literary critics dismissed important social history and writers from their critiques, preferring isolationist, exclusionary narratives.
3. See Mark Noonan, "Re-Writing Ourselves in the Wake of 9/11." Noonan argues that many novels written after 9/11 "were prone to nostalgic excess and reified the very event they were trying to reconstruct." Juxtaposing the unfortunate vicissitudes of reality with characters who do or don't do the right thing saves McCann from overt sentimentalism.
4. Often the domestic is associated, perhaps reflexively, with the sentimental. Susan Faludi writes that the "cultural troika of media, entertainment, and advertising declared the post-9/11 age an era of neofifties nuclear family togetherness, redomesticated femininity, and reconstituted cold warrior manhood" (3–4).
5. *Man on Wire,* directed by James Marsh (2008). Film quotations represent my own transcriptions.
6. Collins writes, "I see you spelled out on storefront windows / And on the bright unfurled awnings of this city / I say the syllables as I turn a corner—/ Kelly and Lee, / Medina, Nardella, and O'Connor" (lines 21–25). He invokes Whitman; the reader may also be reminded of Bartleby's work at the Dead Letters Office.
7. In a literature class at City Tech, my student Noemi Rovirosa made the wise observation that the intentional disparateness of the stiletto and Bible was part of

McCann's democracy: the object from the prostitute and the object from the priest are equal, their lives (and loss of their lives) equal.

8. For a fuller discussion of how the film "reverses the memory" of 9/11, see Martin Randall, *9/11 and the Literature of Terror.*

9. Before Irving, Adriaen van der Donck was a historian of New Netherland. Van der Donck's *A Description of New Netherland,* published in 1655, advertised the Dutch colony to future settlers, including West Indians. Van der Donck's text, which speaks to potential settlers from both the Netherlands and its colonies, is an early acknowledgment of the international nature of New Netherland, one that O'Neill explores centuries later. For further information on this history, see John Easterbrook's "Cosmopolitanism and Adriaen van der Donck's *A Description of New Netherland*" (2014).

10. There is a bit of Irving's Diedrich Knickerbocker, the invented Dutch historian, in Gatsby's invented persona. Prior to the publication of *A History of New York,* Irving placed classified ads concerning the disappearance of his protagonist from a New York hotel. Speculations abounded.

11. Irving's character became synonymous with old New York, and spawned a cottage industry of Knickerbocker products and institutions, including *Knickerbocker Magazine.* For the magazine's editorial and publishing history as well as its cultural and literary significance, see Miller, *The Raven and the Whale.* For more information regarding Knickerbocker's literary descendants, see Elizabeth Bradley, *Knickerbocker: The Myth behind New York.*

12. Snyder notes that similar sentiment exists in *Netherland;* she writes that Hans's vision of the past is informed by "regressive nostalgia" (482).

13. In Kate Brogan's framework, this would be an exorcism, ending the cultural haunting.

14. Snyder reads the act of rewriting in several post 9/11 works, including *Netherland,* differently: "A ghostly 'taint of aftermath' undeniably haunts these melancholic second mowings, but in self-consciously working through the literary history that shapes their imagining of the contemporary national scene, these post-9/11 fictions, and *Netherland* foremost among them, sustain a potential for self-recognition that may permit us to do more than merely repeat the past" (488).

15. For helpful insight contextualizing Fitzgerald, New York, and loss, see Kirk Curnutt's article "Mourning in 'My Lost City.'"

16. Sinead Moynihan in "Upground and Belowground Topographies" discusses McCann's *This Side of Brightness* beside *Let the Great World Spin,* arguing for "the inextricability of time from space in McCann's treatment of trauma, a connection which is illustrated most convincingly through his deployment of the chronotopes of skyscraper and subway" (270).

5. Black Boys and White Whales

1. Baldwin's letter first appeared in *Progressive Magazine* in 1962 and has since been anthologized. Howard Ramsby II points to the Baldwin and Wright allusions as helpful marketing tools for Spiegel and Grau, Coates's publisher, and characterizes the literary conversations in terms of Henry Louis Gates's theory of signifying.

2. Coates has since deleted his Twitter account.

3. Melville lost his father, Allan Melvill, when he was twelve, the same age as the *Rachel*'s missing son.

4. There is a rich body of scholarship on Melville, paternity, and orphanhood. See especially Richard Chase, *Herman Melville,* and Karen Weiser, "Doubled Narratives of Orphanhood in Melville's *Pierre*."

5. In a literary constellation that links the authors I consider in chapters 4 and 5, in 2007 Joseph O'Neill reviewed C. L. R. James's book on cricket and race, *Beyond a Boundary* (1963), which now reads as a preview to *Netherland*. The reader is struck by the similarities between Chuck Ramkissoon and James, who imagined cricket as uniting disparate nationalities, and dreamed of American citizenship.

6. "The Case for Reparations," originally published in the *Atlantic* of June 2014, tells the story of one man, Clyde Ross, to historicize and catalog the number of things taken away from African Americans. "The losses mounted," Coates notes. After Reconstruction, "black people were not left to their own devices. They were terrorized. In the Deep South, a second slavery ruled. In the North, legislatures, mayors, civic associations, banks, and citizens all colluded to pin black people into ghettos, where they were overcrowded, overcharged, and undereducated. Businesses discriminated against them, awarding them the worst jobs and the worst wages. Police brutalized them in the streets. And the notion that black lives, black bodies, and black wealth were rightful targets remained deeply rooted in the broader society," he writes.

7. For further discussion of the literary relationship between Wright and Coates, see Joseph G. Ramsey's two-part essay, "The Petrified and the Proletarian," in *Red Wedge* (2015, 2016).

8. Jesse McCarthy notes that Coates also invokes through association another earlier text, W. E. B. DuBois's *The Souls of Black Folk* (1903), which begins, "Between me and the other world there is ever an unasked question." McCarthy observes, "By writing under the double sign of Du Bois and Wright, [Coates] places his book in the company of the moral and philosophical inquiries of *The Souls of Black Folk* and the lyrical autobiography of Wright's *Black Boy* (1945)."

9. Coates writes about the prevalence of lynch mobs in Mississippi in "The Case for Reparations." Wright's poem begins with an individual victim, but as the abrupt subject switch implies, it is the story of countless murders.

10. In "Between the World and Ferguson," a compelling article that predates Coates's memoir, Jelani Cobb reuses Wright's language: "When I was eighteen, I stumbled across Richard Wright's poem 'Between the World and Me.'"

11. Both *The Beautiful Struggle* and *Between the World and Me* focus predominantly on male texts, communities, and influences. The relative absence of women in Coates's work has attracted criticism.

12. Other writers have used Baldwin's text as a springboard to discuss the state of race, gender, and sexuality issues in the United States. In *The Fire This Time*, Randall Kenan reflects on the lack of progress for African Americans, decades after the civil rights era. *The Fire This Time: A New Generation Speaks about Race* is a collection of essays edited by Jesmyn Ward.

13. If Coates finds refuge in reading—first in his father's assigned texts, later in works of his own choosing at Howard University's library or outside the structure of academia—Baldwin finds temporary refuge in the church. "Letter from a Region in My Mind" chronicles Baldwin's teenage embrace of Christianity, adult curiosity about Islam, and eventual movement away from religion toward secular humanism.

14. Spiegel and Grau, Coates's publisher, made the decision to move up the book's release in response to the murders of African American parishioners. The day after the shooting, on June 18, Coates responded with a blog entry, "Take Down the Confederate Flag—Now," which underscored the state's explicit endorsement of racial violence.

15. The manuscript formed the framework for Raoul Peck's 2016 documentary film about Baldwin, *I Am Not Your Negro*.

16. Part 2 includes Baldwin's essay "Carmen Jones: The Dark Is Light Enough" (*Notes of a Native Son*), in which the author denigrates the all-black musical film adaptation of *Carmen* as offensive for its false, affected portrayal of African Americans. In a dark coincidence, Prince Carmen Jones is Coates's murdered Howard classmate.

17. These pieces are collected in *We Were Eight Years in Power: An American Tragedy* (2017). See Howard Ramsby II's "The Remarkable Reception of Ta-Nehisi Coates" for a helpful gloss on Coates's work for the *Atlantic*. He observes that Coates developed a sizable following through active conversation with readers (a community known as the Horde) in the Comments section online, and from the publication of *Black Panther #1*. Ramsby notes, "A contemporary black book history might also take into account the ways that the digital age reconfigures the activities of African American writers. Coates's abilities to actively engage his readers, previously on his blog and now on Twitter, represent defining qualities of his identity as a writer. . . . Somewhere out there in that vast body of data, we might discover answers to the riddle of why so many black writers are met with indifference, while a select few enjoy receptions that are quite remarkable" (202).

18. For further discussion of President Obama's memoir and literary influence, see Daniel Stein's "Barack Obama's *Dreams from My Father* and African American Literature."

Conclusion

1. For a fuller discussion of Miller's engagement with Emerson and the role of the public intellectual, see Randall Fuller, "Errand into the Wilderness."
2. See Eileen Razzari Elrod's journal article "New Puritans" and Francis T. Butts's essay "The Myth of Perry Miller."

Works Cited

Alexander, Michelle. "Ta-Nehisi Coates's 'Between the World and Me.'" *New York Times,* 17 Aug. 2015.

Alexie, Sherman. "Flight Patterns." *Ten Little Indians.* Grove, 2004.

Alexie, Sherman. *Reservation Blues.* 1995. Grove, 2014.

Alvarez, Julia. *In the Time of the Butterflies.* Workman, 1994.

Bacon, Katie. "The Great Irish-Dutch-American Novel." *Atlantic,* 6 May 2008, https://www.theatlantic.com/magazine/archive/2008/05/the-great-irish-dutch-american-novel/306788/.

Bakhtin, Mikhail. *The Dialogic Imagination: Four Essays.* Edited by Michael Holmquist, translated by Caryl Emerson and Michael Holmquist. 1981. U of Texas P, 1996.

Baldwin, James. "Carmen Jones: The Dark Is Light Enough." 1955. *Notes of a Native Son.* Beacon Press, 2012, pp. 47–58.

Baldwin, James. "Encounter on the Seine." 1950. *Notes of a Native Son.* Beacon Press, 2012, pp. 119–26.

Baldwin, James. "Equal in Paris." 1955. *Notes of a Native Son.* Beacon Press, 2012, pp. 141–62.

Baldwin, James. "Everybody's Protest Novel." 1949. *Notes of a Native Son.* Beacon Press, 2012, pp. 13–24.

Baldwin, James. *The Fire Next Time.* 1963. Vintage, 1992.

Baldwin, James. "Letter from a Region in My Mind." *New Yorker,* 19 Nov. 1962, https://www.newyorker.com/magazine/1962/11/17/letter-from-a-region-in-my-mind.

Baldwin, James. "Many Thousands Gone." 1951. *Notes of a Native Son.* Beacon Press, 2012, pp. 87–118.

Baldwin, James. *No Name in the Street.* 1972. Vintage, 2007.

Baldwin, James. *Notes of a Native Son.* 1955. Beacon Press, 2012.

Baldwin, James. "Remember This House." Manuscript, n.d. *I Am Not Your Negro.* Directed by Raoul Peck, Magnolia Pictures, 2016.

Bell, Michael Davitt. *Hawthorne and the Historical Romance of New England.* Princeton UP, 1971.

Benjamin, Jessica. *Like Subjects, Love Objects: Essays on Recognition and Sexual Difference.* Yale UP, 1995.

Bercovitch, Sacvan. *The American Jeremiad.* U of Wisconsin P, 1978.

Bercovitch, Sacvan. *The Office of the Scarlet Letter.* Johns Hopkins UP, 1991.

Bercovitch, Sacvan. *Reconstructing American Literary History.* Harvard UP, 1985.

Berlant, Lauren. *The Anatomy of National Fantasy: Hawthorne, Utopia, and Everyday Life.* U of Chicago P, 1991.

Binn, Sheldon. "The Fire Next Time." Review of *The Fire Next Time,* by James Baldwin, *New York Times,* 31 Jan. 1963, http://movies2.nytimes.com/books/98/03/29/specials/baldwin-fire.html.

Bloom, Harold. *The Anatomy of Influence: Literature as a Way of Life.* Yale UP, 2011.

Bloom, Harold. *The Anxiety of Influence: A Theory of Poetry.* 1973. Oxford UP, 1997.

Bloom, Harold. *A Map of Misreading.* 1975. Oxford UP, 2007.

Bollinger, Heidi Elisabeth. "The Danger of Rereading: Disastrous Endings in Paul Auster's *The Brooklyn Follies* and Jhumpa Lahiri's *Unaccustomed Earth.*" *Studies in the Novel,* vol. 46, no. 4, 2014, pp. 486–506.

Bradford, William. *Bradford's History of Plimoth Plantation.* Wright and Potter Printing Co., 1898, http://www.gutenberg.org/files/24950/24950-h/24950-h.htm.

Bradley, Elizabeth. *Knickerbocker: The Myth behind New York.* Rutgers UP, 2009.

Brodhead, Richard H. *The School of Hawthorne.* Oxford UP, 1989.

Brogan, Kathleen. *Cultural Haunting: Ghosts and Ethnicity in Recent American Literature.* U of Virginia P, 1998.

Brontë, Charlotte. *Jane Eyre.* 1847. Oxford UP, 1969.

Buell, Lawrence. *New England Literary Culture: From Revolution through Renaissance.* Cambridge UP, 1986.

Buford, Bill. "The Future of American Fiction." Editorial. *New Yorker,* 21 June 1999, pp. 67–68.

Butts, Francis. "The Myth of Perry Miller." *American Historical Review,* vol. 87, no. 3, 1 June 1982, pp. 665–94.

Cain, William. F. O. *Matthiessen and the Politics of Criticism*. U of Wisconsin P, 1988.

Chase, Richard. *Herman Melville: A Critical Study*. Macmillan, 1949.

Cheever, John. "O Youth and Beauty!" *New Yorker*, 22 Aug. 1953, https://www.newyorker.com/magazine/1953/08/22/o-youth-and-beauty.

Cheung, King-Kok. *Articulate Silences: Hisaye Yamamoto, Maxine Hong Kingston, Joy Kogawa*. Cornell UP, 1993.

Coale, Samuel Chase. *In Hawthorne's Shadow: American Romance from Melville to Mailer*. UP of Kentucky, 1985.

Coates, Ta-Nehisi. "And Now for a Much Deserved Moment of Insanity." *Atlantic*, 26 May 2011, https://www.theatlantic.com/entertainment/archive/2011/05/and-now-for-a-much-deserved-moment-of-insanity/239536/.

Coates, Ta-Nehisi. *The Beautiful Struggle: A Father, Two Sons and an Unlikely Road to Manhood*. Spiegel and Grau, 2008.

Coates, Ta-Nehisi. *Between the World and Me*. Spiegel and Grau, 2015.

Coates, Ta-Nehisi. "The Case for Reparations." *Atlantic*, June 2014, https://www.theatlantic.com/magazine/archive/2014/06/the-case-for-reparations/361631/.

Coates, Ta-Nehisi. "A Couple of Thoughts on Melville." *Atlantic*, 26 Apr. 2011, https://www.theatlantic.com/personal/archive/2011/04/a-couple-of-thoughts-on-melville/237869/.

Coates, Ta-Nehisi. "I'm Not Black, I'm Kanye." *Atlantic*, 7 May 2018, www.theatlantic.com/entertainment/archive/2018/05/im-not-black-im-kanye/559763/.

Coates, Ta-Nehisi. "My President Was Black." *Atlantic*, 3 Mar. 2017, https://www.theatlantic.com/magazine/archive/2017/01/my-president-was-black/508793/.

Coates, Ta-Nehisi. "Take Down the Confederate Flag—Now." *Atlantic*, 18 June 2015, https://www.theatlantic.com/politics/archive/2015/06/take-down-the-confederate-flag-now/396290/.

Coates, Ta-Nehisi. Twitter post, 30 Dec. 2016, 9:36 p.m., https://twitter.com/tanehisicoates/status/815069069347094528?lang=en. Account deleted.

Coates, Ta-Nehisi. Twitter post, 31 Dec. 2016, 9:37 p.m., https://twitter.com/tanehisicoates/status/815069417512042496. Account deleted.

Coates, Ta-Nehisi. *We Were Eight Years in Power: An American Tragedy*. One World, 2017.

Cobb, Jelani. "Between the World and Ferguson." *New Yorker*, 26 Aug. 2014, https://www.newyorker.com/news/news-desk/world-ferguson.

Cole, Teju. *Open City*. Random House, 2011.

Collins, Billy. "The Names." 2002. *Aimless Love: New and Selected Poems*. Random House, 2014.

Conrad, Joseph. *Heart of Darkness*. 1899. Knopf, 1993.

Corley, Liam. "Just Another Ethnic Pol: Literary Citizenship in Chang-rae Lee's *Native Speaker*." *Studies in the Literary Imagination*, vol. 37, no. 1, Spring 2004, pp. 61–81.

Cowart, David. *Literary Symbiosis: The Reconfigured Text in Twentieth-Century Writing.* U of Georgia P, 1993.

Cowart, David. *Trailing Clouds: Immigrant Fiction in Contemporary America.* Cornell UP, 2006.

Cowart, David. *The Tribe of Pyn: Literary Generations in the Postmodern Period.* U of Michigan P, 2015.

Curnutt, Kirk. "Literary Friendships, Rivalries, and Feuds." *Ernest Hemingway in Context,* edited by Debra Moddelmog and Suzanne Del Gizzo, Cambridge UP, 2013, pp. 163–72.

Curnutt, Kirk. "Mourning in 'My Lost City': Fitzgerald in the Discourse of 9/11." *F. Scott Fitzgerald Review,* vol. 4, no. 1, 2005, pp. 84–100.

Cutter, M. J. "Multi-Ethnic 'Literature' of the 'United States': Thinking beyond the Borders." *MELUS: Multi-Ethnic Literature of the U.S.,* vol. 40, no. 1, 2015, pp. 13–17.

Danticat, Edwidge. *Brother, I'm Dying.* Knopf, 2007.

Danticat, Edwidge. "Interview with Junot Diaz." *BOMB* 101, 1 Oct. 2007, https://bomb magazine.org/articles/junot-d%C3%ADaz/.

Danticat, Edwidge. *Krik? Krak!* Soho Press, 1995.

Danticat, Edwidge. "New York Was Our City on the Hill." *New York Times,* 21 Nov. 2004, https://www.nytimes.com/2004/11/21/nyregion/thecity/21dant.html.

Danticat, Edwidge. "The Price of Sugar." *Creative Time Reports,* 5 May 2014, http://cre ativetimereports.org/2014/05/05/edwidge-danticat-the-price-of-sugar/.

Danticat, Edwidge, Junot Díaz, Julia Alvarez, and Mark Kurlansky. "Letter to the Editor." *New York Times,* 31 Oct. 2013.

DeLillo, Don. *Falling Man.* New York: Scribner, 2007.

DeLillo, Don. "In the Ruins of the Future." *Harper's Magazine,* Dec. 2001, 33–40.

De Man, Paul. "Introduction." *Toward an Aesthetic of Reception,* by Hans Robert Jauss. U of Minnesota P, 1982, pp. vii–xxv.

Deresiewicz, William. "The Imaginary Jew." *Nation,* 5 May 2007, https://www.thenation .com/article/imaginary-jew/.

Díaz, Junot. *The Brief Wondrous Life of Oscar Wao.* Riverhead, 2007.

Díaz, Junot. *Drown.* Riverhead, 1996.

Díaz, Junot. *This Is How You Lose Her.* Riverhead, 2012.

Dimock, Wai Chee. *Through Other Continents: American Literature across Deep Time.* Princeton UP, 2006.

Donck, Adriaen Van der, C. T. Gehring, W. A. Starna, D. W. Goedhuys, and R. Shorto, editors. *A Description of New Netherland.* 1650. U of Nebraska P, 2008.

Douglass, Frederick. "Self-Made Men." 1859. *Frederick Douglass in Brooklyn.* Edited by Theodore Hamm, Akashic Books, 2017.

Douglas-Fairhurst, Robert. *Victorian Afterlives: The Shaping of Influence in Nineteenth-Century Literature.* Oxford UP, 2009.

Duyckink, Evert. "Nathaniel Hawthorne." *Literary World*, vol. 6, 30 Mar. 1850, pp. 323–25.

Easterbrook, John. "Cosmopolitanism and Adriaen Van der Donck's *A Description of New Netherland.*" *Early American Literature*, vol. 49, no. 1, 2014, pp. 3–36.

Egan, Jennifer. *A Visit from the Goon Squad.* Anchor Books, 2011.

Ellison, Ralph. *Invisible Man.* 1952. Vintage, 1999.

Elrod, Eileen Razzari. "New Puritans." *American Literary History* , vol. 30, no. 1, 2017, pp. 1341–44.

Emerson, Ralph Waldo. *The Annotated Emerson.* Edited by David Mikics, Belknap Press of Harvard UP, 2012.

Emerson, Ralph Waldo. "The American Scholar." 1837. http://digitalemerson.wsulibs .wsu.edu/exhibits/show/text/the-american-scholar.

Engles, Tim. "Visions of Me in the Whitest Raw Light: Assimilation and Doxic Whiteness in Chang-rae Lee's *Native Speaker.*" *Hitting Critical Mass: A Journal of Asian American Cultural Studies*, vol. 4, no. 2, 1997, pp. 27–48.

Entzminger, Bettina. *Contemporary Reconfigurations of American Literary Classics: The Origin and Evolution of American Stories.* Routledge, 2013.

Falkoff, Marc, editor. *Poems from Guantánamo: The Detainees Speak.* U of Iowa P, 2007.

Faludi, Susan. *The Terror Dream: Fear and Fantasy in Post-9/11 America.* Metropolitan Books, 2007.

Fisher Fishkin, Shelley. *Was Huck Black? Mark Twain and African-American Voices.* Oxford UP, 1994.

Fitzgerald, F. Scott. *The Great Gatsby.* 1925. Scribner, 2004.

Fleissner, J. L. "Symptomatology and the Novel." *Novel: A Forum on Fiction*, vol. 42, no. 3, 2009, pp. 387–92.

Flora, Joseph M. *Ernest Hemingway: A Study of the Short Fiction.* Twayne, 1989.

Foer, Jonathan Safran. *Extremely Loud and Incredibly Close.* Houghton Mifflin Harcourt, 2005.

Fuller, Randall. "Errand into the Wilderness: Perry Miller as American Scholar." *American Literary History*, vol. 18, no. 1, March 2006, pp. 102–28.

Fuss, Diana. *Dying Modern: A Meditation on Elegy.* Duke UP, 2013.

Gay, Roxane. *Bad Feminist: Essays.* Harper Perennial, 2014.

Genette, Gerard. *Palimpsests: Literature in the Second Degree.* 1982. U of Nebraska P, 1997.

Golimowska, Karolina. "Cricket As a Cure: Post-9/11 Urban Trauma and Displacement in Joseph O'Neill's Novel *Netherland.*" *Journal of American Culture*, vol. 36, no. 3, 2013, pp. 230–39.

Graulund, Rune. "Generous Exclusion: Register and Readership in Junot Díaz's *The Brief Wondrous Life of Oscar Wao.*" *MELUS: Multi-Ethnic Literature of the United States*, vol. 39, no. 3, 2014, pp. 31–48.

Greven, David. "Hawthorne and Influence." *Nathaniel Hawthorne Review,* vol. 42, no. 1, Spring 2016, pp. 1–15.

Hai, Ambreen. "Re-Rooting Families: The Alter/Natal as the Central Dynamic of Jhumpa Lahiri's *Unaccustomed Earth.*" *Naming Jhumpa Lahiri: Canons and Controversies.* Edited by Lavina Dhingra and Floyd Cheung, Rowman & Littlefield, 2012, pp. 181–209.

Harford Vargas, Jennifer. "Dictating a Zafa: The Power of Narrative Form in Junot Díaz's *The Brief Wondrous Life of Oscar Wao.*" *MELUS: Multi-Ethnic Literature of the United States,* vol. 39, no. 3, 2014, pp. 8–30.

Hawthorne, Nathaniel. *The English Notebooks, 1856–1860.* 2 vols. Edited by Thomas Woodson and Bill Ellis, Ohio State UP, 1997.

Hawthorne, Nathaniel. *The House of the Seven Gables, and the Snow Image.* Boston, 1876.

Hawthorne, Nathaniel. *The Marble Faun.* Wheeler, 1902.

Hawthorne, Nathaniel. *Mosses from an Old Manse.* Wiley and Putnam, 1852.

Hawthorne, Nathaniel. *Passages from the French and Italian Notebooks of Nathaniel Hawthorne.* Houghton, Osgood, 1880.

Hawthorne, Nathaniel. *The Scarlet Letter and Other Writings: Authoritative Texts, Contexts, Criticism.* Edited by Leland S. Person, Norton, 2004.

Hawthorne, Nathaniel. *Septimius Felton, or, the Elixir of Life.* 1872, http://www.gutenberg.org/files/7372/7372-h/7372-h.htm.

Hemingway, Ernest. *Death in the Afternoon.* Charles Scribner's Sons, 1932.

Hemingway, Ernest. "The Short Happy Life of Francis Macomber." *The Complete Short Stories of Ernest Hemingway: The Finca Vigía Edition.* Scribner, 1998, pp. 5–28.

Hemingway, Ernest. "The Snows of Kilimanjaro." 1936. *The Complete Short Stories of Ernest Hemingway.* Scribner, 1998, pp. 39–56.

Hemingway, Ernest. "Ten Indians." *Men Without Women.* Charles Scribner's Sons, 1927.

Hoffman, Jan, N. R. Kleinfield, Maria Newman, Janny Scott, Robin Finn, Glenn Collins, and Anthony DePalma. "Portraits Redrawn: Living with Loss." *New York Times,* 11 Sept. 2011, https://archive.nytimes.com/query.nytimes.com/gst/fullpage-9904E4DE1F3BF932A2575AC0A9679D8B63.html.

Hughes, Evan. *Literary Brooklyn: The Writers of Brooklyn and the Story of American City Life.* Henry Holt, 2011.

Hughes, Langston. "Let America Be America Again." 1936. *The Collected Poems of Langston Hughes.* Knopf, 1996.

I Am Not Your Negro. Directed by Raoul Peck, Magnolia Pictures, 2016.

Idol, John L., and Buford Jones, editors. *Nathaniel Hawthorne: The Contemporary Reviews.* Cambridge UP, 1998.

"Interview with Michiko Kakutani: President Obama on What Books Mean to Him." *New York Times,* 16 Jan. 2017, https://www.nytimes.com/2017/01/16/books/transcript-president-obama-on-what-books-mean-to-him.html.

Irr, Caren. *Toward the Geopolitical Novel: U.S. Fiction in the Twenty-First Century*. Columbia UP, 2014.

Irving, Washington. *A History of New York*. 1809. Penguin, 2008.

Jacobs, Harriet. *Incidents in the Life of a Slave Girl: Written for Herself*. Thayer and Eldridge, 1861.

James, C. L. R. *Beyond a Boundary*. Stanley Paul/Hutchinson, 1963.

James, Cyril Lionel Robert. *Mariners, Renegades, and Castaways: The Story of Herman Melville and the World We Live In: The Complete Text*. UP of New England, 2001.

James, Henry. *Hawthorne*. Harper and Brothers, 1879.

Jauss, Hans Robert. *Toward an Aesthetic of Reception*. U of Minnesota P, 1982.

Jay, Paul. *Global Matters: The Transnational Turn in Literary Studies*. Cornell UP, 2010.

Jewett, Sarah Orne. *Deephaven*. James R. Osgood, 1877.

"Jhumpa Lahiri: By the Book." *New York Times*, 5 Sept. 2013, https://www.nytimes.com/2013/09/08/books/review/jhumpa-lahiri-by-the-book.html.

Jimoh, A. Yemisi, and Angelo Rich Robinson. "Guest Editors' Introduction: Twenty-First-Century Perspectives on U.S. Ethnic Literatures." *MELUS: Multi-Ethnic Literature of the U.S.*, vol. 43, no. 4, Winter 2018, pp. 1–5.

Johnson, Reed. "Rethinking Hemingway 50 Years after His Death." *Los Angeles Times*, 2 July 2011, https://www.latimes.com/entertainment/la-et-hemingway-20110702-story.html.

"Jonathan Lethem, The Art of Fiction No. 177." Interview by Lorin Stein. *Paris Review*, Summer 2003, https://www.theparisreview.org/interviews/228/jonathan-lethem-the-art-of-fiction-no-177-jonathan-lethem.

Joyce, James. *A Portrait of the Artist as a Young Man: Complete, Authoritative Text with Biographical, Historical, and Cultural Contexts, Critical History, and Essays from Contemporary Critical Perspectives*. Edited by R. B. Kershner, Bedford/St. Martin's Press, 2006.

Kachka, Boris. "The Confidence Artist." NYMag.com, 31 Mar. 2008.

Kakutani, Michiko. "Obama's Secret to Surviving the White House Years: Books." *New York Times*, 16 Jan. 2017, https://www.nytimes.com/2017/01/16/books/obamas-secret-to-surviving-the-white-house-years-books.html.

Kakutani, Michiko. "Wonder Bread and Curry: Mingling Cultures, Conflicted Hearts." *New York Times*, 3 Apr. 2008, https://www.nytimes.com/2008/04/04/books/04Book.html.

Kazin, Alfred. *A Walker in the City*. 1951. Harcourt Brace Jovanovich, 1969.

Kazin, Alfred. "On Perry Miller." *New York Review of Books*, 25 Nov. 1965, https://www.nybooks.com/articles/1965/11/25/on-perry-miller/.

Kenan, Randall. *The Fire This Time*. Melville House, 2007.

Kesey, Ken, and Robert Stone. "Blows to the Spirit." *Esquire*, vol. 105, no. 6, June 1986, pp. 266–78.

Kim, Daniel. "Do I, Too, Sing America?: Vernacular Representations and Chang-rae Lee's *Native Speaker*." *Journal of Asian American Studies,* vol. 6, no. 3, October 2003, 231–60.

Kingston, Maxine Hong. *Tripmaster Monkey: His Fake Book.* Vintage, 1989.

Kingston, Maxine Hong. *The Woman Warrior: Memoirs of a Girlhood Among Ghosts.* Knopf, 1976.

Kopley, Richard. "Hawthorne's Transplanting and Transforming 'The Tell-Tale Heart.'" *Studies in American Fiction,* vol. 23, no. 2, 1995, pp. 231–41.

Kravitz, Bennett. "The Culture of Disease or the Dis-ease of Culture in *Motherless Brooklyn* and *Eve's Apple*." *Journal of American Culture,* vol. 26, no. 2, 2003, pp. 171–79.

Kristeva, Julia. *Semeiotike: Recherches pour une semanalyse.* Editions du Seuil, 1969.

Lahiri, Jhumpa. "Jhumpa Lahiri Talks about *Unaccustomed Earth*." Random House Audio Interview. Sept. 2013, https://www.randomhouse.com/kvpa/jhumpalahiri/audio_interview.php.

Lahiri, Jhumpa. "Trading Stories: Notes from an Apprenticeship." *New Yorker,* 6 June 2013, http://www.newyorker.com/magazine/2011/06/13/trading-stories.

Lahiri, Jhumpa. *Unaccustomed Earth: Stories.* Knopf, 2008.

Larson, Kelli A. "On Safari with Hemingway: Tracking the Most Recent Scholarship." *Hemingway and Africa,* edited by Miriam B. Mandel, Camden House, 2011, pp. 323–82.

Las Casas, Bartolomé de. *A Brief Account of the Destruction of the Indies.* 1552. Echo Library, 2007.

Lee, Chang-rae. *Native Speaker.* Riverhead Books, 1995.

Lethem, Jonathan. *Dissident Gardens.* Doubleday, 2013.

Lethem, Jonathan. *Fortress of Solitude.* Doubleday, 2003.

Lethem, Jonathan. *Motherless Brooklyn.* Random House, 1999.

Lewis, Nghana Tamu. "Race and Ethnicity: Africans." *Ernest Hemingway in Context,* edited by Debra Moddelmog and Suzanne Del Gizzo, Cambridge UP, 2013, pp. 315–22.

Lopate, Phillip. *Waterfront: A Walk around Manhattan.* Anchor Books, 2004.

Man on Wire. Directed by James Marsh, Magnolia Home Entertainment, 2008.

Mardorossian, Carine M. "From Literature of Exile to Migrant Literature." *Modern Language Studies,* vol. 32, no. 2, 2002, p. 15.

Mason, Anthony. Interview with Junot Díaz. *CBS News,* June 8, 2008.

Matthiessen, Francis Otto. *American Renaissance: Art and Expression in the Age of Emerson and Whitman.* Oxford UP, 1941.

Mathis, Ayana. "Black Male Writers for Our Time." *New York Times,* 30 Nov. 2018, https://www.nytimes.com/interactive/2018/11/30/t-magazine/black-authors.html.

McCall, Dan. *Citizens of Somewhere Else: Nathaniel Hawthorne and Henry James.* Cornell UP, 2010.

McCann, Colum. *Let the Great World Spin*. Random House, 2009.

McCann, Colum. "Walking an Inch Off the Ground: Reader's Guide to *Let the Great World Spin*." *Let the Great World Spin*, pp. 358–60.

McCann, Colum. "A Conversation with Colum McCann and Nathan Englander," http://www.randomhouse.com/rhpg//rc/library/display.pperl?isbn=9780812973990&view=qa.

McCarthy, Jesse. "Why Does Ta-Nehisi Coates Say Less Than He Knows?" *Nation*, 15 Nov. 2015.

McFarland, Philip James. *Hawthorne in Concord*. 1970. Grove Press, 2004.

McGann, Jerome. "Washington Irving, a History of New York, and American History." *Early American Literature*, vol. 47, no. 2, 2012, pp. 349–76.

Melville, Herman. *Mardi, and A Voyage Thither*. 1849. Northwestern-Newberry, 1998.

Melville, Herman. *Moby-Dick*. 1851. Edited by Harrison Hayford and Hershel Parker, Norton, 2002.

Milder, Robert. *Hawthorne's Habitations: A Literary Life*. Oxford UP, 2013.

Miller, Arthur. *A View from the Bridge: A Play in Two Acts*. Penguin, 1960.

Miller, Edwin Haviland. *Salem Is My Dwelling Place: A Life of Nathaniel Hawthorne*. U of Iowa P, 1992.

Miller, Nancy K. "Portraits of Grief: Telling Details and the Testimony of Trauma." *differences: A Journal of Feminist Cultural Studies*, vol. 14, no. 3, Fall 2003, pp. 112–35.

Miller, Perry. *Errand into the Wilderness*. Harvard UP, 1956.

Miller, Perry. *The New England Mind: The Seventeenth Century*. Harvard UP, 1939.

Miller, Perry. *The Raven and the Whale: The War of Words and Wits in the Era of Poe and Melville*. 1956. Greenwood, 1973.

Miller, Stephen. *Walking New York: Reflections of American Writers from Walt Whitman to Teju Cole*. Fordham UP, 2015.

Mong, Adrienne. "A Writer's Life: Interview with Chang-rae Lee." *Far Eastern Economic Review*, 9 Nov. 2000, pp. 22–26.

Moraru, Christian. "Speakers and Sleepers: Chang-rae Lee's *Native Speaker*, Whitman, and the Performance of Americanness." *College Literature*, vol. 36, no. 3, Summer 2009, pp. 66–91.

Moynihan, Sinead. "Upground and Belowground Topographies: The Chronotopes of Skyscraper and Subway in Colum McCann's New York Novels before and after 9/11." *Studies in American Fiction*, vol. 39, no. 2, Fall 2012, pp. 269–90.

Mukherjee, B. "Immigrant Writing: Changing the Contours of a National Literature." *American Literary History*, vol. 23, no. 3, 2011, pp. 680–96.

Mukherjee, Bharati. *The Holder of the World*. Ballantine Books, 1993.

"Portraits of Grief." *New York Times*, 8 Dec. 2002, B54.

Myerson, Joel, editor. *Selected Letters of Nathaniel Hawthorne*. Ohio State UP, 2002.

Ng, Fae Myenne. *Bone.* Hachette, 2014.

Noonan, Mark. "Re-Writing Ourselves in the Wake of 9/11." *Reconstruction,* vol. 11, no. 2, 2011.

Obama, Barack. *The Audacity of Hope: Thoughts on Reclaiming the American Dream.* Crown/Three Rivers Press, 2006.

Obama, Barack. *Dreams from My Father: A Story of Race and Inheritance.* Times Books, 1995.

O'Neill, Joseph. "All over America." Interview with Travis Elborough. *Netherland.* Fourth Estate, 2008.

O'Neill, Joseph. "Bowling Alone: *Beyond a Boundary* by C. L. R. James." Review, *Atlantic,* 11 Sept. 2007.

O'Neill, Joseph. *Netherland.* Pantheon, 2008.

O'Rourke, Meghan. "An Interview with Pulitzer Prize–Winning Author Junot Díaz." *Slate,* 8 Apr. 2008.

Orr, Mary. *Intertextuality: Debates and Contexts.* Polity, 2003.

Patell, Cyrus R. K. *Emergent U.S. Literatures: From Multiculturalism to Cosmopolitanism in the Late Twentieth Century.* New York UP, 2014.

Peacock, James. "We Learned to Tell Our Story Walking: Tourette's and Urban Space in Jonathan Lethem's *Motherless Brooklyn.*" *Diseases and Disorders in Contemporary Fiction: The Syndrome Syndrome,* edited by T. J. Lustig and James Peacock, Routledge, 2013, pp. 67–82.

Pease, Donald E. "Introduction." *Mariners, Renegades, and Castaways: The Story of Herman Melville and the World We Live In: The Complete Text,* by Cyril Lionel Robert James, UP of New England, 2001.

Pease, Donald E. "Introduction." *Reframing the Transnational Turn in American Studies,* edited by Winfried Fluck, Donald E. Pease, and John Carlos Rowe, Dartmouth College P, 2011.

Pease, Donald. *Visionary Compacts: American Renaissance Writings in Cultural Context.* U of Wisconsin P, 1987.

Pinckney, Darryl. "The Anger of Ta-Nehisi Coates." *New York Review of Books,* 26 Jan. 2016, https://www.nybooks.com/articles/2016/02/11/the-anger-of-ta-nehisi-coates/.

Poe, Edgar Allan. "The Murders in the Rue Morgue," 1841, https://www.poemuseum.org/the-murders-in-the-rue-morgue.

Prescott, Orville. "Books of the Times: *A Walker in the City* by Alfred Kazin." Review, *New York Times,* 7 May 1978.

Ramsby, Howard II. "The Remarkable Reception of Ta-Nehisi Coates." *African American Review,* vol. 49, no. 3, 2016, pp. 196–204.

Ramsey, Joseph G. "The Petrified and the Proletarian (part 1)." *Red Wedge,* 28 Dec. 2015, http://www.redwedgemagazine.com/online-issue/coates-baldwin-wright.

Randall, Martin. *9/11 and the Literature of Terror*. Edinburgh UP, 2011.

Reising, Russell. *The Unusable Past: Theory and the Study of American Literature*. Routledge, 1987.

Remnick, David. "Ten Days in June." Interview with Barack Obama. *New Yorker*, 26 June 2015, https://www.newyorker.com/news/news-desk/ten-days-in-june.

Reynolds, David S. *Beneath the American Renaissance: The Subversive Imagination in the Age of Emerson and Melville*. Oxford UP, 1988.

Reynolds, David S. *Walt Whitman's America: A Cultural Biography*. Knopf, 1995.

Reynolds, Michael S. *Hemingway: The 1930s through the Final Years*. Norton, 2012.

Rhys, Jean. *Wide Sargasso Sea*. Norton, 1992.

Romano, John. "Just above My Head." *New York Times*, 23 Sept. 1979, http://movies2.nytimes.com/books/98/03/29/specials/baldwin-above.html.

Rowe, John Carlos. *The Theoretical Dimensions of Henry James*. Wisconsin Project on American Writers. U of Wisconsin P, 1984.

Sáez, Elena Machado. "Dictating Desire, Dictating Diaspora: Junot Díaz's *The Brief Wondrous Life of Oscar Wao* as Foundational Romance." *Contemporary Literature*, vol. 52, no. 3, 2011, pp. 522–55.

Saldívar, Ramón. "The Second Elevation of the Novel: Race, Form, and the Postrace Aesthetic in Contemporary Narrative." *Narrative*, vol. 21, no. 1, 2013, pp. 1–18.

Sale, Roger. *Literary Inheritance*. U of Massachusetts P, 1984.

Schiff, James A. "Updike's *Scarlet Letter* Trilogy: Recasting an American Myth." *Studies in American Fiction*, vol. 20, no. 1, 1992, pp. 17–31.

Schuessler, Jennifer. "Ta-Nehisi Coates's 'Visceral' Take on Being Black in America." *New York Times*, 17 July 2015, https://www.nytimes.com/2015/07/18/books/ta-nehisi-coatess-visceral-take-on-being-black-in-america.html.

Schillinger, Liesl. "American Children." *New York Times*, 5 Apr. 2008, http://www.nytimes.com/2008/04/06/books/review/Schillinger3-t.html.

Smith, Betty. *A Tree Grows in Brooklyn*. 1943. Harper, 1947.

Snyder, Katherine V. "Gatsby's Ghost: Post-Traumatic Memory and National Literary Tradition in Joseph O'Neill's *Netherland*." *Contemporary Literature*, vol. 54, no. 3, 2013, pp. 459–90.

Sollors, Werner. *Beyond Ethnicity: Consent and Descent in American Culture*. Oxford UP, 1986.

Sollors, Werner. "A Critique of Pure Pluralism." *Reconstructing American Literary History*, edited by Sacvan Bercovitch, Harvard UP, 1986, pp. 250–79.

Solnit, Rebecca. *Wanderlust: A History of Walking*. Viking, 2000.

Sova, Dawn B. *Edgar Allan Poe: A to Z*. Checkmark Books, 2001.

Spiegelman, Art. *In the Shadow of No Towers*. Pantheon, 2004.

Spiller, Robert Ernest, editor. *Literary History of the United States*. Macmillan, 1948.

Srikanth, Rajini. "What Lies Beneath: Lahiri's Brand of Desirable Difference in *Unaccustomed Earth*." *Naming Jhumpa Lahiri: Canons and Controversies,* edited by Dhingra, Lavina, and Floyd Cheung, Lexington Books, 2012.

Stein, Daniel. "Barack Obama's *Dreams from My Father* and African American Literature." *European Journal of American Studies,* Spring 2011, pp. 6–1.

Strout, Elizabeth. *Olive Kitteridge.* Penguin Random House, 2008.

Takaki, Ronald. *A Different Mirror: A History of Multicultural America.* Back Bay Books, 1993.

Thoreau, Henry David. "Walking." 1862. *Walden, and Other Writings of Henry David Thoreau.* Random House, 1992, pp. 625–64.

Tolchin, Neal L. *Mourning, Gender, and Creativity in the Art of Herman Melville.* Yale UP, 1988.

Trapp, Erin. "The Enemy Combatant as Poet: The Politics of Writing in *Poems from Guantánamo*." *Postmodern Culture,* vol. 21, no. 3, 2011, pp. 269–90.

Turpin, Zachary. "Hawthorne the Unreliabilist: His Epistemology in "The Custom-House" and Other Prefaces." *ESQ: A Journal of the American Renaissance,* vol. 60, no. 4, 2014, pp. 487–520.

TuSmith, Bonnie. *All My Relatives: Community in Contemporary Ethnic American Literatures.* U of Michigan P, 1993.

Walcott, Derek. "The Schooner Flight." *Collected Poems, 1948–1984.* Noonday, 1988, pp. 345–61.

Ward, Jesmyn, editor. *The Fire This Time: A New Generation Speaks about Race.* Scribner, 2016.

Weiser, Karen. "Doubled Narratives of Orphanhood in Melville's Pierre." *Leviathan,* vol. 18, no. 1, 2016, pp. 22–40.

West, Cornel. "In Defense of James Baldwin—Why Toni Morrison (a literary genius) Is Wrong about Ta-Nehisi Coates." Facebook post, 16 July 2015, https://www.facebook.com/drcornelwest/posts/in-defense-of-james-baldwin-why-toni-morrison-a-literary-genius-is-wrong-about-t/10155807310625111/.

West, Cornel. "Ta-Nehisi Coates Is the Neoliberal Face of the Black Freedom Struggle." *Guardian,* 17 Dec. 2017, www.theguardian.com/commentisfree/2017/dec/17/ta-nehisi-coates-neoliberal-black-struggle-cornel-west.

Whitehead, Colson. *Sag Harbor: A Novel.* Doubleday, 2009.

Whitehead, Colson. *The Underground Railroad: A Novel.* Doubleday, 2016.

Whitehead, Colson. "The Year of Living Postracially." *New York Times,* 3 Nov. 2009, https://www.nytimes.com/2009/11/04/opinion/04whitehead.html.

Whitehead, Colson. *Zone One.* Doubleday, 2011.

Whitman, Walt. *Walt Whitman: The Complete Poems.* Edited by Francis Murphy, Penguin, 2005.

Wilhite, Keith. "Introduction." *The City since 9/11: Literature, Film, Television*. Edited by Keith Wilhite, Fairleigh Dickinson UP, 2016, pp. 1–22.

Williams, Dana A. "Everybody's Protest Narrative: *Between the World and Me* and the Limits of Genre." *African American Review*, vol. 49, no. 3, Fall 2016, pp. 179–83.

Wilson, Michael T. *The Sentimental Mode: Essays in Literature, Film and Television*. McFarland, 2014.

"The Wondrous Life of Junot Díaz." Interview with Junot Díaz. *CBS News*, 8 June 2008.

Wood, James. "Beyond a Boundary." *New Yorker*, 26 May 2008, https://www.newyorker.com/magazine/2008/05/26/beyond-a-boundary.

Wright, Richard. "Between the World and Me." *Partisan Review*, 1935, pp. 18–19.

Wright, Richard. *Native Son*. 1940. New York: Harper Perennial, 1996.

Index

Alexander, Michelle, 131

Alexie, Sherman, 4–5, 141

allegory, 52

All My Relatives: Community in Contem-porary Ethnic American Literatures (TuSmith), 12

Alvarez, Julia, 79

American Jeremiad, The (Bercovitch), 141

American literary canon, 2, 6, 13, 17. *See also* literature

American Renaissance: definition of, 7; invocation of, 49–50, 143; new, 1, 7–9, 142–44; second, 7; third, 19

American Renaissance: Art and Expression in the Age of Emerson and Whitman (Matthiessen), 1, 7, 13, 119

"American Scholar, The" (Emerson), 15, 140

Anxiety of Influence, The (Bloom), 10–11

Arnolfini Portrait, The (van Eyck), 61–62

Atlantic, 103, 113, 119, 136–38

Audacity of Hope, The: Thoughts on Reclaiming the American Dream (Obama), 137

Bacon, Katie, 103

Bad Feminist (Gay), 4

Bakhtin, Mikhail, 81

Baldwin, James, 4, 18, 113, 122, 127–36, 153n1, 154n13

Baltimore, 123

Barnum, P. T., 26

Beautiful Struggle, The (Coates), 112–13, 127–28, 134

Bell, Millicent, 56

Beneath the American Renaissance (Reynolds), 3

Benjamin, Jessica, 34–35

Bercovitch, Sacvan, 54, 141

Between the World and Me (Coates), 14, 18, 113–14, 118, 120–25, 128–29, 131, 133–38

"Between the World and Me" (Wright), 125–27

Beyond Ethnicity: Consent and Descent in American Culture (Sollors), 5, 7

Binn, Sheldon, 132

Black Boy (Wright), 127

Black Lives Matter, 129

"Black Male Writers for Our Time" (Mathis), 142–43

Bloom, Harold, 10, 146n6

"Blows to the Spirit" (Kesey and Stone), 76

Bollinger, Heidi Elisabeth, 63, 149n13

Bone (Ng), 141

Bradford, William, 51

Bradley, Elizabeth, 107–8

Brando, Marlon, 25

Brief Account of the Destruction of the Indies, A (de las Casas), 71

Brief Wondrous Life of Oscar Wao, The (Díaz), 14, 66–85, 150n11

Brodhead, Richard, 7–8, 12, 54–55

Brogan, Kathleen, 110

Brother, I'm Dying (Danticat), 14, 142

Buell, Lawrence, 55

Buford, Bill, 9

Cain, William, 13–14

catharsis, 96

Chase, Richard, 7

Cheever, John, 75–76

Cheung, King-Kok, 31, 34

"City of Ships" (Whitman), 99

City since 9/11, The (Wilhite), 89

City University of New York (CUNY), 83, 100, 143, 155n3

Clayton, Jay, 11

Coale, Samuel Chase, 49, 62

Coates, Ta-Nehisi, 4, 14, 18, 112–38, 142, 153n8, 154n17; gender in work of, 154n11; on religion, 120–21

Cobb, Jelani, 126

Collins, Billy, 97

colonialism, 102–3, 107; twentieth-century, 104

Concord, 45, 50–51

Cowart, David, 12, 33, 39–40, 65, 77, 84, 86, 146n10

"Critique of Pure Pluralism, A" (Sollors), 5, 14

"Crossing Brooklyn Ferry" (Whitman), 17, 21–22, 25, 29–31, 38, 109

Curnutt, Kirk, 67

Danticat, Edwidge, 7, 14, 70–71, 79, 142

Davitt Bell, Michael, 49

death, 62

Deephaven (Jewett), 4

de las Casas, Bartolomé, 71

DeLillo, Don, 89, 98

de Man, Paul, 9–10, 50–51

democracy, 7, 9, 14, 115, 141

Dialogic Imagination, The (Bakhtin), 81

Díaz, Junot, 4, 8, 14, 17, 64, 66–87

Dimock, Wai Chee, 15

domestic fiction, 74. *See also* literature

Dominican Republic, 69–72, 78–79, 81–83

double entendre, 57

Douglas-Fairhurst, Robert, 10

Douglass, Frederick, 15, 143

Dreams from My Father: A Story of Race and Inheritance (Obama), 137

Dreiser, Theodore, 7

Drown (Díaz), 71

Dublin, 91

Du Bois, W. E. B., 37

Dutch Nursery Rhymes in Colonial Times (Ferris), 107

Duyckink, Evert, 8, 43, 47

Dying Modern (Fuss), 126

Egan, Jennifer, 89

Ellison, Ralph, 41, 115

Emergent U.S. Literatures: From Multiculturalism to Cosmopolitanism in the Late Twentieth Century (Patell), 13

Emerson, Ralph Waldo, 7, 15, 50, 140

"Encounter on the Seine: Black Meets Brown" (Baldwin), 134

"Equal in Paris" (Baldwin), 135

era de Trujillo, La: Un estudio casuístico de dictadura hispanoamericana (Galíndez), 83

Errand into the Wilderness (Miller), 141

ethnic American literature, 80, 84–86, 141, 145n2. *See also* literature

ethnicity: and immigration, 30–36, 102; religion and, 29, 59, 109. *See also* race; religion

"Everybody's Protest Narrative" (Williams), 129

"Everybody's Protest Novel" (Baldwin), 127

Extremely Loud and Incredibly Close (Foer), 89

Falkoff, Marc, 89

Falling Man (DeLillo), 89

fantasy fiction, 69–70. *See also* literature

Faulkner, William, 7

Fire Next Time, The (Baldwin), 18, 128, 131, 133

Fisher Fishkin, Shelley, 5

Fitzgerald, F. Scott, 3, 7, 17, 89, 104–6, 109, 111

Flaubert, Gustave, 75

"Flight Patterns" (Alexie), 4

Florence, 1, 53

F. O. Matthiessen and the Politics of Criticism (Cain), 13

Foer, Jonathan Safran, 89

freedom, 27

Frost, Robert, 7

Fuss, Diana, 126

Galíndez Suárez, Jesús de, 83

"Gatsby's Ghost" (Snyder), 89–90

Genette, Gerard, 11–12; transtextuality of, 25

geography, 21–42; and literary inheritance, 23; and the self, 22

Global Matters: The Transnational Turn in Literary Studies (Jay), 8

Godey's Lady's Book, 47

"Going Ashore" (Lahiri), 59–60, 62–63

Golimowska, Karolina, 105

Graulund, Rune, 82

Great Gatsby, The (Fitzgerald), 17, 89, 95–96, 101–10, 137

Greven, David, 59

Hai, Ambreen, 59

Haiti, 79, 142

Harford Vargas, Jennifer, 68

Harvard University, 1, 139

"Hawthorne and His Mosses" (Melville), 2

Hawthorne and the Historical Romance of New England (Davitt Bell), 49

Hawthorne, Nathaniel, 1, 3, 7–8, 15, 17, 43–65, 116, 120–21, 142, 148n8

Heart Is a Lonely Hunter, The (McCullers), 4

Heart of Darkness (Conrad), 79

"Hell-Heaven" (Lahiri), 49–50, 60

Hemingway, Ernest, 3–4, 7, 17, 66–87,
150n13
Henry IV (Shakespeare), 38
heteroglossia, 81
Hispaniola. *See* Dominican Republic;
Haiti
historical fiction, 89. *See also* literature
history: American intellectual, 139–40;
of colonialism, 78, 105–8; of immigration, 106; and literary inheritance,
23; of New England, 49; of New York,
88–111; of race relations, 135; traumatic, 18; of violence, 126
History of New York, A (Irving), 17, 89,
101–2, 104, 106–7, 110, 148n4, 152n10
House of the Seven Gables, The (Hawthorne), 63
Hudson, Henry, 103
Hudson River School, 52
Hughes, Evan, 23
Hughes, Langston, 9
humor, 52, 70

identity: American, 14, 49, 108, 139;
black, 117, 134; communal, 59, 113;
crisis of, 17, 30–42; cultural, 13;
destruction of, 126; hyphenated, 82;
individual, 59, 113; multiple, 39, 134;
search for, 30–42; and the self, 21–22,
32; spectrum of, 17. *See also* language
"I Hear America Singing" (Whitman), 17,
22, 25–26, 31, 94
immigrant literature, 6, 12–14, 50, 64–65,
84–85, 151n14. *See also* immigrants;
literature
immigrants: communities of, 105; dreams
of, 109–10; ethnicity and, 30–36, 50;
experience of, 17, 30–42, 48–50, 64–65,
69–70, 86, 122

Incidents in the Life of a Slave Girl
(Jacobs), 4
"In Defense of James Baldwin—Why
Toni Morrison (a Literary Genius)
Is Wrong about Ta-Nehisi Coates"
(West), 130
India, 58
individualism, 12
*Influence and Intertextuality in Literary
History* (Rothstein and Clayton), 11
inheritance, 18
intertextuality, 10–12, 16, 18, 142; inten-
tional, 77; and literary colonialism, 68;
theories of, 12, 142
"In the Ruins of the Future" (DeLillo), 98
Invisible Man (Ellison), 41, 115
irony, 62, 104
Irr, Caren, 81
Irving, Washington, 17, 89, 101–8, 111,
148n4, 152nn10–11

Jacobs, Harriet, 143
James, C. L. R., 122–23
James, Henry, 2, 48–49
Jane Eyre (Brontë), 79
Jauss, Hans Robert, 9–10, 50
Jay, Paul, 8, 70, 82
Johnston, Kenneth, 72–73
Joyce, James, 35
Just above My Head (Baldwin), 131

Kakutani, Michiko, 64, 109–10
Kazin, Alfred, 22, 27–29, 36, 139–40
Kesey, Ken, 76
Kim, Daniel, 41
King, Martin Luther, Jr., 132
Kingston, Maxine Hong, 34
Knickerbocker: The Myth behind New York
(Bradley), 107–8

Kogawa, Joy, 34

Kravitz, Bennett, 26

Krik? Krak (Danticat), 142

Kristeva, Julia, 11

Kurlansky, Mark, 79

Lahiri, Jhumpa, 2, 4, 6, 8, 15, 17, 43–44,
    49–51, 53–65, 149n13

language: absence of, 30; dialogic, 68;
    experimentation with, 22; of grief,
    35; of Hemingway, 84; loss of, 57; of
    Melville, 120; and multiple identity,
    39; and occupations, 26; search for, 30;
    of silence, 31–32, 34; similarity in, 67.
    See also identity

Leaves of Grass (Whitman), 16, 30

Lee, Chang-rae, 4, 8, 15, 17, 30–42

"Let America Be America Again"
    (Hughes), 9

Lethem, Jonathan, 4, 17, 22–30, 33–34,
    36, 39–40, 42, 145n1, 147n5

"Letter from a Region in My Mind" (Bald-
    win), 128

"Letter to My Nephew on the One Hun-
    dredth Anniversary of Emancipation"
    (Baldwin), 113, 122, 128–29, 132–33

Let the Great World Spin (McCann), 17,
    88–111

*Life of the Mind in America, The: From the
    Revolution to the Civil War* (Miller), 139

Like Subjects, Love Objects (Benjamin), 35

Lincoln, Abraham, 18–19

Literary Brooklyn (Hughes), 23

literary colonialism, 17. *See also* literature

literary criticism, 2, 12–13, 140; American,
    151n2; history of, 14. *See also* literature

literary history, 5, 142. *See also* literature

Literary History of the United States
    (Spiller), 7

Literary Inheritance (Sale), 4

*Literary Symbiosis: The Reconfigured Text
    in Twentieth-Century Writing* (Cowart),
    12, 40, 77

literature: African American, 41, 127,
    129, 131, 134, 137; Asian American,
    13, 31, 41; British, 12, 146n9; early
    American, 139; gay and lesbian, 13;
    Hispanic American, 13; multiethnic,
    5–7; national, 8, 10; Native American,
    13; New York, 18, 24, 89–91, 93, 111,
    147n3; and planting, 51–58; plurality
    of American, 143; postmodern, 68;
    traditions of, 131, 137, 143. *See also*
    ethnic American literature; immigrant
    literature; transnational literature;
    writing

Longfellow, Henry Wadsworth, 46

Lopate, Phillip, 24, 30

Machado Sáez, Elena, 71

"Mannahatta" (Whitman), 93–94, 99

Man on Wire (documentary film), 99–100

"Many Thousands Gone" (Baldwin), 127

Map of Misreading, A (Bloom), 11

Marble Faun, The (Hawthorne), 2, 64

Mariners (Pease), 122

*Mariners, Renegades, and Castaways: The
    Story of Herman Melville and the World
    We Live In* (James), 122–23

masculinity: crisis of, 17, 69–72; and
    homophobia, 70; Hemingway and, 76;
    issues of, 18, 69–75. *See also* sexuality

Massachusetts Bay Colony, 45

Mathis, Ayana, 142–43

Matthiessen, F. O., 1, 7, 9, 119, 143

McCall, Dan, 146

McCann, Colum, 4, 17–18, 88–111

McCarthy, Jesse, 130, 132

McGann, Jerome, 103

Melville, Herman, 2–3, 7–8, 18, 51–52, 113–25, 131, 140, 142; readership of, 6; religion of, 120–21

Mengestu, Dinaw, 14

Men Without Women (Hemingway), 4

Milder, Robert, 45, 64

Miller, Arthur, 22

Miller, Edwin Haviland, 60, 116

Miller, Nancy K., 96

Miller, Perry, 2–3, 6, 139–40

Moby-Dick (Melville), 2–3, 78, 113–25, 130

modernism, 7, 74

Moraru, Christian, 30, 40

Morrison, Toni, 128

Mosses from an Old Manse (Hawthorne), 2, 45, 47, 51, 56

Motherless Brooklyn (Lethem), 16, 21–29, 31–32, 37, 39–42, 147n2

Mourning, Gender, and Creativity in the Art of Herman Melville (Tolchin), 124

Mukherjee, Bharati, 84–85, 148n5

multiethnic literatures of the United States. *See* ethnic American literature

"Murders in the Rue Morgue, The" (Poe), 40

"My President Was Black" (Coates), 136–37

"Names, The" (Collins), 97

Native Americans, 103

Native Son (Wright), 40–41, 127

Native Speaker (Lee), 15–16, 22, 27, 30–31, 37–42

"Nature" (Emerson), 51

Netherland (O'Neill), 17, 89–111

New England Mind, The: The Seventeenth Century (Miller), 141

New York, 16–17, 21–42, 88–111; Brooklyn, 22–24, 27–29, 36–37, 54, 98, 105–8, 110; Manhattan, 88, 91, 93–94, 106; myths of, 101–2; physical structure, 29, 41; postapocalyptic, 89; streets, 22, 27, 31, 41–42, 93–94, 147n6

New Yorker, 8, 18, 102, 128, 142

New York Review of Books, 139

New York Times, 142–43

"New York Was Our City on the Hill" (Danticat), 7

Ng, Fae Myenne, 141

9/11, 88–111; Family Room at One Liberty Plaza, 98; loss of, 101, 110; victims of, 96–97. *See also* World Trade Center

No Name in the Street (Baldwin), 134–35

North American Review, 47

Notes of a Native Son (Baldwin), 127, 133, 135

"Notes of a Native Son" (Baldwin), 134

novel: contemporary, 89; postnational, 110; traditions of, 7. *See also* literature

Obama, Barack, 18–19, 64, 117, 130, 132, 136–38

"Of Plimoth Plantation" (Bradford), 51

"Old Manse, The" (Hawthorne), 52

Olivarez, José, 14

Olive Kitteridge (Strout), 4

"Once in a Lifetime" (Lahiri), 58, 60–61

O'Neill, Joseph, 4, 8, 17–18, 89–111

"Only Goodness" (Lahiri), 55, 59, 61

Orr, Mary, 109

"O Youth and Beauty!" (Cheever), 75–76

palimpsest, 3, 66–87, 141

Palimpsests: Literature in the Second Degree (Genette), 11

Paris, 134–35

Patell, Cyrus, 13, 85–86

Peacock, James, 23

Pease, Donald, 122, 148n10

Perdomo, Willie, 14

Petit, Philippe, 90–91, 94, 97, 99–100

physicality, 21

Pinkney, Daryl, 136

Poe, Edgar Allan, 3, 40–41, 47

*Poems from Guantánamo: The Detainees
    Speak* (Falkoff), 89

Portrait of the Artist as a Young Man, A
    (Joyce), 35

postcolonialism, 80

postmodernism, 80

post-9/11 fiction, 88–111. *See also*
    literature

Prescott, Orville, 28

"Price of Sugar, The" (Danticat), 79

Proust, Marcel, 9

race, 18, 117, 132, 136–37, 154n12; history
    of relations of, 135; primacy of, 77;
    violence and, 120, 128. *See also* Black
    Lives Matter; ethnicity

*Raven and the Whale, The: The War of
    Words and Wits in the Era of Poe and
    Melville* (Miller), 2, 139–41

realism, 80

religion: and blasphemy, 122; criticism
    of, 120–21; and ethnicity, 29, 59, 109;
    of Melville, 120–21; salvation in, 74,
    154n13; skepticism and, 121; and tradi-
    tion, 59. *See also* ethnicity

"Remember This House" (Baldwin), 129

Remnick, David, 18

Reservation Blues (Alexie), 141

Reynolds, David S., 3, 27

Reynolds, Michael, 75

Rhys, Jean, 79

"Rip Van Winkle" (Irving), 108

Romano, John, 131

Rothstein, Eric, 11

Rowe, Juan Carlos, 48

Sag Harbor (Whitehead), 137

Saldívar, Ramón, 80

Sale, Roger, 4

Salem, 43–49, 53–55, 63, 65

Scarlet Letter, The (Hawthorne), 15, 43–45,
    47–48, 50–58, 62–65

Schillinger, Liesl, 49

School of Hawthorne, The (Brodhead),
    8, 12

science fiction, 87. *See also* literature

secular humanism, 7, 154n13

Selby, Hubert, 22

"Self-Made Men" (Douglass), 15–16

self-reliance, 50, 54

Semeiotike (Kristeva), 11

semiology, 56–57; structuralist, 85

Sentimental Education (Flaubert), 75

sentimentalism, 74–75, 80, 151n3

Septimius Felton, or, the Elixir of Life
    (Hawthorne), 60

sexuality, 154n12; experience of, 72–74;
    masculinity and, 69–74. *See also*
    masculinity

Shakespeare, William, 38; tragedies of,
    131

"Short Happy Life of Francis Macomber,
    The" (Hemingway), 67–82

"Sleepers, The" (Whitman), 22, 30,
    38–39, 42

Smith, Betty, 23

Snyder, Katherine V., 89–90

Sollors, Werner, 5, 7, 12, 14

Solnit, Rebecca, 28–29, 37

"Song of Myself" (Whitman), 31, 39, 94–95

"Song of Prudence" (Whitman), 21

Spiegelman, Art, 89

Spiller, Robert, 7

Stone, Robert, 76

Stowe, Harriet Beecher, 127

subjectivity: affirmation of, 75; criticism of, 129; destruction of, 126; elucidation of, 22; and ethnicity, 32

Subtlety, A, or the Marvelous Sugar Baby, an Homage to the unpaid and over-worked Artisans who have refined our Sweet tastes from the cane fields to the Kitchens of the New World on the Occasion of the demolition of the Domino Sugar Refining Plant (Walker), 78–79

Tamu Lewis, Nghana, 77

temporality, 22; and the self, 22

Ten Little Indians (Alexie), 4

This Is How You Lose Her (Díaz), 71

Thoreau, Henry David, 7, 26–27, 50–51, 56

Through Other Continents: American Literature across Deep Time (Dimock), 16

Tolchin, Neal, 124

Toward an Aesthetic of Reception (Jauss), 9, 50

Toward the Geopolitical Novel (Irr), 81

tragedy, 70, 131

Trailing Clouds: Immigrant Fiction in Contemporary America (Cowart), 12

transcendentalism, 46–47, 54

transnational literature, 82. *See also* literature

Tree Grows in Brooklyn, A (Smith), 23

Tribe of Pyn, The: Literary Generations in the Postmodern Period (Cowart), 12

Tripmaster Monkey: His Fake Book (Kingston), 4

Trujillo, Rafael, 69–70, 73, 79, 82–83. *See also* Dominican Republic

TuSmith, Bonnie, 12–13

Ulysses (Joyce), 91

Unaccustomed Earth (Lahiri), 15, 43–44, 49, 54–55, 58–65

"Unaccustomed Earth" (Lahiri), 44, 50, 57

Uncle Tom's Cabin (Stowe), 127

Underground Railroad, The (Whitehead), 4, 137

United States: civil rights movement in, 135–36; colonialism of, 78; criticism of, 120; identity of, 6; mythologies of, 123; nature of, 10, 110; project of, 138; race relations in, 118, 125, 136–37; transformation of, 105

Victorian Afterlives (Douglas-Fairhurst), 10

View from the Bridge, A (Miller), 23

violence: and black men, 124, 126, 132, 153n6; colonial, 71; domestic, 71; and masculinity, 71–72; and race, 120, 124–28, 132, 153n6; of terrorism, 89

Visit from the Goon Squad, A (Egan), 89

Walker in the City, A (Kazin), 22, 27–28, 36

"Walking" (Thoreau), 26

Was Huck Black? Mark Twain and African-American Voices (Fisher Fishkin), 5

Waterfront: A Walk around Manhattan (Lopate), 24

West, Cornel, 129–30

Whitehead, Colson, 14, 89, 137

Whitman, Walt, 3, 7, 16–17, 23–24, 38–42,
    97, 99, 109, 111, 116; cartographic
    legacy of, 21–42; democratic vision,
    100; everyman persona, 32; homage
    to, 89, 93, 100
Wide Sargasso Sea (Rhys), 79
Wilde, Oscar, 70
Wilhite, Keith, 89
Williams, Dana A., 129–30
Williams, Raymond, 13, 85–86
Wilson, Michael T., 74
Wood, James, 102
World Trade Center, 88, 90, 95, 97,
    99–101. *See also* 9/11

Wright, Richard, 4, 18, 40, 113, 125–28,
    135, 153n9
writing: ethnic American, 80, 85, 128,
    141–42; and gender, 74; immigrant,
    80; standards of, 74; theory of,
    149n2; tradition of, 128. *See also*
    literature

Yamamoto, Hisaye, 34
"Year of Living Postracially, The" (White-
    head), 137
"Year's End" (Lahiri), 59, 61

Zone One (Whitehead), 89

CPSIA information can be obtained
at www.ICGtesting.com
Printed in the USA
LVHW092145130120
643535LV00006B/85/P

9 780813 943596